Saint George and the Dragon

Saint George and the Dragon

Text by
Jan Svanberg

Photographs by
Anders Qwarnström

Translated from Swedish by David Jones

RABÉN PRISMA

ℜℜ
Bokförlaget Rabén Prisma
Besöksadress: Kungstensgatan 49
Box 45022
104 30 Stockholm
e-postadress: raben.prisma@raben.se

© TEXT *Jan Svanberg*
© PHOTOGRAPHS *Anders Qwarnström*
All the photographs except those listed on page 214.
The cover photograph depicts Saint George and the Dragon in Stockholm
City Church and is the work of Anders Qwarnström.
The other cover pictures are reproduced in the book as well.
The English translation of the Legend of St George
According to Jacobus de Voragine
on page 176 is by William Granger Ryan.
(In Jacobus de Voragine, The Golden Legend –
Readings on the Saints, Princeton 1993.)
Published by agreement with Princeton University Press, USA.
Set in Monotype Bembo (PostScript)
COVER AND GRAPHIC DESIGN *Christer Hellmark*
REPRO *Offset Kopio Oy, Helsinki*
PRINTED & BOUND BY *New Interlitho, Milan* 1998
ISBN 91-518-3392-1

Contents

- 6 Foreword
- 9 Saint George – Martyr and Dragon-slayer
- 11 The International Background
- 29 The Cult of Saint George in Sweden

- 33 The Battle of Brunkeberg and its Aftermath

- 43 Saint George and the Dragon in Stockholm City Church
- 45 Sten Sture's Altar Foundation
- 51 The Knight, the Dragon and the Princess
- 67 The City of Silene
- 73 The Martyrdom of Saint George on the Reliefs on the Plinth

- 103 Bernt Notke – The Saint George Master
- 105 From Antwerp to Lübeck
- 111 From Dance Macabre Wall-hangings to a Large Signed Group of Sculptures
- 119 The Reredoses at Århus, Tallinn and Uppsala
- 127 A Portrait of a Swedish King
- 133 The Saint George Statue in Stockholm

- 141 A Perennial Motif

- 173 Documentation
- 175 The Legend of St George According to Jacobus de Voragine
- 183 The Mediaeval Swedish Versions of the Legend of Saint George
- 186 The Original Position of the Saint George Group
- 191 Saint George from the Reformation to the Present Day
- 195 Strindberg on Finding the Relics
- 199 Strindberg's Report
- 200 Notes
- 214 Illustrations
- 215 Bibliography
- 219 Index of Individuals, Places and Objects

Foreword

During the Middle Ages, Saint George, the great martyr and dragon-slayer, became one of the most popular figures throughout Christianity. He has been depicted as the national saint of England and as the patron saint of Moscow and Barcelona, for instance, as well as in countless pictures right up until the present day. Remarkably enough, however, the most pre-eminent representation of Saint George is to be found in Stockholm. This is because, more than five centuries ago, Sweden's ruler granted the leading artist in the Baltic countries unique resources so that he could produce something exceptional. It was a votive offering to the saint invoked before the decisive victory in 1471 in the struggle for national autonomy. The elaborate sculptural group with its larger-than-life statues was inaugurated in Stockholm's City Church, now its cathedral, on the Eve of the New Year of 1490 by a Papal nuncio.

The first scholar to devote attention to this internationally famous sculpture was Johnny Roosval, who from 1901 wrote several articles and after the first world war two books in Swedish on the work. In 1962 Max Hasse published a pamphlet in German and it has also been the subject of many articles and chapters in many books, mainly by Swedish and German scholars, but also by Danish and Russian ones. Since the days of Roosval and Hasse research findings have cast new light on many aspects of the statue, our knowledge has increased and photographic techniques have developed.

The core of this work, first published in 1993 in Swedish, consists of the first thorough presentation in words and in colour illustrations of the group of sculptures in Stockholm City Church with all its details and relief panels. But the work also contains chapters that place the monument in a wider context both chronologically and geographically. One of them presents the long history of the motif of Saint George before the creation of the statue, another the vitality with which it has survived up until the present – not least thanks to the powerful example set by the statue in the City Church. An extensive chapter is also devoted to its originator, Bernt Notke, which presents him in the light of recent findings about his other major works.

This book is based on long-standing research that I began in 1971 shortly before the 500th anniversary of the victory commemorated by the monument. It is also based on Anders Qwarnström's assiduous photographic documentation, some of it shot from a specially erected scaffold so that details that are difficult or impossible to see from floor-level could be illustrated. Before the 500th anniversary of the inauguration of the monument in 1989, the relics and the inaugural document were removed from the reliquary so that they could be examined and photographed.

This edition has been published to coincide with Stockholm's designation as the Cultural Capital of Europe for 1998 and this is the first volume in English devoted to the capital's internationally most celebrated work of art. We should like to express our gratitude to the Swedish Council for Research in the Humanities and Social Sciences which provided the funding to make the translation possible and to David Jones for the skill and enthusiasm with which he has rendered not only the work itself but also the many excerpts from mediaeval rhyming chronicles into English.

To avoid a maze of confusing references to illustrations, these are only provided when an illustration referred to in the text cannot be found on the same page or the facing pages.

The main body of the book is followed by a documentary section which contains no illustrations. It begins with the text of the section of "The Golden Legend" about Saint George, both in Latin and in an English translation. The following chapter deals with different mediaeval versions of the legend in the different vernacular languages – a German version, an English one and four in Swedish – to try to establish which version Notke used for his distinctive rendering of the Saint's combat with the dragon. There then follows a discussion of the complicated problem of where and how the different items that form the group as a whole may originally have been arranged in the City Church. A third chapter is devoted to the history of the sculpture from the Reformation up until the present day, the movements and the various restorations it has undergone. Then follows Strindberg's dramatic report on how he rediscovered the lost relics in the attic of the City Church one cold day in February 1880. The work ends with the notes to the main text (the documentary section has its own footnotes), a bibliography, the provenance of the illustrations and an index.

Anyone who is interested in more details about the ten coats-of-arms painted on the monument and their owners (see illustrations 71-80 and the relevant captions which contain the main information about them) should consult the heraldic analysis in the Swedish edition of this work (page 196–198) which has not been translated for inclusion in this volume. The same is true of the list of medieval images of Saint George that have been preserved in Sweden and Finland, which are listed in tables in the Swedish edition (page 199–210).

In carrying out our research and taking photographs, we have been assisted by many willing helpers and we should like to acknowledge our gratitude to all of them – they are too numerous to be mentioned by name here. We should like to express our gratitude in particular to the representatives of the Stockholm City Church, the Central Board of National Antiquities and the Numismatic Collection. I should also like to extend my personal thanks to Ingrid Hemgren, who in recent years has been responsible for the conservation of the monument and who has generously shared her observations with me.

Without the active interest of our publisher, Uno Palmström, neither the English edition of this work nor the second edition in Swedish would ever have seen the light of day. We should like to conclude by acknowledging the debt we owe both to him, and to our editor, Eva-Maria Westberg, who has dedicated so much time and care to this and to the previous edition.

Stockholm December 1997
Jan Svanberg

Abstract

Svanberg, Jan, Saint George and the Dragon. Department of the History of Art, Stockholm University, S-101 91 Stockholm. Stockholm 1998, 224 pages. Monograph. ISBN 91-518-3392-1. Colour photographs by Anders Qwarnström.

The late-Gothic Saint George group in Stockholm City Church is examined from the point of view of iconography, style and function. The knight, his horse and the princess are executed as larger than life polychrome wooden sculptures together with the enormous dragon, whereas eleven reliefs depicting different scenes from the life of the saint, eight of them of his martyrdom, are smaller. The work was dedicated in 1489 and had been commissioned by Sten Sture Senior, then Governor of the Realm of Sweden, as a votive offering after a decisive victory in his struggle for Sweden's autonomy. For this reason the group is not only a devout altar foundation with a reliquary for relics on the saint's chest, but also a victory monument embodying both personal and national symbolism, indicated by the fact that Saint George's horse bears the donor's coat of arms and Sweden's national colours.

One chapter presents the long history of the Saint George motif before the creation of the statue, another the vitality with which it has survived up until the present - not least thanks to the powerful example set by the statue in Stockholm. One chapter is devoted to its originator, Bernt Notke, which presents him in the light of recent findings about his other major works in the Baltic region.

At the end of the volume Latin and Swedish versions of the Saint George legend, together with Strindberg's own account of his discovery of the relics, are provided in an English translation.

Saint George – Martyr and Dragon-slayer

1. The executioners bind Saint George to a cross, lacerate him with iron claws and singe the wounds with torches. Seated on the right is the governor, Dacianus, sceptre in hand, making a commanding gesture, while behind him is the devil. One of eleven scenes from the dreadful martyrdom of the saint painted with Spanish expressiveness on the great altar of Saint George in Valencia. From around 1410 and attributed to Marzal de Sas. Now in the Victoria & Albert Museum, London.

The International Background

Saint George is in every way an international figure. Since the earliest days of Christianity the blessed George has been venerated both in the East and the West – as Hagios Georgios in the Greek-Orthodox communion and as Sanctus Georgius by Roman-Catholics. During the first eight centuries he was recognised as the pre-eminent martyr. It was only after the first crusade that he became known in the 12th century as the dragon-slayer and it has been in this capacity that he has remained popular during the following eight hundred years. Indeed, so great was his repute that his name was quickly adopted by the different vernacular languages. In Italian it became Giorgio, Jorge in Spanish, Georges in French, George in English, Georg or Jürgen in German, Jurij in Russian, and Göran, Jörgen, Örjan, Jörn or Yrjö in Scandinavia, to mention just a few examples. In Catholic countries he has been venerated up until the present as a saint and elsewhere he is used in different contexts as a well-known symbol – the champion of the good and vanquisher of the monstrous, an archetypal image.[1]

Gods and heroes that kill dragons or other evil monsters have been worshipped since time immemorial in different religions and cultures. We seem to have a great and constant need of such superhumanly powerful dragon-slayers. Saint George first acquired this dominant and archetypal function during the High Middle Ages but before that in Western Europe it had been attributed to a number of predecessors both in the Early Christian period and considerably earlier.

One of the gods that overwhelmed monsters was Horus, who in prehistoric Egypt fought against Set, the great adversary of the gods. In one battle, Set assumed the form of a crocodile, in another that of a snake and in the final conflict that of a large red hippopotamus, which Horus, in the guise of a handsome youth, kills with a well-aimed blow of a harpoon. In a great battle, the greatest of the Babylonian gods, Marduk, vanquished the original chaos of rain, winter and night in the shape of the awesome dragon Tiamat. He hurled lightning and hurricanes at her so that Tiamat had to close her fearsome jaws, and he could then cut her open with his scimitar to bring light, life and order into the world. Marduk was a solar god, like the Greek Apollo, whose arrows, according to mythology, killed the dragon Python at the sacred spring of Delphi when the god became master of the site of his oracle. In the Old Testament, the prophet Isaiah (27:1) described how the Lord with sword, "sore and great and strong", shall punish Leviathan, the piercing crooked serpent and slay the dragon that is in the sea.[3]

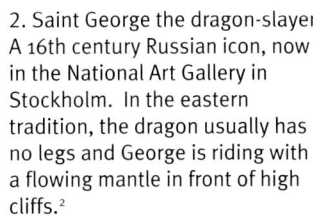

2. Saint George the dragon-slayer. A 16th century Russian icon, now in the National Art Gallery in Stockholm. In the eastern tradition, the dragon usually has no legs and George is riding with a flowing mantle in front of high cliffs.[2]

3. Horus in conflict with Set. Egyptian sculpture from the New Empire or the Late Period.

4. Perseus releasing Andromeda. The sea monster and the head of Medusa used to petrify it have been depicted in minuscule. A mural from the House of the Dioscuri in Pompeii, now in the Museo Nazionale, Naples. Ist century A.D.

Among heroes, in classical Greece and Rome, Perseus was the pre-eminent dragon slayer. The son of Zeus and Danaë, he had just decapitated the witch Medusa, whose glance turned all to stone, and was on his way home. He arrived in Ethiopia, where King Kefeus and his queen, Cassiopeia, held sway. The queen claimed to be more beautiful than the fair daughters of the god of the sea. As punishment for this hybris, the realm was ravaged by a sea-monster whose depredations, according to the oracle, could only be forestalled if the queen's beautiful daughter Andromeda were sacrificed to the dragon. She had already been taken to a cliff on the shore and chained there, when Perseus arrived in the nick of time, was seized with love for Andromeda and conquered the dragon. In one version, he used the head of Medusa to petrify it, in another he hews it to death with his scimitar (cf. Marduk). Thus he gained the princess as his bride.[4]

For the Germanic tribes, the great dragon-slayer was Siegfried (in Scandinavia he was called Sigurd). He laid an ambush for the dragon Fafner, guardian of the great treasure, and killed it with his sword as it slithered down to drink. However, the gold thus acquired was subject to a curse which would lead to many deaths, and eventually to Sigurd's.[5]

This hero from the pagan *Völsungasagan* (in German *Nibelungenlied*) was

5. Siegfried drives his sword through Fafner, runic script on the dragon's long body. Detail from a 5-metre wide stone inscription from the 11th century at Ramsundsberg in Södermanland, Sweden.

so popular in Scandinavia that he continued to be represented in Christian art during the early Middle Ages.

He is mainly to be found in the carved decoration on the porches of the Norwegian "stave" churches, as in Hylestad. Sigurd's struggle with the dragon could be seen as a parallel to the battles of biblical heroes with the powers of darkness in the form of dragons or evil monsters.[6]

In the Bible, from the Fall onwards, the great serpent remains a perpetual threat. According to the Book of Revelations (12:7 ff.) finally there is to be a great battle in heaven between Michael and the dragon: "And the great dragon was cast out, that old serpent called the Devil, and Satan". Now the heavens can rejoice but "Woe to the inhabiters of the earth and of the sea! for the devil is come down unto you." (verse 12). The Archangel Michael therefore became the great dragon-slayer of the early Middle Ages, venerated in a powerful cult found in both the eastern and the western Church. Evidence of this can be found, for instance, in innumerable representations of Michael vanquishing the dragon, usually with a spear but sometimes with a sword, most often as it crawls at his feet. In Swedish mediaeval art images like this of St. Michael are also frequent.[7]

For many years, in other words, the archangel Michael fulfilled the

6. Siegfried has concealed himself in a hollow from which he thrusts his sword through the dragon. Relief in the porch of the "stave" Church in Hylestad, now in the University of Oslo collection of antiquities.

7. Michael's battle with the dragon. The archangel is wearing chain mail and carrying a large shield but the sword in his right hand has now disappeared. The dragon is spewing flames or poison from the second head at the end of its tail. Ironwork on the door of the church at Rogslösa in Östergötland dating from around 1200.

function that Saint George was not to assume until the High Middle Ages. In fact, the oldest written version of the legend of Saint George, in Greek, contains no battle with a dragon but depicted him as the great martyr (*megalo-martyr* in Greek). This version contains details recorded much later in *Legenda aurea* (the Golden Legend) in its account, presented below, of the martyrdom. In the early Christian legend, however, this was a long drawn-out process and contained many more ordeals. There the saint is tortured to death time after time with increasingly sophisticated and horrifying methods, but then revived by God. Finally he was beheaded in 303 A.D. after having converted the Governor's wife and 30,900 heathens to Christianity.[8]

When, where and how the legend arose is clouded in obscurity. It is most likely that it dates from the 4th century somewhere in Asia Minor, perhaps in Cappadocia itself, where the saint is said to have originated from. Strongholds of the cult of Saint George were soon to be found in the neighbouring areas. One of them was the city of Antioch, which at times at least was accounted the site of the Saint's martyrdom. Another was Palestine, where the later so famous Church of Saint George in Lydda-Diospolis was held to possess the remains of the saint, as is witnessed by a pilgrim from North Africa as early as the 520s. It did not take long before the cult had become intensive in Egypt as well, and in other parts of the Eastern Empire, not least in the capital Byzantium, where a number of churches were dedicated to Saint George.[9]

The Greek legend soon gave rise to variants, and eventually translations into a number of languages, among them Coptic, Ethiopian, Syrian, Armenian and Georgian. The legend also passed from Greek to the Slavic languages and to Arabic and Turkish, because Saint George was also adopted by the Muslim world. In the 5th century two mutually independent translations had already been made into Latin before a third was produced in Rome in the 8th century, which was to become the version dominant in the West. During the same period Rome adopted from Byzantium – as eventually did the whole of the Roman Church – April 23rd, the day of his death, as the date on which to celebrate Saint George. Outside Italy, the cult of Saint George quickly spread to France and southern Germany, for instance. Eventually the legend was translated into the various Western European vernacular languages and different variants arose while, at the same time, the legend was retold in verse in several languages, the first in German as early as the end of the 9th century.

What was it that led to the dissemination of the legend and cult of Saint George and the strength of their impact during these early and crucial centuries, long before his dramatic battle with the dragon had been invented? It was first and foremost his unusually dreadful martyrdom which enabled him to stand out among the countless martyrs competing for in-

8. George in combat with the dragon. San Girorgio Martire at Petrella Tifernina in Abruzzo was one of the first churches dedicated to the martyr saint. Around 1200 it was rebuilt and provided with new reliefs in a primitive but expressive Romanesque style. At that time, Saint George's combat with the dragon was a new motif.

terest. The "great martyr" outdid them all in endurance and emerged as the "saint of indestructible life" embodying in this way the principle of the vitality of Christianity. Another reason for his popularity was that even in the early Christian version the legend concludes with George extracting God's promise that he may come to the assistance of those who call upon him in adversity.

These two attributes of the saint would exert a powerful influence during the later Middle Ages as well. Then St George was called upon as one of the "fourteen aids in adversity", an enormously popular and effective constellation of saints who provided collective protection against most of the ills one could incur. Saint George, whose body during his martyrdom was destroyed and dismembered in various ways and then miraculously healed, became during the Middle Ages the patron saint of lepers. Their hospitals and chapels, dedicated to Saint George, were erected outside the walls of cities because of the risk of infection with the dreaded disease. This can still be seen in Visby on the island of Gotland, where the medieval ruins of the chapel of Saint George's Hospital lie well outside the city, 300 yards north of Norderport, the northern gate in the city wall.

George possessed a third quality, however, even in the early Christian legend, which, although not emphasised, was to prove increasingly significant – he was an officer. This was to contribute substantially to the success of his cult and to his eventual evolution into the champion who is the object of our interest in this work. It did not take long before he had become the patron saint of Byzantine officers and soldiers and during the 6th century, according to a number of accounts, he came to the aid of different commanders in battle. During this century, the cult of the soldier saint was promoted principally by the Emperor Justinian, the founder of the military and administrative Byzantine state, and there is evidence of his having founded at least two Churches dedicated to Saint George. The cult was also espoused by his courtiers, and their seals show that George was one of the most popular saints.

From the 6th century onwards, Saint George was depicted in Byzantine art in many images that have been preserved, for instance on icons, frescoes and mosaics. He is always portrayed as young and beardless, sometimes as an eminent courtier but more often as an officer in armour standing, weapons in hand, in full or half-figure. He is often rendered together with other, similarly depicted Byzantine military saints, mainly the black-bearded Theodor and/or Demetrius. Eventually a version of the legend developed, which became popular in Western Europe as well, in which all three were brothers. In this version they are all sons of the Count of Antioch, the two elder brothers so admire the youngest, George, that they give him their shares of their inheritance. Then all three set off into the world to fight for Christianity in different areas.

This typical image of Saint George – alone or with his "brothers" – standing in armour with his weapon in his hand was to survive in the conservative art of Byzantium for more than a thousand years and is also encountered on medieval Russian coins and icons. During the High Middle Ages, this image was also adopted in Western Europe. The most famous examples consist of two statues of the saint as a knight standing in full armour.

One of these statues is from the High Gothic period and can be found in the "porch of the martyrs" at Chartres (the statue has been mistaken for that of his bearded brother Theodor, as the consoles each depict a scene from the martyrdom of the other).[11] The other is Donatello's statue in marble from Or San Michele in Florence, carved in 1416 as one of the pioneering works of the Renaissance. In relief on the base, there is a representation of George in mounted combat with the dragon, a motif that admittedly by then had been common all over Europe for several centuries, but which was, after all, not part of the original legend. Let us examine how this motif arose.

It is not unusual to portray an officer on horseback. Like the other Byzantine military saints, in particular Theodor and Demetrius, George could also be depicted as a victorious knight. The first time this occurs is in a Coptic tapestry in the 6th century. And in an icon in Saint Catherine's Monastery in Sinai, probably from the 9th century, he is thrusting his lance into a small bearded man under his horse's hoofs. This motif is common in the many images of the saint in Georgia. One of these Georgian

Saint George. The wording is "o Georgio" in Greek. Russian coin found on Gotland. Minted by Prince Jaroslav of Kiev (died 1054).[10]

silver icons, from the beginning of the 11th century, states that the bearded man George is riding over and killing is the "godless King Diocletian" the Emperor of Rome who had him executed.[12]

It is also in the region in which the cult of Saint George first originated in Asia Minor that the first pictures of George as a dragon slayer appear. One is a small mould from Smyrna, probably from the 6th century, which shows him thrusting his lance into a serpent-like dragon beneath his horse: the other is a small Byzantine gold plate, where both George and Demetrius appear as mounted dragon-slayers. In other cases, Theodor is similarly represented. If the small figure George is shown defeating in a group of images is his evil pagan opponent, a more general symbol for the evil which the saint resists is the serpent or the dragon. At any rate, the images seem to have predated words, as it is not until much later that George's combat with the dragon is described in writing, the first time being in a collection of miracles in Greek from the 11th century.

The new motif arrived in Western Europe in connection with the First Crusade in 1099. Legend has it that when the crusaders besieged Antioch, where St George is said to have endured his martyrdom, he together with the two other Byzantine military saints, Demetrius and Merkurius, appeared on a white horse to the Frankish army and then led them to victory over the Muslims. According to *Legenda aurea* George also appeared to them outside Jerusalem and led the crusaders as they stormed the city to recover it from the Saracens.

9A & B. A statue of Saint George from around 1220 in the southern porch of Chartres Cathedral. On the left can be seen the correct console with George undergoing torture on the wheel of knives. It was mistakenly installed under the statue of his brother in the same porch.

This is what laid the foundation for the popularity of this combative, victorious, equestrian saint in the Europe of the crusades and knightly chivalry. It led to his breakthrough as the dragon-slayer in legend, cult and visual art and to his increasing importance as a saint for the remainder of the Middle Ages. He became the symbol of the Knights of Malta, stamped on their coinage, as he naturally also became for the Brotherhood of Saint George. Indeed, he became the favourite patron of most knights, whose aid was repeatedly besought in various battles. At the battle at Puig in Huesca in Spain in 1237 he was seen fighting alongside the Christians aiding them to victory over the Moors. He was the foremost example of a *miles Christi*, a soldier of Christ.[13]

It is not until the 12th century that the earliest known legend with a description of Saint George's combat with the dragon appears in the West (the first is in a collection of miracles at the Monastery of St. Emmeram in Regensburg). The first version has Saint George meeting the dragon on foot and vanquishing it merely by calling on God and making the sign of the cross. In another version, he kills the dragon with a cross, as "can be read in other books" as the author of *Legenda aurea* laconically informs us. But such use of pure magic to conquer the dragon did not go down well with the imagination of the feudal world, which preferred to envisage George fighting like a real knight.

The result was that another version of the legend, characterised by knightly practice and influenced by the typical images that the Byzantine

10A & B. Saint George in Donatello's marble statue from 1416 in Or San Michele at Florence. The relief on the base by the same sculptor depicts George's combat with the dragon (on the right). The original is now in Bargello, Florence.

world had already developed, soon arose and gained mastery. This describes how George engages the dragon on horseback and it is this account which is given prominence in *Legenda aurea*.

Among the earliest pictorial representations of this kind is a coin minted in the 12th century for the Frankish Count of Antioch, who had been installed by the crusaders. The saint's name written in Greek makes it clear that the knight with the halo thrusting his spear into a serpent-like dragon on the ground beneath his horse really is George (and not one of the other Byzantine knightly saints like Theodor). This was to continue to predominate as the typical image in the Greek Orthodox Church's many depictions of Hagios Georgios. This is how he appears in Russian icons from the late Middle Ages and onward, astride a rearing white horse thrusting his lance into the sinuous serpent-like dragon (figure 2).[14] In Western Europe, as well, Saint George is often depicted on horseback thrusting a spear or a lance into the dragon. Here, however, the various representations differ to a greater extent when it comes to the stage of the combat depicted or how the Saint is armed.

11. Mould from Smyrna for a pilgrim's badge. It dates probably from the 6th century and is therefore the oldest known representation of George's battle with the dragon. The name in Greek to the left of the halo is reversed in the mould.

The first monumental picture in Western Europe of George's struggle with the dragon is the relief created by Master Nikolaus in 1135 over the main porch of the cathedral in Ferrara. Here George is riding over the dragon, who has been thrown on its back by a blow from the lance, which then broke so that the knight is now raising his sword against the monster.[15]

Here already we see the type of representation which is later to predominate and culminate in the great statue of Saint George and the Dragon in Stockholm.[16]

The most famous medieval free-standing group representing Saint George and the dragon previous to this is the one cast by the brothers Martin and George von Klausenburg in bronze in 1373, which can be seen in Prague (the knight is half life-size). He has now lost both his shield (on which the signatures and the date were inscribed) and the lance that had once been raised and thrust into the jaws of the small lizard-like dragon on the ground (his sword is still hanging in the sheath attached to his belt). The statue was erected on the castle mount in Prague, initially outside Saint George's monastery, but later moved to surmount a renaissance well in one of the castle's courtyards.[17]

12. George and Demetrius killing an evil man and a dragon. Byzantine gold plate from the 6th or 7th century.

There are many variants in Western European art, as has already been made clear. George may be fighting with lance in his hand, or he may already have used this weapon and be drawing his sword. He may be wielding the sword over his head, he may be brandishing it sideways from left to right or from right to left.

Innumerable images of the saint can be found spread throughout the countries of Europe and executed in every conceivable material and tech-

13. George in combat with the dragon. Relief by Master Nicolaus carved in 1135 on the porch of the cathedral in Ferrara. This photograph was taken after conservation in 1989, when the original colouring appeared, for instance the dapple-grey horse.

nique. You can come across him on a Romanesque bronze door in Sicily, in a Gothic pattern book for artists on Iceland, or as a large stone sculpture on the facade of a Gothic cathedral as in Angoulême or Basle. Saint George and his combat with the dragon remained a favoured motif during the Renaissance, when it was depicted by famous artists, for instance in sculpture by Donatello, paintings by Uccello, Carpaccio and Rafael, and engravings and woodcuts by Dürer.[18]

The motif has continued to enthral artists of later periods as well, among them Tintoretto and Rubens in the 16th and 17th centuries and Eugène Delacroix, Gustave Moreau and Hans von Marées during the 19th, to mention only a few famous examples.

Saint George was therefore one of the major international saints. Nevertheless, the warrior saint became a national symbol in several different places. First and foremost this is true of England, where Saint George became the national patron saint as early as in the 13th century, and his banner with a red cross on a white background is still the country's flag. In certain countries during specific periods Saint George became a cohesive national symbol in the battle against foreign invaders. This is how the rebellion of the Estonians began against the overlordship of the Danes and the Teutonic Order on the night of Saint George, 1343. The way in which the saint functioned as a national symbol in Sweden during the latter half of the 15th century will be the subject of the next chapter. An interesting contemporary parallel can be found in Moldavia in what is now Romania, where "Gheorge" was also enlisted both in warfare and as a cult to produce remarkable and unique visual art.

14. A copper coin minted in Antioch 1112-19. To the right Saint George's name can be seen, and the city's initial on the left.

21

In his struggle against the advancing Turks, the Prince of Moldavia, Stefan the Great (1457-1504), adopted Saint George as the protector of his troops, emblazoning him on the standard of the Moldavian army as a symbol of Christianity and its victory. Even more churches than previously were dedicated to Saint George. After Stefan's death, his son Petru Rares developed an ecclesiastical iconic programme which would symbolise the continued struggle against the Turks and the spiritual values that were being defended. He decided that the exterior walls of the churches were to be painted with frescoes just as the interiors were – Moldovita 1537 and Voronet 1547 are good examples. In these remarkable exterior frescoes in the Byzantine style, Saint George plays an important role. He normally occupies a prominent place at the southern porch so that he can be seen by people entering the church, and a considerable number of the images derive from his legend. A total of 33 scenes from his life adorn the church at Arbore, painted in 1541, including an unusual one of Saint George celebrating a feast. After the middle of the 16th century, when Moldavia lost its sovereignty, the iconographic role played by Saint Ge-

15. George in combat with the dragon. Bronze statue in Prague, cast in 1373 by the brothers Martin and Georg von Klausenburg. Today the original forms part of the collection of art at Saint George's Monastery, Prague.

orge diminished and once again he was portrayed as merely one among many military saints on the interior walls of the churches.[19]

What was it that endowed Saint George's battle with the dragon with such popularity all over Europe – from Georgia in the east to England in the west, from Ethiopia in the south to Scandinavia in the north? Several explanations have been put forward, which attempt in different ways to

16. George in combat with the dragon. Relief on the 12th century porch of the Church of St. John the Baptist at Ruardean, Gloucestershire, England.[20]

17. George vanquishes the dragon, now about to be led by the princess into the city, from which her parents, the king and queen, are following the drama. This fresco was painted in 1547 on the facade of the church at Voronet, Romania.

explain the deeper implications of the motif that have turned it into so central a symbol. Historians of religion have drawn attention to the many predecessors the dragon-slaying saint has had among heroes, angels and gods that have already been mentioned.

When the sun gods Horus, Marduk and Apollo contend with monsters, their combat symbolises not only the victory of good over evil but also the conquest of night by day, of winter by spring. From this perspective, it hardly seems a coincidence that the Feast of Saint George is celebrated on April 23, a day that still bears his name in the Swedish almanac.

One of the most eminent pioneers of modern psychology has interpreted the struggle with the dragon as an archetype in the collective unconscious. The victory of the hero over the monster exemplifies, according to C.G.Jung, an important stage in the process of individualisation, the triumph of the ego over the dominance of the unconscious and, particularly for boys, liberation from the all-consuming mother. These interpretations provide food for thought and need not exclude each other. There can be no doubt, however, that Saint George, venerated ever since the

18. Painting by Paolo Uccello from ca. 1435, in the National Gallery, London. The dragon has emerged from his lair into a garden of clipped bushes and there encounters George's lance. The princess has already placed her belt around the dragon's neck to lead it into the city.[21]

early Christian period as the most steadfast of all the martyrs and also, since the 12th century, as the great dragon-slayer was a figure charged with import.[22]

19. Europe's rulers praying to Saint George. From left to right, Charles VIII of France, the Emperor Fredrik III of Germany, Maximilian, as King of Rome, Archduke Philip the Fair of Burgundy, Ferdinand II of Aragon (above) and Henry VII of England (far right). Their contemporaries Christian I of Denmark, and Sten Sture the Elder of Sweden could also have joined those kneeling in front of the altar with the image of Saint George. Miniature from a prayer-book made in the Netherlands around 1500.

20. Poster for a puppet theatre in Cefalù from 1967 which displays the archetypal motif in Ariosto's renaissance version of the legend, still popular in Sicily. In *Orlando furioso* Roger is travelling on his hippogriff (a creature with a Griffin's head and wings and the body of a horse), when he catches sight of Angelica, like Andromeda, in chains and about to be devoured by a sea-monster. He rescues her after a savage battle.[23]

21. An illustration in the Duke of Bedford's Breviary, illuminated in Paris around 1420 by the "Bedford Master", an inspired visual story-teller. The king and queen watch from the city of Silene ("Sylene") as their daughter goes out to meet George. "Fair youth, flee!" ("Bone iuuenis fuge") she says, and he responds "Lass, why do you tarry?" ("Filia quid prestolaris"). When the dragon emerges from the lake, he attacks it, with the princess kneeling close by. She can then be seen in the foreground using the belt she has removed to lead the dragon towards the city, while George, now dismounted, continues to wound it and goad it with his lance and the people flee in terror. The manuscript is now in the Bibliothèque Nationale in Paris.

puincia huc aduenusti: uel quo   imortalis dei impio deseruire. Ite-
nomine uoceris. Sanctus ge-   acianus dixit. Erras
orgius dixit. Epianus † de-   georgi: accede † im-
seruus sum: georgius nuncu-   mola deo apollini

22. A painting from around 1470 by the young Albertus Pictor in the church at Ösmo in Södermanland in Sweden. His presentation is dramatic with a telling use of form – compare the straps on the white horse here and in figure 25. Here the knight has a helmet with the visor lowered and a shield with the red cross of Saint George, while his cloak is flowing behind him. The lance is striking a winged dragon whose tail has tied itself into a well-formed knot. Note the king and queen looking down from the city of Silene as spectators of their daughter's fate.[24]

The Cult of Saint George in Sweden

When did the cult of Saint George arrive in Scandinavia? As early as in 1126 one of the altars in Lund Cathedral was dedicated to him (along with a number of other saints) while the building was still under construction as the seat of the Archbishop for the whole of Scandinavia. And in the calendar dated 1198 from the church at Vallentuna in Uppland, April 23 is designated as the Saint George's Day, which it still is both in Sweden and abroad. In both these cases he is referred to as "George the Martyr".[25]

The oldest known Swedish visual representations of the saint also date from the latter half of the 12th century. On Gotland, which was trading actively with Russia, an eastern-looking Saint George makes an appearance in the thoroughly Byzantine wall-paintings in the church at Källunge. In the painting to the right of the triumphal arch which has now almost entirely disappeared, the saint has dismounted from his horse, which is

23. Saint George charges at an unusually large dragon. Relief on a font from the latter half of the 12th century originally in the church at Vättlösa in Västergötland, now in SHM.

standing in the background, and is sticking his spear into the sinuous serpent.²⁶

On a font from the church at Vättlösa in Västergötland, on the other hand, there is a typically Western representation, in a form that is most closely reminiscent of contemporary parallels in England. It depicts a rider equipped with a helmet, shield, spurs and handsome stirrups charging, sword in hand, at an enormous dragon that is brandishing its forked tongue threateningly at the saint. It is portrayed as dragons usually are in Western Romanesque art with two legs and with wings – here the wings are folded to form a hump on the dragon's back.²⁷

Pictures of the equestrian saint are still equally rare in Swedish art of the High Gothic period. He is depicted on only two imported works – a chalice and a chasuble – and as a dragon-slayer on fragments of wall-paintings from the 14th century in two manorial churches in the area around Lake Mälaren (Ängsö and Vendel).²⁸ As a martyr, Saint George, as has already been mentioned, became the patron saint of lepers and the object of a cult, which in the 14th century gave his name to the hospitals and churches erected for their succour, in, for instance, Turkku (Åbo), Visby, Kalmar, Skänninge and Stockholm.²⁹ The cult venerating him as the patron of knights and warriors intensified, however, during the 15th century, when the traditional chivalric ideals, virtues and ceremonies once again came into fashion.

The resurgence of this interest also found artistic expression in most countries. Among the many Northern European examples, one that is particularly interesting from a Swedish point of view is the famous "Artushof" in Danzig (Gdansk), where the brotherhood of Saint George was accounted the most eminent, and where large wooden statues of the knight, the dragon and the princess stood in the Artushall.³⁰

The cult of Saint George the knight was introduced into Sweden by Karl Knutsson, who according to the chronicler, travelled far and wide on the continent and learnt there how battles were fought. Moreover, he spent the seven years between his first and second regency in Danzig and it was there that, using Artushof as his model, "he built his court within the town/to Sweden's fame and great renown". In Sweden, while still a marshal before a battle in 1438 he called on "Saint George the holy martyr knight/to assist him in this present fight". And when as king of Sweden, Karl drew up his armies before the winter campaign in Scania in 1452 – with the help of his experience from abroad, as the chronicler explicitly states – his advance guard bore a banner with the image of Saint George ("Saint George's visage was plain to see").³¹

During Karl Knutsson's lifetime, we also find the first references to Guilds of Saint George in Sweden, in 1443 in Stockholm and 1460 in Uppsala. They soon spread to other places in Sweden, such as Strängnäs,

24. Saint George thrusting a now lost lance into a small dragon at his feet. A characteristic late-Gothic wooden statuette of the saint. This forms part of the large reredos completed in Lübeck for Stockholm City Church in 1468, now in SHM.

25. This picture forms part of the wall-painting in the church at Vendel in Uppland, which was signed by Johannes Ivan in 1451. Saint George is wearing a circlet of ostrich feathers in his hair and his horse a cross on its brow. His spear is striking an enormous four-legged reptile, while the princess is waiting close by with a fettered sheep. The city they have left can be seen in the background.

Västerås, Visby and Stora Kopparberg in Dalecarlia. Here Saint George became the patron saint of the miners.[32]

During the 15th century Göran (the Swedish form of George) also became a common Christian name in Sweden. The saint's breakthrough in Swedish visual art also took place during the Karl Knutsson's lifetime. More than twice as many images of Saint George have been preserved from this period as from all the previous periods together.[33]

In 1470, from his death bed Karl Knutsson appointed his nephew Sten Gustavsson Sture (from the Tre Sjöblad family) to safeguard what he had achieved. What Sten Sture inherited was not merely the dying king's castles and estates but above all the responsibility for a policy of nationalism which, as Governor of the Realm, he would successfully maintain for over a quarter of a century. He also took over the cult of Saint George, which he was to exploit in this political struggle to much greater effect than his uncle. He was to turn the cult into a cohesive national symbol as a result of the Battle of Brunkeberg.

The aim of this policy was to keep Sweden outside the Scandinavian union that the three kingdoms of Denmark, Norway with Iceland and Sweden with Finland had agreed to established in 1397. But from the 1430s Sweden broke away for periods to withdraw definitely in 1523, while Denmark went on dominating Norway in a union lasting until 1814.

26. The heat of the battle at Brunkeberg Ridge. A gouache in the frame below a portrait of Gustav Vasa, now at Gripsholm, painted after 1560 and ascribed to William Boy or J. Baptista van Uther. Although it depicts the liberation of Stockholm from the Danes by Gustav Vasa it could just as easily have been the battle of Brunkeberg, half a century earlier.

The Battle of Brunkeberg and its Aftermath

After several raids on the Swedish border territories, in 1471, Christian I of Denmark decided on a major and decisive venture to compel Sweden to rejoin the Union. During his preparations for war he had, admittedly, negotiated with Sten Sture and the Swedish Council of the Realm, but he soon violated the agreements that had been made. Rearmament continued and the king managed to persuade a group of Hansa cities to promise to blockade trade with Sweden.

With a well-equipped army and mercenary German cannoneers and their cannons, he set sail for Stockholm, arriving with his fleet on July 18. During the following two months he ordered his troops to strengthen their positions on the top of the Brunkeberg ridge and could thus lay siege to the Swedish capital from the north. At the same time Christian also assembled his supporters from Uppland, where he received homage in various places, either by proxy or during a personal visit to Uppsala in September. Many of the major landowners, among them the Oxenstierna and Vasa families and Lord Trotte Karlsson of Eka, had aligned themselves with the Union king, so that his adherents included both their many tenants and some of the yeomen of Uppland.[1]

During the same period Sten Sture and his supporters, such as the Tott and Trolle families, gathered together their men-at-arms and the peasantry from Småland, Götaland and Sörmland. Nils Bosson Sture (a member of the Natt och Dag family) raised the miners and the men of Dalecarlia and joined Sten Sture's forces, as they rounded Lake Mälaren to the north near Köping. The combined armies then marched eastwards along the northern shore of Lake Mälaren and on October 9 they had reached Järva, immediately north-west of the capital. Sten Sture now issued an ultimatum to the king calling on him to withdraw. This was ignored.

Before the battle, which took place on October 10, Christian probably had around 5,000 men at his disposal, including the Swedes from Uppland. He had the major advantage of having his main force positioned on the crown of the steep Brunkeberg ridge behind fortifications that consisted of woven baskets filled with sand and stones and also wooden palisades. He had placed another force down by the convent at Klara (now the site of the church) to prevent Sten Sture's main forces, advancing from the north, to establish contact with his men inside the city. A third force had been detailed to guard the ships at Käpplingeholmen (today Blasieholmen, then an island but now a peninsula). He had, however, failed to set a guard on the bridge linking this island with Norrmalm, so that it was possible to row there from Stockholm and saw off the stanchions suppor-

27. A good impression of the city for which the battle was waged in 1471 can be gained from the Sundog picture, in Stockholm City Church. It was admittedly painted because of a remarkable heavenly phenomenon in 1535 but no major changes had been made to the city's building during the intervening period. The city island rises from the shore of Lake Mälaren towards the City Church in front of the Three Crowns Castle in the centre of the picture. Small suburbs, consisting mainly of "cabbage farms" lie at the foot of the Brunkeberg ridge and the cliffs to the south. Behind the city is the sea.

ting the bridge, an oversight that was later to have fateful consequences.

Sten Sture's troops outnumbered his opponent's. He had twice as many men, according to the Sture Chronicle, the primary source of our information about the battle, together with the Lay of Brunkeberg and Olaus Petri's Swedish Chronicle. But they were not as well equipped or trained as the bulk of the king's army, and they were fighting the battle at a disadvantage in having to storm a fortified position from below.

Sten Sture had also divided his men up into three forces. He was to lead his main army himself in its attack from the west up the ridge. Nils Sture was to make a circling manoeuvre with his troops so that he could eventually attack from the east. And his own men were to make a sally from Stockholm under the command of Knut Posse, warden of the castle, and use hundreds of sloops and small boats to cross the channel called Strömmen so that they could storm the ridge from the south. Sten Sture's wife, who had recently improved morale in the city by distributing free food and alms to the poor, was standing with other women and "looked out through the castle's lofty wall /to see how well the struggle would befall".

Before the battle, both commanders delivered inflammatory speeches to their troops, in accordance with an age-old military tradition. King Christian finished his speech by commending his army to the protection of "the knight Saint George" in the coming battle. Sten Sture said among other things that he wanted to save Sweden from harm and neither spare nor fear the enemy and he persuaded his men to confirm with upraised arms that they all wanted the same. Full of confidence, they all began to sing "the Lay of Saint George". In other words both armies called upon the same saint to protect them during the battle. During the battle the men fighting for the Swedish Governor of the Realm bore twigs and tufts of straw to identify themselves, an important detail in the days before uniforms existed.

When Sten Sture's troops had marched up to Norrmalm and the city clocks struck 11, there began a battle that was to be long and bloody. The Sture Chronicle provides dramatic descriptions of the fighting.

It began with a mutual exchange of fire from longbows, crossbows and muskets. There is, however, no mention of what use the King put his cannons to, and they may well have caused more psychological damage with their flames and noise than material destruction. Then the attempts to storm the ridge began, with fierce close combat with swords, spears and axes. Weapons splintered, shields and mail gave way, horses and men fell, and the sound of battle mixed with war-cries and the wailing of the wounded. According to the Sture Chronicle, "a poor peasant, Björn Starke was his name" ran ahead of Sten Sture's horse wielding his two-handed sword ferociously to make way for his commander.

The course of the battle seems to have been as follows. In one of the early sallies from Stockholm, a successful attempt was made to burn the screen, the wooden palisade, that provided cover for the Danish troops at the convent at Klara. But Sten Sture's repeated attempts to storm the main Danish force from below were repulsed time and again by the strong Danish defences at the top of the ridge. During one of the attacks, however, both King Christian and his foremost Swedish supporter were struck in the face by a bullet. The effects of these bull's-eyes are described by the Sture Chronicle with unrestrained glee:

> *Then suddenly at once there blows*
> *Lead from a musket on King Christian's nose*
> *Four of his teeth the lead removed*
> *From nose and mouth flowed streams of blood*
> *Lord Trötte Karlsson was hot and tired*
> *So to some rest he then aspired,*
> *Sat on the ground, and bared his head.*
> *He got the reward that he should dread*
> *For drawing King Christian in this plight,*
> *No better fate befell the wight,*
> *Between his eyes there struck hot lead*
> *Down he fell and lay there dead.*

In other words, Lord Trotte was killed while the injured king had to be borne away from the battle.

When Sten Sture's third attempt to storm the ridge had been rebuffed, the Danes pursued his men down the ridge to Klara. With their backs to the convent, however, the Governor's men rallied shouting

> *The Danes from Denmark have come down*
> *To meet us here on level ground*
> *If you want to stay in Sweden any longer*
> *Now's the time to show you're stronger.*²

Now the banners of the two armies were facing each other and in the fierce close combat that ensued the Danes first lost theirs but then managed to regain it and retire with it up to the top of the ridge, having sustained heavy losses (500 dead according to the chronicler).

Finally the combination of Nils Sture's circling manoeuvre, the fourth attempt by the main Swedish force under Sten Sture's command to storm the ridge and a sally from Stockholm led by the warden Knut Posse – in which he was injured – forced the Danes to quit their positions at the top of the ridge. Several hundred fleeing soldiers died in the water and the marshy area between Norrmalm and Käpplingeholmen, as the supports of the bridge leading to the Danish moorings had been secretly sawn in two by the Swedes. Christian managed to get on board his ships with roughly half of his original army and returned to Denmark, leaving the peasants from Uppland to come to terms with the victors as best they could. The King's army sustained enormous losses, according to the Sture Chronicle 1,800 men, of whom half fell in battle and half drowned, and to this must be added 900 who were taken prisoner, among them the Danish Marshall of the Realm, Klas Rönnow.

After decades of conflict both internally and with enemies abroad, the decisive victory at Brunkeberg inaugurated a period of nearly thirty years of peace in Sweden, in which mining, trade and handicrafts flourished. This economic prosperity combined with increasing self-confidence – the victorious army had, after all, to a large extent been made up of peasants – has left its obvious mark on many churches in central Sweden. A large number of them were now modernised with elaborate stellar vaults, the vaulting and the walls embellished with lavish paintings by Albertus Pictor and other Swedish painters. In addition, a big number of reredoses were commissioned either in Sweden or abroad.

One effect of the victory was that Sten Sture's nationalistic propaganda began to gain ground outside the peasantry. Only four days after the battle, it was decided that the capital's magistrates – and those of other towns as well – of whom half had previously been German, were in the future only to consist of Swedish-born men. Archbishop Jakob Ulfsson, who before and during the battle had maintained a strictly neutral stance, was prepared on the day following the battle to claim that its outcome was a national victory dependent on the exceptional grace of God and the support of his own cathedral's particular saint, Saint Erik.[3] Indeed, according to the chronicler's verse, people had seen how "Sweden's patron" had wielded his burning sword in the sky every time Sten Sture's men had rallied for a new attack. Within the ecclesiastical province of Sweden, it was decided in 1474 that the feasts of both Saint George and St. Erik should be celebrated with the greatest of ceremony as were the feasts of the other two patron saints of the realm, Sigfrid and Birgitta.[4] All four were often depicted in works of art and Saint George considerably more often than during any other era. Almost half of all the mediaeval pictures of the saint that have been preserved stem from the time of Sten Sture the Elder (more than 80, of 171 in all).

The powerful archbishop collaborated for many years with Sten Sture and the most important result of their joint national endeavours was the foundation of a Swedish university, the first in Scandinavia, at Uppsala in 1477. In wall paintings and reredoses, in which hitherto the major international saints had predominated totally, the early Swedish saints from the period of Sweden's conversion, Sigfrid, Eskil, Botvid, Elin of Skövde, etc.

28. Albertus Pictor signed the wall painting in the church at Kumla in Västmanland in 1482. In one of the new stellar vaults he has portrayed the death of Saint Olov at the battle of Stiklastad in 1030, but as was then customary, has depicted contemporary armour and weapons.

reappear, in addition to St. Erik, to whom prominence had already been given during the the first national uprising against the Scandinavian Union led by Engelbrekt in the 1430s. This is how the church, by breathing life into ancient local cults and spreading them over the country, participated in Sten Sture's evocation of a national consciousness.

Salient expression was given to this mood in the large reredos procured by Archbishop Jakob Ulfsson for the high altar of Uppsala Cathedral during the decades following the great victory. The reredos was destroyed in a disastrous fire in 1702 but we know what most of the visual decoration looked like thanks to drawings that had previously been made and which formed the basis of the engravings published shortly after the fire in Peringskiöld's book on Uppsala.[5] The reredos depicted the history of St. Erik in numerous scenes up until the moment when he was defeated

Tab. III.   Monumen

29. Swedish and Danish knights in combat and the capture of St. Erik. Panel painting from the reredos of the high altar in Uppsala Cathedral, created after 1471 and destroyed by fire in 1702. An engraving based on drawings made by Johan Peringskiöld 1696-97 and printed in his *Monumenta Ullerakerensia* 1719.

and beheaded outside Uppsala by a Danish claimant to the throne. On the extreme right, one of the pictures shows how St. Erik is seized by a Danish army marching forward in serried ranks. But the time-honoured national saint, who, according to the oft-cited legend, was killed by the Danes in 1160, is standing pointing at the picture of knights in combat that occupies the major part of both panels and records how vengeance was visited on the arch-enemy three centuries later. It shows the Swedish knights approaching from the right. They can be recognised by the tufts of straw in their helmets, an echo of the Battle of Brunkeberg, as they ride forward, the Swedish flag with its three crowns fluttering aloft..

In the foreground rides Sten Sture, three water-lily leaves on his shield, using his lance to unhorse a Dane carrying a crossbow. His horse's trappings differ from the others' with small bells hanging everywhere, a detail that will be found on Saint George's horse in the City Church. The second rank is led by Karl Knutsson, who can be identified by the ship that forms his coat of arms, and his horse bears the insignia of the realm. His lance is striking a knight with Denmark's three leopards on his shield.

Here, in other words, the Swedes are successful – one of them has even reached the Danish National Standard. The fact that not only Sten Sture but also Karl Knutsson are leading the Swedish army shows that this is not a historical rendering of a specific battle but more of a summarisation, a symbolic representation of the nation's struggle during the preceding decades. There can, however, be no doubt that the painting was inspired by the most recent and decisive victory in 1471.

Saint George and the Dragon in Stockholm City Church

30. Saint George. Note the knight's chain with the cover of the reliquary in the middle of his chest and the support for his lance under the right pouldron or shoulder plate.

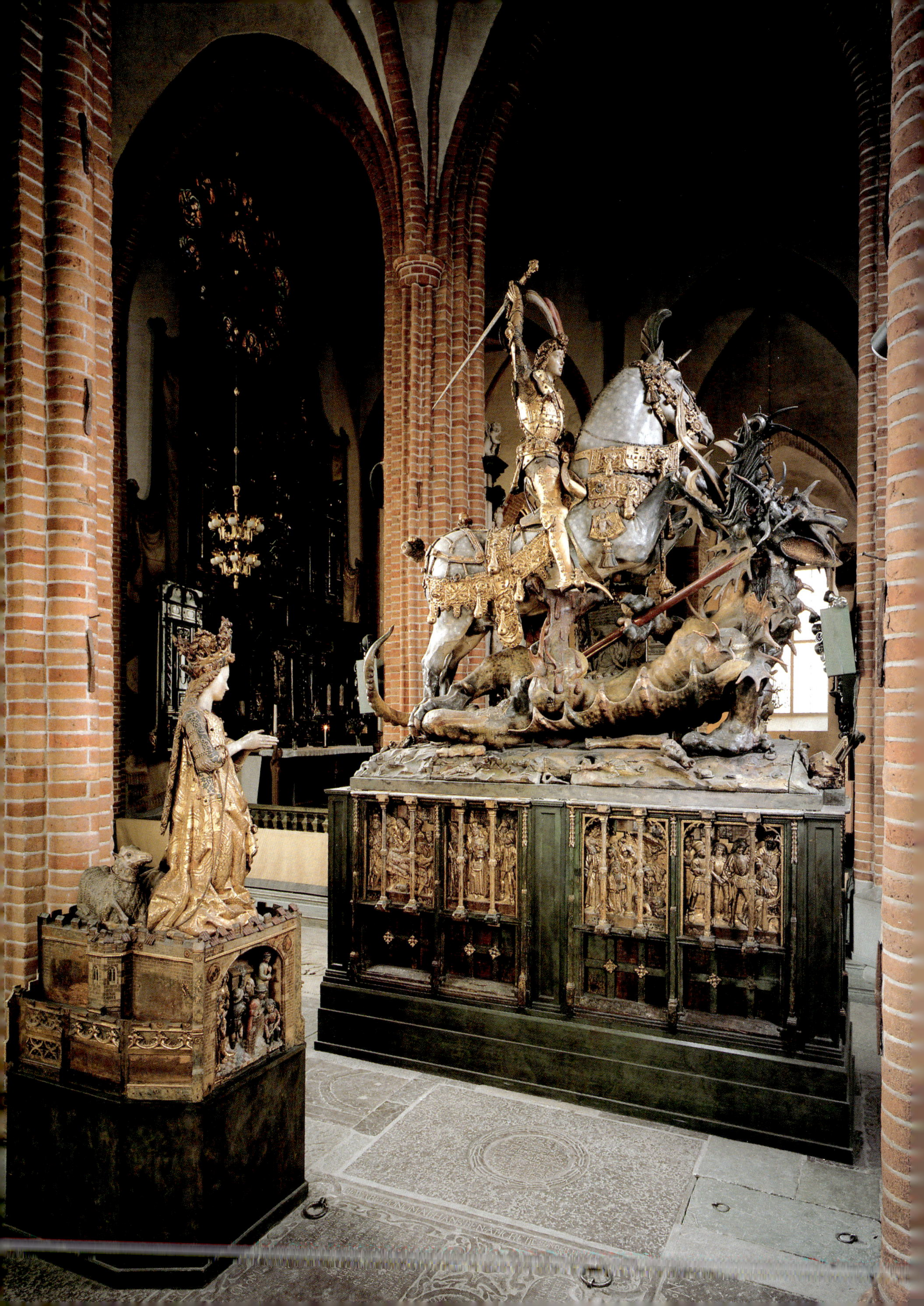

Sten Sture's Altar Foundation

The nationalism described in the previous chapter found literary expression in the verse chronicle and the Lay of Brunkeberg. It was, however, to be given its fullest and most eminent artistic embodiment in the altar that Sten Sture himself founded in honour of Saint George, the saint to whom his troops, according to these sources, had appealed before the battle. The chronicler relates that on the morning before the battle Sten Sture had entered the city and had mass said for himself and for the populace in the City Church.* This mass was celebrated at the altar dedicated to the Holy Cross in the centre of the church, which was also the site of the cult of Saint George. After the battle, Sten Sture wished to give thanks to the saint who had brought them victory by dedicating a new and richly decorated altar to him. Some time was to elapse, however, before all the arrangements could be completed and the imposing work erected. This was such a great event that in both the Greyfriars' diary and the Sture Chronicle, and later in Olaus Petrus' Chronicle – sources which otherwise make no mention of reredoses or other works of art – there is a record of the arrival in 1489 of "ye great George in Stockholm's town church".[1]

* *The City Church, dedicated to Saint Nicholas, was and still is often referred to as "Storkyrkan" (the Great Church). Since 1942 it has served as the Cathedral of the Diocese of Stockholm.*

The unanimous agreement of this information about the year in which it was installed has been confirmed by the monument itself. Among the relics lodged in a special receptacle in Saint George's chain, including fragments of bone with the inscription *De Sancto Georgio*, there was also a parchment. This, along with the bundle of relics, was removed in 1880 from the City Church to the Royal Library by August Strindberg, at that time an employee of the library, who has given us an evocative description of his sensational find in a newspaper article (included in the documentation at the end of this volume). The bundle of relics, however, was mislaid at the Library and only found some decades later, when the relics were also described in a scholarly article.[2]

Much later they were returned to the City Church and, in a small ceremony in 1954, replaced in the reliquary in the knight's chain on Saint George's chest.[3]

The Latin text of the document found with them reads in translation "In this year of grace 1490. On the Feast of St. Sylvester (New Year's Eve 1489) I, Antonius Mast, Protonotary Apostolic and Nuncio or Emissary to this realm of Sweden, dispatched with letters of indulgence for this year of jubilee, entombed these venerable relics in the image of Saint George, which also on this day was erected at this place. The stern knight and lord, Lord Sten Sture, the Governor of the Blessed Realm of Sweden, and his

31. The entire Saint George group in its present position in the northern aisle of the chancel of Stockholm City Church. This photograph was taken before the iron railings were erected around the work.

wife, the noble and generous lady, Lady Ingeborg, ordained this joyfully for the sake of their salvation."[4]

The Vatican archives have preserved summaries of several appeals addressed by Sten Sture through his ecclesiastical emissary in Rome, Hemming Gad, in 1492 to the Pope together with the replies. This exchange of letters in Latin concludes on November 17 with papal confirmation of the establishment of a prebend by the Governor of the Realm and his wife on behalf of the altar to Saint George in Stockholm City Church, with the donor as its patron and with the reservation of certain rights for the Archbishop in Uppsala. In the two preceding documents, dated February 6 and November 3 of the same year, Sten Sture had requested additional relics for the cult of Saint George and pointed out that he had himself spent more than 4,000 silver marks, which would correspond to millions, in today's currency.[5]

An appeal dated November 3 1492 is of particular interest. This mentions that Lord Sten and Lady Ingeborg (in Latin termed *vicerex,* vice-King, and *principissa*, Princess) "intend to endow a special chapel and altar to the knight and martyr Saint George and to St. Gereon" another martial saint, on whose feast, October 10, the Battle of Brunkeberg had been fought. What Sten Sture wanted, therefore, was to acquire relics, particularly those of the saint and also of other saints. Finally it is stated "that the same vice-King and his subordinates have spent more than 4,000 silver marks on completion of the image of Saint George and that every year it was his custom to walk in ceremonial procession with the Princess, the assembled clergy, the Blessed Sacrament and all the city's relics to the Brunkeberg Ridge on St. Gereon's day", i.e. the anniversary of the battle.

32. The reliquary in the pendant on Saint George's chest originally contained a bundle of relics in each of the four compartments and was covered by a pane of glass, which was replaced in 1700 with the present wooden cover (see Illustration 30) after the relics had been removed. Only one bundle remains, together with the bone belonging to another, which Strindberg wrapped in paper on which he wrote "St. Cyriakus". When opened on October 5 1989, the left-hand upper compartment contained a sheet of parchment and the right two folded sheets of paper, one containing Strindberg's hand-written report, the other the names of those present when the relics were returned in 1954.

33. A cloth bag in red and gold velvet brocade, 15th century Italian work, contains the fragments of bone wrapped in cotton. According to the paper labels in the bag and a joint parchment label outside they are "from Saint George, St. Blasius and St. Germanus" ("de scto Georgio et sancto Blasio et scto Germano"). The other fragment of bone was the only relic in a bag that has now disappeared and is said to come from St. Cyriakus. Two other bags, which contained bones from St. Leo and St. Martin and from Donatus and ten thousand knights, have disappeared completely. In addition to the relics, the bag that has been preserved also contained the parchment document with Antonius Mast's declaration (size 56 x 92 mm).

This is as good a testimony as any to the link between Sten Sture's great victory, his statue of Saint George and the symbolic value he ascribed to it.[6]

It has been assumed that even the great figure of George was carried in procession, as were smaller images of saints. The equestrian figure was, after all, a reliquary. While the large horse is firmly attached to its base, the rider can be detached from the saddle and raised or lowered, by means of an iron ring which still forms part of the head, from the vault above or from a special scaffold. It is possible that on these special occasions, the rider was detached to be placed on a special smaller processional horse on wheels – similar moveable wooden horses on which saints could be borne in procession have been preserved in other places. We also know from abroad that images of George were customarily carried in procession on the Saint's feast-day.[7]

Antonius Mast, who placed the relics in the image of Saint George, was one of the emissaries sent by Pope Innocent VIII to different countries to promote a planned international crusade against the Turks. His task was to win Sten Sture, like other rulers, over to the cause, and preach the crusade to the common people while collecting money for it. For this purpose Mast was furnished with parchment documents called Roman Jubilee Indulgences, which granted an unusually long period of remission from punishment for sin both in this life and from the ordeals that could be expected in Purgatory.

He had already arrived in Stockholm in the Autumn of 1489 with a large number of these indulgences, and even more were printed for him in Stockholm. On October 28, next to the high altar in the City Church, he had a cross erected of the kind that denoted that an indulgence campaign for the crusades was taking place there.[8]

Two months later, he immured the relics, ceremoniously dedicating the image of Saint George in the presence of Sten Sture and his wife, who had travelled up from Gripsholm. Mast undoubtedly took advantage of this occasion to remind the congregation in his inaugural address that Saint George was the crusading saint *par excellence*.

On the following day, January 1 1490, the indulgence cross was removed from the City Church and Mast went on to continue his campaign in other towns. Although a great deal of money was raised, the Pope was unable to initiate a crusade against the Turks. Sten Sture was, however, to exploit the crusading enthusiasm that had been aroused for his own and the nation's ends, directing it against an enemy nearer to home, the encroaching power of Moscow. In this context his statue of the saint was to play an important symbolic role.

The next time there is mention of Sten Sture's altar foundation for Saint George, we learn that it was revered as a source of national ferrour.

The verse chronicler tells us that in 1495 Sten Sture had St. Erik's banner brought from Uppsala Cathedral so that it could be borne in the war against Russia and that he caused it to be conveyed into Stockholm City Church:

> *The people surrounded him like a forest*
> *both monks and clergy,*
> *knights and brave fighting men*
> *flocked the town's church within*
> *many with pallid skin*
> *and the banner was set at Saint George's altar*
>
> *— — —*
>
> *Sir Sten on both his knees bowed then*
> *God in heaven have grace on Swedish men*
> *and the banner received in solemn state*[9]

This elaborate ceremony in the City Church was intended, in other words, to charge the symbol carried by the earlier national saint of Sweden with the protective and victorious might with which Saint George had previously imbued Sten Sture's army. With both the national saints enlisted in the defensive war about to take place on Sweden's eastern borders, it could be considered as a Swedish crusade against the Russians.

When Sten Sture returned from the war in the east, which concluded in the restoration of the status quo, strong opposition to his authority led by the Archbishop had developed in the Council of the Realm. But when Sten Sture was asked to relinquish his title as Governor of the Realm, his response was to raise the peasantry and burn the Archbishop's estates, resulting in his excommunication by this dignitary. In this situation, the Council of the Realm preferred the authority of the King of Denmark, the monarch of the union. Sten Sture, however, reached a rapid and favourable agreement with King Hans, who had succeeded his father Christian I in 1481. He gave up the title of Governor of the Realm to become the Royal Steward ("rikshovmästare") and was granted large estates. In this newly assumed dignity, he was present at the coronation of King Hans in Stockholm City Church in 1497. After four years, however, the Swedish magnates, led by Sten Sture, rose in revolt against the king. Once again they elected Lord Sten as Governor of the Realm and he spent his final years leading the war of liberation so successfully that all that was left to the Danes when he died in 1503 were Kalmar, Öland and Gotland. In order to keep Sten Sture's death secret, which occured when he was returning from the Danish border, Hemming Gad ordered one of his men to continue the journey in Sten Sture's clothes and with his knight's chain around his neck (cf. Saint George's knight's chain). This was to ensure that in the confusion of the moment and despite the wishes of the Archbishop it would be possible to elect Svante Nilsson Sture (Natt och Dag) to succeed Sten Sture as Governor of the Realm.[10]

In connection with the death of Sten Sture, the verse chronicler describes yet another function of the monument that he had founded in the City Church. Here, Sten Sture is imagined describing the events following his death in 1503, when his body had been brought from Jönköping to Stockholm:

> *My corpse then in the City Church shall lie*
> *In Saint George's altar*[11]

In other words, his coffin was placed in Saint George's altar, which appears to have been below the group of sculptures, i.e. inside the base, which is composed of a number of screens decorated with bas-relief carvings. Originally, there were openings, both above and below the relief carvings. Not long afterwards, however, all of these openings were blocked with planks of wood, the sides facing outwards painted to resemble stonework (see below page 78 and fig. 82). The inside surface of these planks, however, are unpainted, unlike the rest of the interior of the base, which is painted green and decorated with stars and flowers (see fig. 83). This is where the altar to the saint must have been placed, with spaces provided for the graves of the two founders, Sten Sture and his wife.

In many English churches similar burial chapels, *chantries*, were erected during the same period, their sides pierced to allow the tombs and altar to be seen. But burial monuments in which pierced screens surrounding the graves themselves are surmounted by equestrian statues which betoken the occupiers were most often seen in Italy in the 15th century, and have been likened to the arrangement in the City Church. At any rate, this space in the base of the statue, which had obviously been envisaged as a chantry, is where we should imagine Sten Sture's coffin lying during the New Year of 1504, when the verse chronicle tells us that it was placed inside Saint George's altar.[12]

After a short time, however, Sten Sture's coffin was removed and taken in solemn procession to its final resting place in the abbey church of Mariefred. He had himself founded this abbey towards the end of his life, when he probably also decided that this was where his grave should lie, the spot where he could be most certain of repose and masses for his soul. The daring Renaissance idea of making the newly founded altar in an urban church a monument to the victories and life of its benefactor, which he had manifestly entertained for some time, had finally yielded to the traditional mediaeval belief that an abbey provided the best final resting place. Once the original plans had been altered and his remains conveyed to Mariefred, the natural thing to do was to seal the openings at the top and bottom of the base of the statue in Stockholm.

34. St. Erik with his banner. A wooden sculpture in the reredos in the church at Knivsta outside Uppsala, where it was probably carved by Master Olof in 1502, as his name and this date are carved inside the reredos. St. Erik is usually shown carrying a sword but in this image he is also holding his banner. It has the three crowns painted on a piece of parchment, representing a pennant attached to the staff of a lance. St. Erik's banner was kept in Uppsala Cathedral and Sten Sture was reluctantly permitted to borrow it for his war against Russia. The little sneering man at St. Erik's feet represents Magnus Henrikssen, who had the saint killed with a sword (the weapon has now partially disappeared).

The end walls of the base of the equestrian statue consist of large panels with reliefs of the armorial bearings of the founder and his wife. The forward facing panel displays Sten Gustavson Sture's three water-lily leaves in black, and underneath in minuscule "Sten Stur ridd." ("Sten Sture Esq."). The other panel has Ingeborg Åkesdotter Tott's quartering in gules and or – red and yellow – and underneath the words "vroue ingeborch" (Lady Ingeborg). These coats-of-arms were probably placed on or above the doors allowing entrance to the interior of the base to emphasise that their owners had not only endowed the foundation of the altar but also owned the burial-place.

35. Sten Sture's coat-of-arms on the front of the base of the main statue is finely carved and painted and equipped with mediaeval iron bars. At the bottom is the inscription "Sten sture riddare" (Sten Sture Esq.). His shield with three water-lily leaves in black on a yellow field is surmounted by a helmet with the badge of its owner stamped into it in the form of three interlinked water-lily leaves, and each horn also bears three water-lily leaves.

36. Ingeborg Tott's coat-of-arms on the rear of the base of the main statue has been created in the same way. At the bottom is the inscription "vroue ingeborch" (Lady Ingeborg). Her shield with the red and yellow quarters of the Tott family is surmounted by a helmet with no mark of ownership and is decorated with an acanthus in the same way as her husband's. Both panels measure 49 x 27 inches (123 x 69 cm.).

The Knight, the Dragon and the Princess

Let us now focus on the group of statues themselves rather than the sources. The group portrays with unique clarity Saint George's most popular exploit as it is described in *Legenda aurea*. A lake outside the pagan city of Silene in Lydia (for details about the position of this country see page 175) was the home of a terrifying dragon. Every day the inhabitants of the city were obliged to give the dragon two sheep to eat. When they began to run out of sheep, each day one of the inhabitants of the city, chosen by lot, took the place of one of the sheep. One day the lot fell to the king's only daughter, and she walked out towards the lake leading a sheep. At that moment, the Cappadocean knight Saint George came riding by and learnt from the princess what she was about to encounter. When the dragon arrived, he attacked and defeated it, but did not kill it straight away. Instead he persuaded the princess to tie her belt round the cowed monster and lead it into the city. With the help of the persuasive power of the wounded but still terrifying dragon, Saint George converted the princess's father and the whole of his city to Christianity. Only then did the knight kill the dragon before continuing his travels (see the legend, page 176).

The main group, which is nearly 12 feet tall (about 3.5 metres), shows the knight in combat with the dragon. The artist has portrayed the dragon so that the spectator is convinced of its reality and its overwhelming ferocity. The numerous spiny outgrowths give the four-legged reptilian monster with its two wings an unusually frightening appearance. Both the size of the representation of the dragon and its monstrous spines are unique in European art, but counterparts can be found in China. It has been assumed that impulses from such a distance could have been conveyed to the artist via northern Italy, which was trading vigorously with the East at this period.

One example of this kind of influence may be found in a drawing of a large dragon of the Chinese type by the 15th century Venetian master Jacopo Bellini. It is quite possible for the northern European sculptor to have been inspired in this way by the form of Chinese dragons – even though the eastern dragon, a creature representing fertility, rain clouds, good luck and fortune, is the very opposite of the western dragon in its symbolic import.[13]

As we have seen, the western dragon is a creature of evil and death not only in the Saint George legend but in the Bible itself and in all subsequent Christian traditions. The enormous dragon in the City Church has been portrayed according to mediaeval zoological beliefs with both male

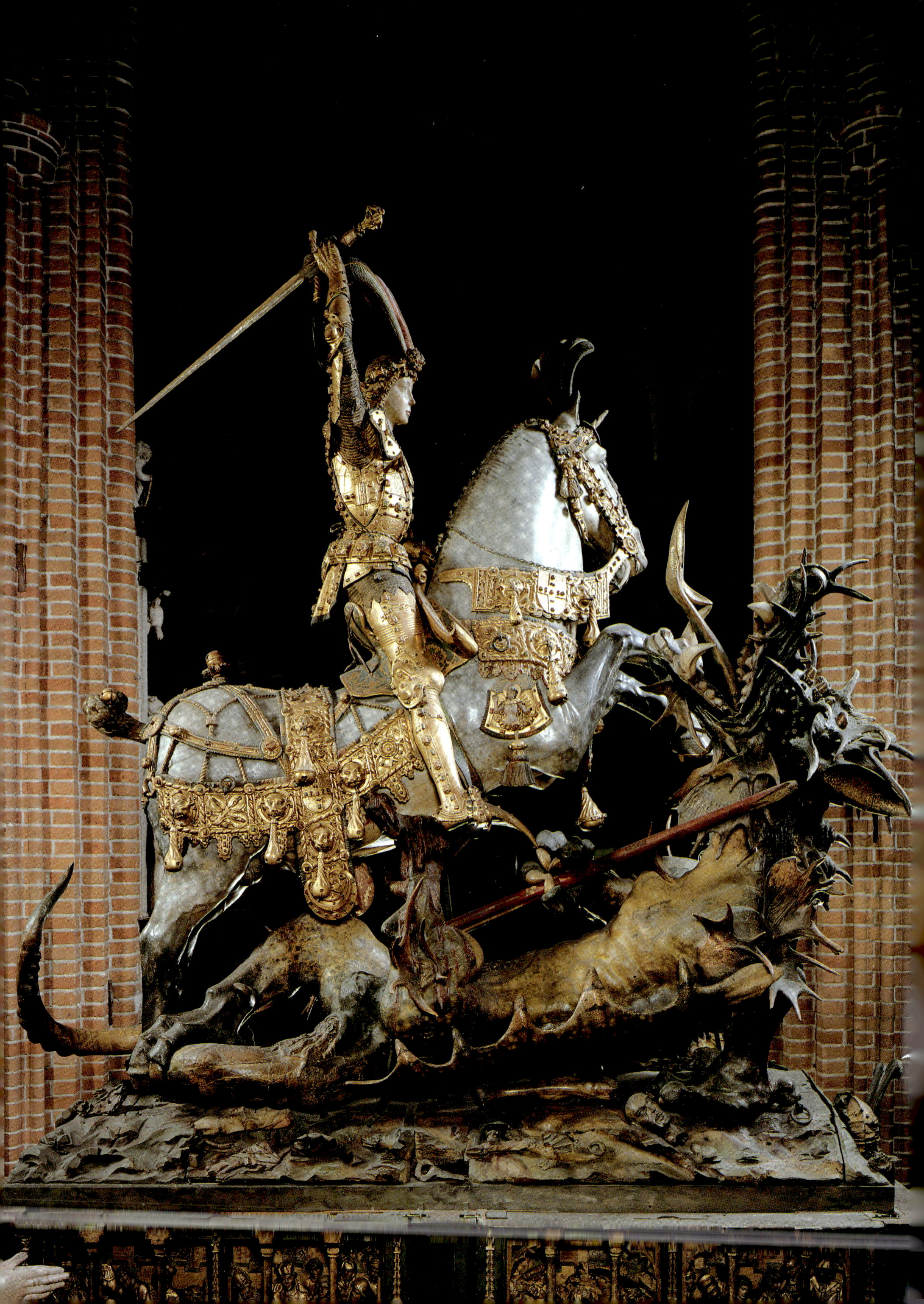

and female sexual organs. Evil has therefore no difficulty in reproducing itself, and on the ground beneath the great dragon the dragon's issue can be seen peering from holes and darting forward to eat what scraps of food remain. Some of these consist of the legs and heads of sheep, but the majority are the more or less gnawed arms, legs and heads of human beings.

In one place there is a skull with only a few scraps of flesh left on it, elsewhere there is the more or less intact head of a man, its features frozen in rictus. These are depicted with such chilling realism that they must have been based on studies from nature, perhaps beneath the Stockholm gallows. The same is true of a complete bust of a dead man, standing on the base of the statue, its head drooping as if it were modelled on the head of a man recently cut down from the hangman's rope. Here the naked realism is composed with an expressiveness that creates a cogent image of sudden, violent death.[14]

The enormous spiny dragon, its offspring and its victims in the barren setting of rugged cliffs are contrasted with the knight, who, clad in golden armour, rises, fearless and erect, in the stirrups of his charger to deliver the decisive blow with his upheld sword. The grouping of the statues shows clearly how the artist envisaged the progress of the struggle up to the moment of this final blow. The knight has set to work as if fighting in a traditional tournament. He has galloped, lance lowered, towards the advancing dragon, rearing up on its hind legs beating its wings, its jaws spouting venom. In the encounter Saint George's lance has struck and penetrated the dragon's throat, so that the creature has fallen backwards into its present position. The head of the lance has lodged in the wound, but the shaft has broken and is now gripped in one of the dragon's front claws, the other claw thrusting against the ground to raise the dragon's jaw with its barbed tongue, towards the horse and its rider. The monster is defecating, as some reptiles do when attacked, furiously brandishing its tail, and at the same time clenching one of its back claws, in pain or impotent fury.

The dragon has prevented the horse from moving by jabbing its other back claw into the horse's stomach to force it backwards and upwards in what seems to be a rearing movement. Allowing the dragon's leg to lift the horse like this has enabled the artist to solve the difficult problem that

38. Bust of a dead man. The open coat with lapels has been made of parchment and only one side of it has been preserved. The undergarment laced across the chest has been painted on to the figure. There are traces of real hair that have been attached to the skull.[15]

37. The combat seen from the knight's right-hand side – the main point of view which enables the knight's sword-arm and face and the dragon's head to be seen.

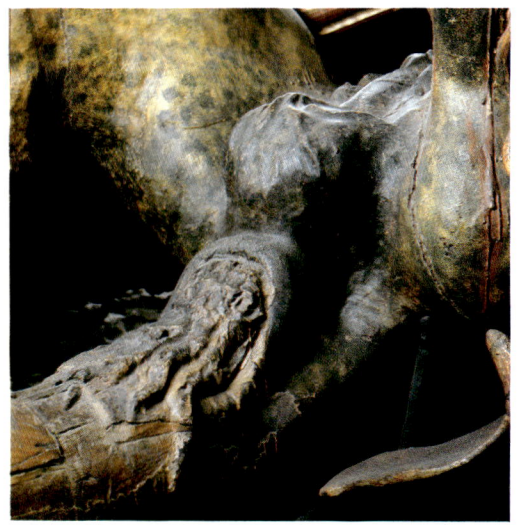

39-40. The hermaphrodite dragon's genitals and anal opening.
41-46 The dragon's victims and offspring. The details in the first four illustrations are from the right hand side of the base plate, the last two from the left (from the rider's position).

41. Two severed right arms – the upper arm has been contrived of parchment and a snake is creeping through the lower one, which is a carving.

42. Two unfledged dragons tearing at the leg of a sheep below a severed human leg.

43. The severed but relatively intact heads of a human being and a sheep.

44. A toad.

45. A skull which still has some remnants of flesh and the lower jaw.

46. A hand, a skull with no lower jaw and a young dragon.

his contemporary, Leonardo da Vinci, unsuccessfully contended with for so long – how to portray a horse rearing dramatically on its hind legs in a monumental sculpture without having to resort to devices that did not fit in naturally with the motif such as supporting tree-trunks or the like.[16]

After the lance had done good service and been broken, obedient to the rules of the chivalric tournament, the knight then engages his foe in close combat with his other weapon, the sword. He is raising it above his head to strike a vertical blow.[17] This is exactly how the combat is described in Örjansvisan (the Lay of Saint George), which tells us that when the lance splintered, Saint George quickly drew his sword (see page 185). *Legenda aurea* and other continental and Swedish versions of the legend only describe him using a lance.

Close to the knight is the princess – in some versions of the legend her name is Elya, in others Kleodolinda – awaiting the outcome of the struggle that is to affect her fate. Her face reveals the same unwavering calm, is as unconcerned by the clamour of combat as Saint George's is. Like him, she is portrayed larger than life.[18] With her tall crown and a robe of richly patterned gilt brocade, she is kneeling with her hands clasped in prayer, holding the unfortunate sheep who is to share her fate by a lead. These two form a group sharing a common base, which was subsequently erroneously placed on top of the castle – to enable it to fit the train of her gown together with part of the base had to be sawn off. She had, after all, left the town leading the sheep and according to the legend was "on a stone" out by the dragon's lake, when, after the knight has arrived, the monster revealed itself and battle could commence. The princess and sheep must therefore originally have been placed on a stone-like support close to the main group.

The saint's great dapple-grey charger has Sten Sture's water-lily leaves

41

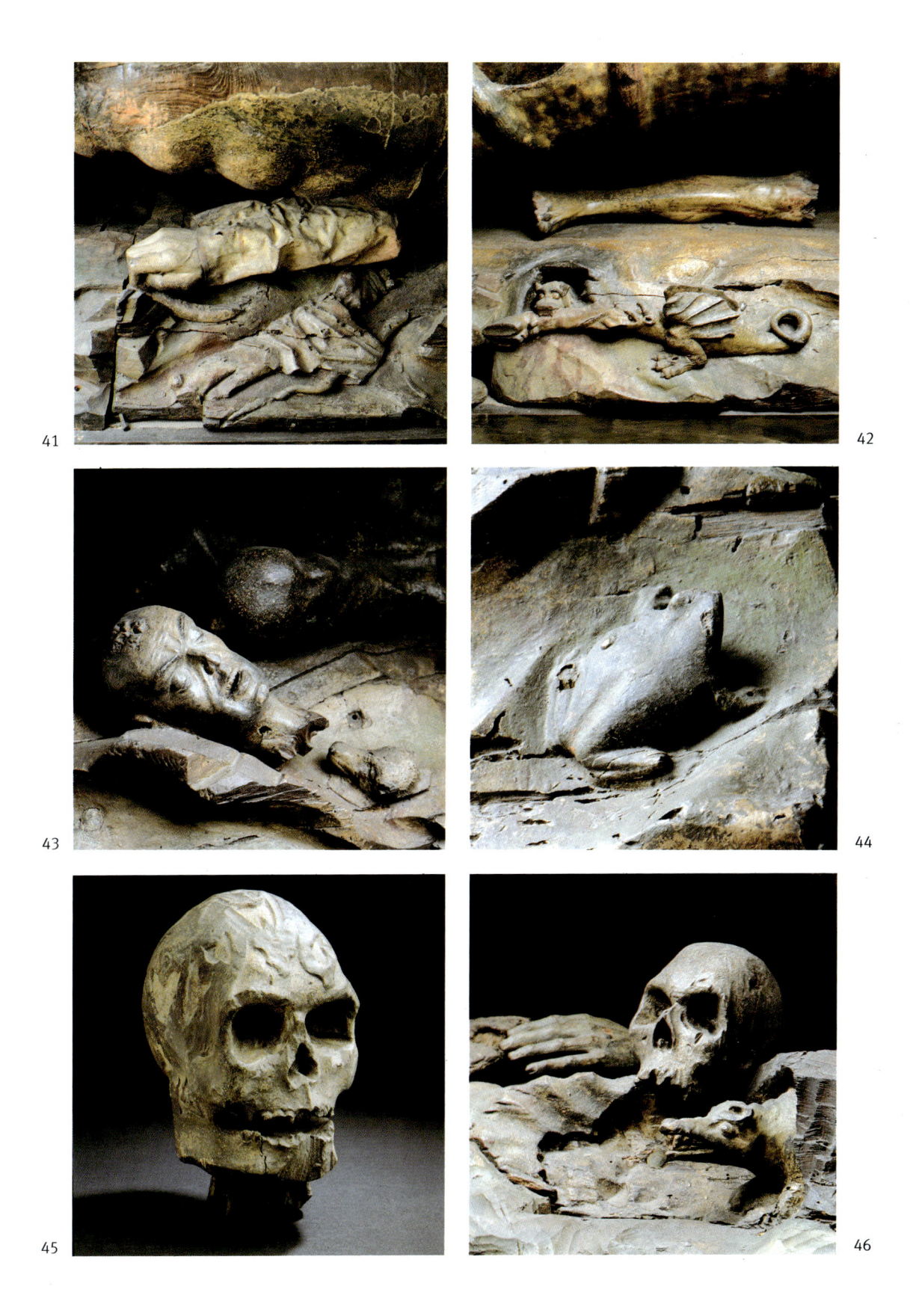

42

43

44

45

46

branded high on its loin as a mark of ownership. From a letter that still exists, we know that Sten Sture's horses were actually branded in this way.[19] In addition, the Sture coat-of-arms and the coat-of-arms of Saint George can be found in numerous places on the horse's harness. The words of the speech that the verse chronicle describes him delivering to his army before the battle of Brunkeberg can give us some idea of how important this horse was to Sten Sture:

> *And you will see that I shall do my utmost*
> *And risk my life, my men and even my horse*[20]

This is an exceptionally realistic portrayal of a noble, well-proportioned horse. For instance, the bulges on the inside of the legs and the veins that stand out because of the effort the horse is making have been portrayed

47-50. The head of the horse with its harness of small bells, tassels, the spiral horn on its brow and a plume of three ostrich feathers. Two of these are in the Swedish colours, one blue and one yellow, and the third in Saint George's colours, red and white. The rest of the horse's harness bears numerous examples of Saint George's coat of arms with the cross, and of Sten Sture's three water-lily leaves. His proprietary brand, a water-lily leaf, is branded on the horse's left loin.

51. The princess is wearing a sleeveless over-garment of gold brocade decorated with pomegranates. Her close-fitting green under-garment can be seen through the large openings beneath her arms and its sleeves are slit to reveal a delicate, shirred fabric below. Her costume, like the tall crown, is richly adorned with jewels. She and the lamb are mounted on the same base plate which has been erroneously placed on the roof of the castle, so that her train had to be sawn off (the fracture can be seen above the pinnacles of the tower).

with great naturalism, and the head is extraordinarily life-like. The docked tail has been bound, as it would have been in a real battle. The horse's magnificent harness is lavishly adorned with small bells hanging from lion masks and with two pendants with miniature reliefs of Christ as the Man of Sorrows and Our Lady on a crescent moon. The horse is bearing a twisted horn on its brow, transforming it symbolically into a unicorn. These were believed to be impossible for a man to capture, and their horns were said to remove the venom from poison, which was the dragon's most dangerous weapon.[21]

The symbolism in the horse's plumes has not previously been observed. One plume is blue, one yellow and half of the third is red, the rest white. Saint George's colours have to share one plume while the Swedish colours (blue and yellow) have been given a plume each.

The saint is attired in a faithful reproduction of a sumptuous suit of armour from the late-mediaeval period.[22] There is mention in the 16th century of his shield, but this has since disappeared. His helmet now lies at the front of the base plate. It has been hollowed out sufficiently to encompass Saint George's head. Instead, however, he is wearing a diadem of two ostrich feathers in his own colours, red and white. The helmet may originally have been carried by a hovering angel (hanging from the vault above) – similar devices were found abroad – which would be an allusion to the legend's assertion that Saint George received his armour and weapons from heaven.[23] This is also reflected in the gilt armour with its exaggeratedly opulent embellishment with precious stones and in the miniature relief in the centre of the back of the belt of Our Lady in a crescent moon. The saint's main adornment is his knight's chain, with the reliquary incorporated in its centre on his chest. Apart from such special features, however, the realistic detail suggests that both the horse and its harness and the saint's armour and weapons have been modelled on real examples which belonged to Sten Sture.

The Sture family crest on the horse and harness, where moreover it has been combined with Saint George's coat-of-arms, suggests that the portrayal of the knight has more than one meaning – personal and political symbolism in addition to the religious significance. Is the image of Saint George vanquishing the dragon also meant to show us Sten Sture defeating the Danish army at the battle of Brunkeberg? The statue of the knight has, admittedly, few of the individual characteristics of a portrait but reveals rather the idealised image of a youthful knight full of faith and vigour. But this matches completely the idealised chivalric image of himself that Sten Sture expressed in his words. When in a moment of anger he was accused by the Archbishop of having broken his promise he replied, "I

52. The pendant on the horse's right shoulder (left-hand illustration) portrays the half-length figure of Christ as the Man of Sorrows above a cloud. Note how the rays of sunshine and the drops of rain have been painted emerging from the cloud above Christ's halo.

53. The pendant on the horse's left shoulder (right-hand illustration) portrays Mary with the Infant Jesus wreathed in rays of sunshine. Both pendants are framed by precious stones and a fringe painted alternately in blue, red and gold, like the three tassels below.

54. The combat seen from the knight's left, which gives the best view of the horse. The iron strut under its stomach is a 20th century addition.

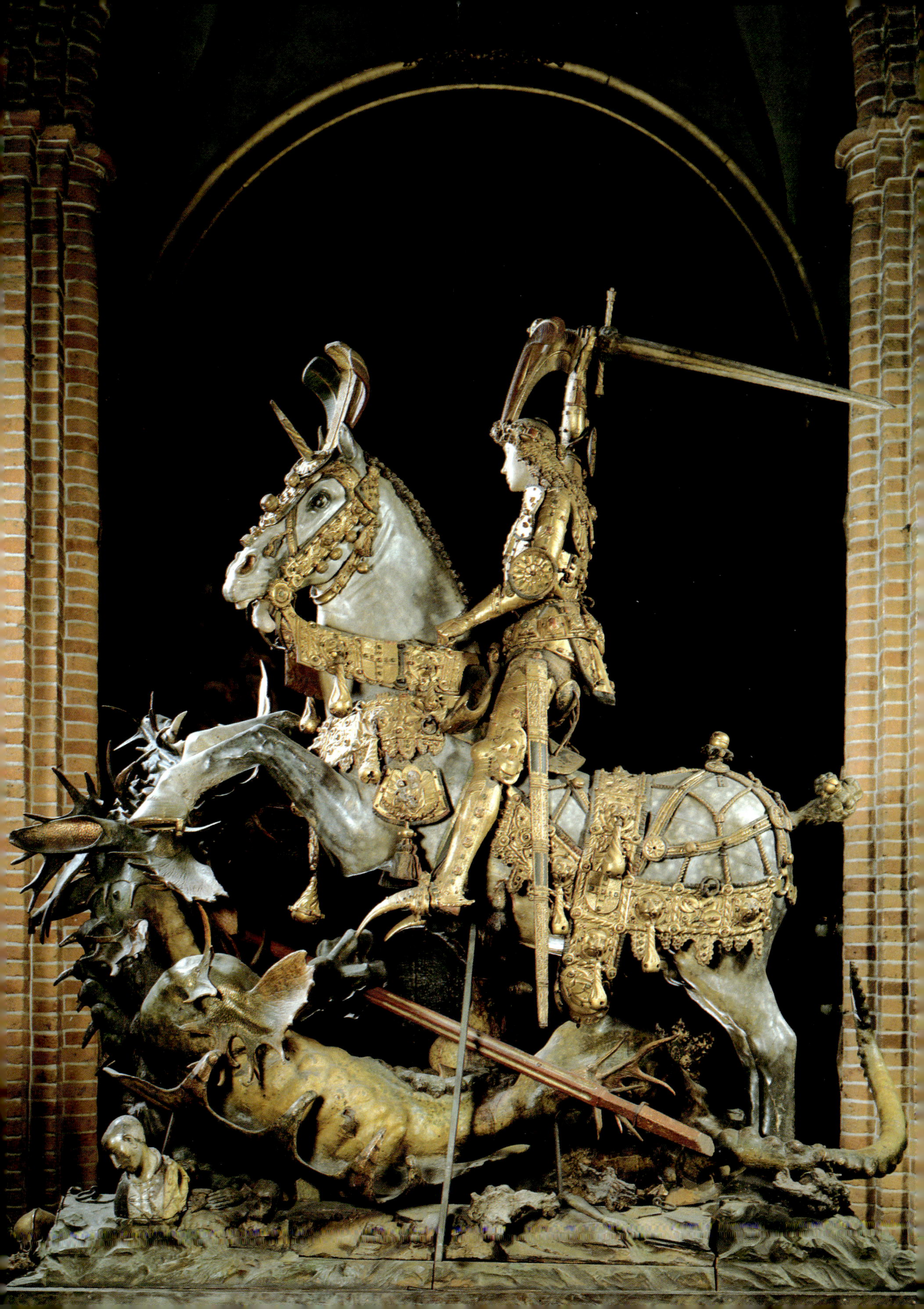

55-56. All that the knight is wearing on his head is a bejewelled diadem crowned with two ostrich feathers, red and white, George's colours. He has steel gauntlets and leather thongs fasten the plates of armour over the chain mail on his arms. There is a substantial hinge to enable his cuirass to be opened, which, like the projecting lance support, looks as if it is riveted below the arm to the exposed plate of the cuirass. Elsewhere, this is covered by a close-fitting golden tunic decorated with patterns of vegetation, fringes and a large cross of Saint George front and back. At the back the tunic finishes in a stiff tail. Both the cuirass and the tunic are lavishly decorated with rubies and emeralds in raised settings. Everything is reproduced realistically in wood which has been painted or gilt – even the sword and its sheath – while the high pommels of the saddle and the chains of the reins are made of metal.

57. The saint's helmet is placed at the front of the base plate, its visor lowered, with a plume of ostrich feathers. The riband in the colours of Saint George is made of parchment.

have up until this day, by the grace of God, borne my crest of water-lily leaves like a true Christian knight." And in the verse chronicle, chivalry is presented as characterising him:[24]

> Lord Sten, the Governor of the Realm
> Rode in dignity and probity
> A very model of true chivalry

Youthfulness also formed part of the idealised image of the knight. For that reason he is continually referred to as "the young Lord Sten" even when the chronicler is describing the events of the 1480s when he was over 40 and therefore in contemporary terms far from young. This ideal found consummate expression in the equestrian saint with its young, noble and comely features.[25]

This idealisation of chivalry had developed during the feudal period as the ideological underpinning of a militaristic social order and found expression in chivalric literature and art which was characterised by a congenial rigour and idealised shapes, as in the famous 13th century Bamberg Rider. During the 15th century, when knights in armour met their match in troops of peasants armed with new weapons like crossbows and canon, and when the feudal aristocracy had to yield to the new princely power of the emerging nation-states, paradoxically the chivalric forms and ideals were revived at their rulers' courts, now ensuring the loyalty of the magnates to the demands of their rulers. This was the transitional period that Sten Sture belonged to, although he was one of the first Swedish advocates of strong centralised power and outspoken *realpolitik*, he was able at the same time to describe himself as "a true Christian knight". These ambiguities endow the monument to his victory with unusual tension: it is both a personal memorial to a new and more purposeful type of ruler and the ultimate expression of the mediaeval concept of the Christian knight. Added to this is the fertile contrast of this high-flown idealism with the detailed realism in which it finds expression.

It is with methods like these that the artist has managed to make the dragon and the saint as convincing as the horse, which plays a key role in the group as a whole. The horse alone can be compared with real life and therefore in turn verify the realism of the group as a whole. And it is on the horse that the personal and national symbolism have been concentrated. As we have seen, on its loin it bears Sten Sture's water-lily leaf, on its harness his emblem is combined with that of Saint George, and the plumes are in the saint's colours and those of Sweden.[26] The horse thus branded with the Sture device probably depicts the horse Sten Sture rode at the battle of Brunkeberg and is in this case the first and also the greatest portrait of a horse in the history of Swedish art.

58. On his hips hangs the heavy belt with its large, bejewelled clasp and in the middle of the back a relief of Our Lady in a wreath of five roses. The belt around the waist of the tunic is made of real rope.

59. Leg-plate, armoured shoe, spur and stirrup give the illusion of being metal but are made of wood, while the stirrup-leather really is leather.

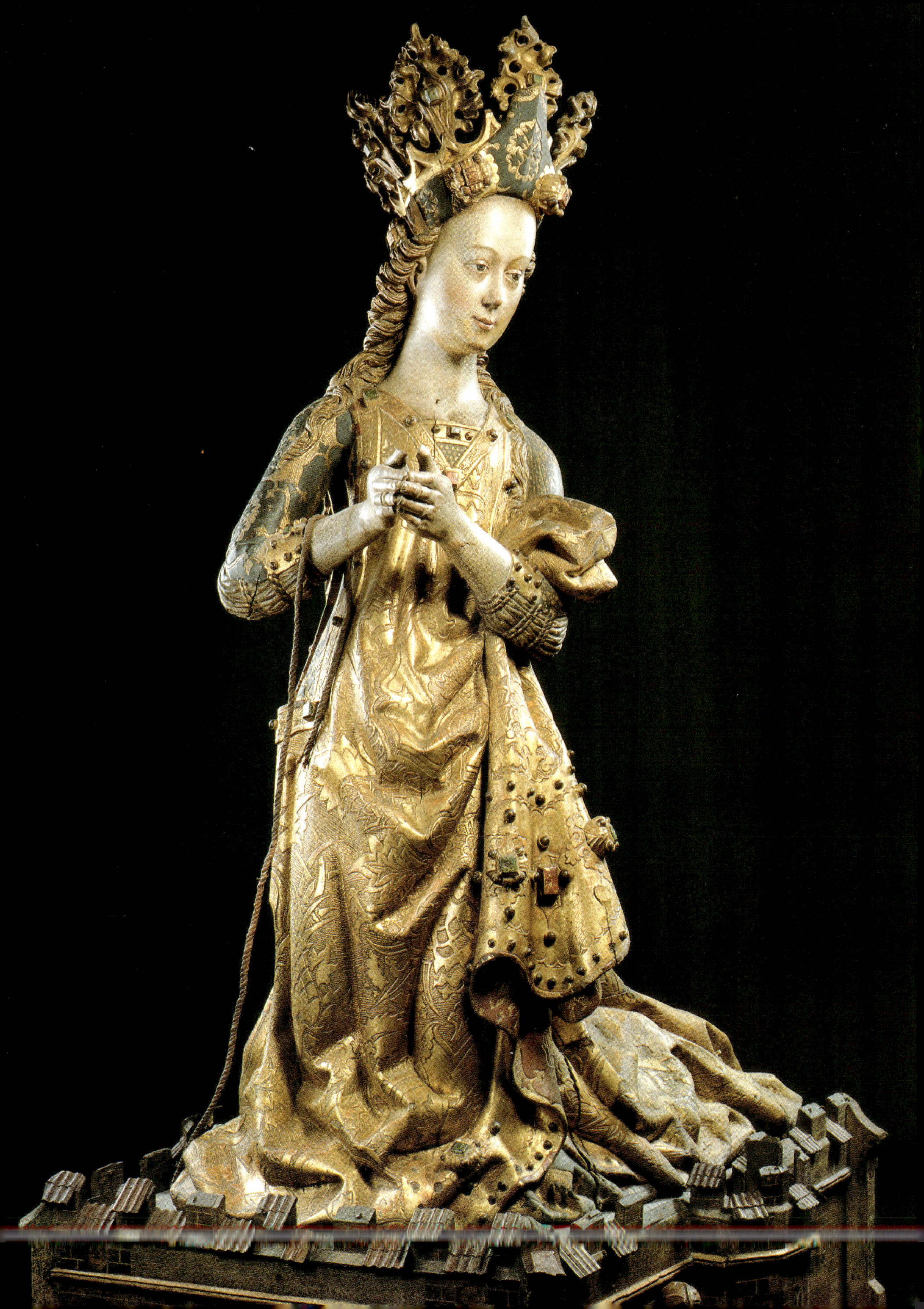

The knight, on the other hand, bears only the cross of Saint George on his tunic and chain and only the colours of Saint George figure in the plumes on his brow. And his noble, youthful face is of exactly the same type as in other statues of George, for instance Donatello's (compare illustrations 10A and 30). This can hardly therefore represent a covert portrait of Sten Sture. This of course would not prevent his contemporaries from seeing a likeness between "the young knight, Lord Sten", as he is presented in the chronicle, and the prototype of idealised chivalry in the sculpture.

What the heraldic signs are saying, therefore, is that at the fateful moment Saint George was riding Sten Sture's horse with the Swedish colours to vanquish a dreadful enemy. This means that there is no difficulty in interpreting the roles of the remaining figures in the group on the basis of the personal and national symbolism so clearly revealed by the horse.

The princess, saved by Saint George's combat from being devoured by the dragon, stands for Sweden in Sten Sture's symbolic system, which he saved at the Battle of Brunkeberg from being swallowed up by the union with Denmark. It has also been assumed that she could represent his wife, Ingeborg Tott. But no portrait has been preserved of either of the founders to which the knight or the princess could be compared. The figure also lacks the relevant coat-of-arms and colours (the Tott family's red is missing). One could possibly discern certain personalised traits in the upturned nose and the broad forehead, but even there idealisation has the upper hand. Nor, as far as Sten Sture's wife is concerned, who he referred to in one of his more intimate letters as "beloved companion", do we have any literary idealisation of her appearance to compare with.[27]

One of the scales on the dragon's back has the form of a standard late-Gothic escutcheon. It bears no markings, however, but is painted in the same green colour as the rest of the dragon. It has been assumed that it was intended to paint the Danish flag or the three leopards of the Danish national emblem to drive home the obvious political symbolism of the dragon, but that this idea was finally abandoned in view of the fact that political circumstances could alter and it could then appear to be too provocative. If so, this was well-considered as only eight years after the inauguration of the national monument, Sten Sture was obliged to relinquish his position as Governor of the Realm and witness the coronation of Hans of Denmark as the Union King in the City Church (cf. page 48). It was just as well that it was not made too obvious to the new monarch that the dragon was meant to depict his father and his Danish army, vanquished by Saint George – Sten Sture.[28]

Despite the political symbolism that the Saint George group more or less clearly expressed, it must not be forgotten that its primary significance was religious. It was primarily a cult image portraying the victory of

60-61. The princess kneeling, her hands clasped in prayer and the train of her dress gathered in the fold of one arm. An imposing crown surmounts an abundant head of hair. The rows of locks covering her back have been sculpted from a plank of wood placed there specially. The hair was once a dull gold, but it has proved impossible to restore the original colour fully.

62-63. All that remained of the original paintwork on the face of Saint George were a few patches around the mouth and chin. The rest of the face was repainted during restoration in the 20th century with a pointillism which distinguishes these surfaces from the smoother and glossier original. The princess's face on the other hand still has the relatively well preserved and well restored original polychromy. This was missing only on the lower left section of the face, where during the 20th century new gesso (see page 116) has been added and painted over. A necklace, which is now lost, was attached by the nail that can be seen above the base of the throat. Contemporary fashion dictated that women should wear their hair high off the forehead.

the saint over evil. And despite its function as a monument to a victory or a funeral memorial, it must not be forgotten that what the two founders established was primarily an altar, endowed according to the custom of the time and to the words of the foundation document for the sake of their salvation.

Page 66:
64. The main group seen from the front. Note the point of the lance which is protruding from the dragon's throat to the right, and that one of the scales on its back has the form of a late-gothic shield. Immediately below it can be seen the helmet, to the right the bust of the dead man and to the left a shoulderblade.

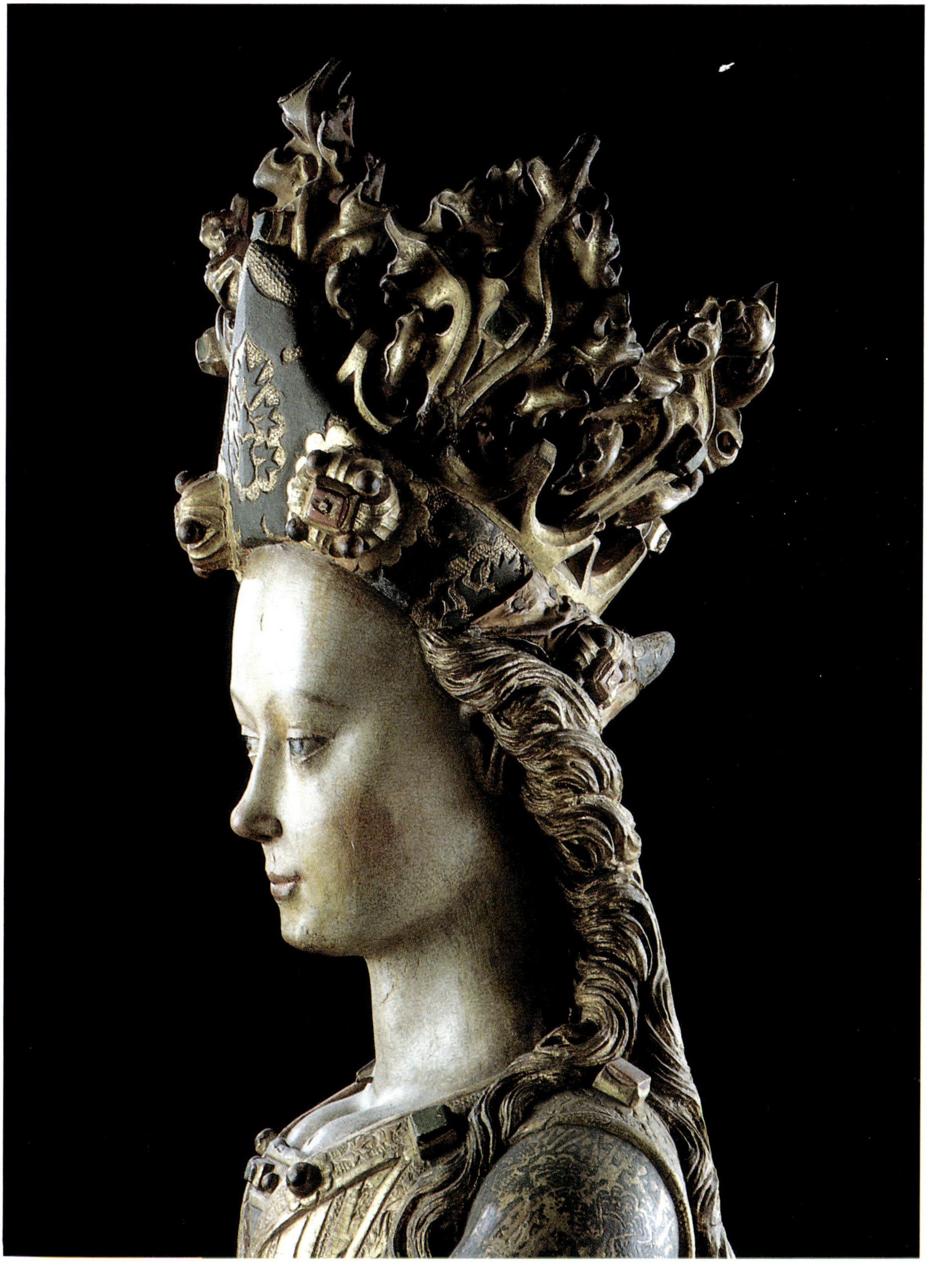

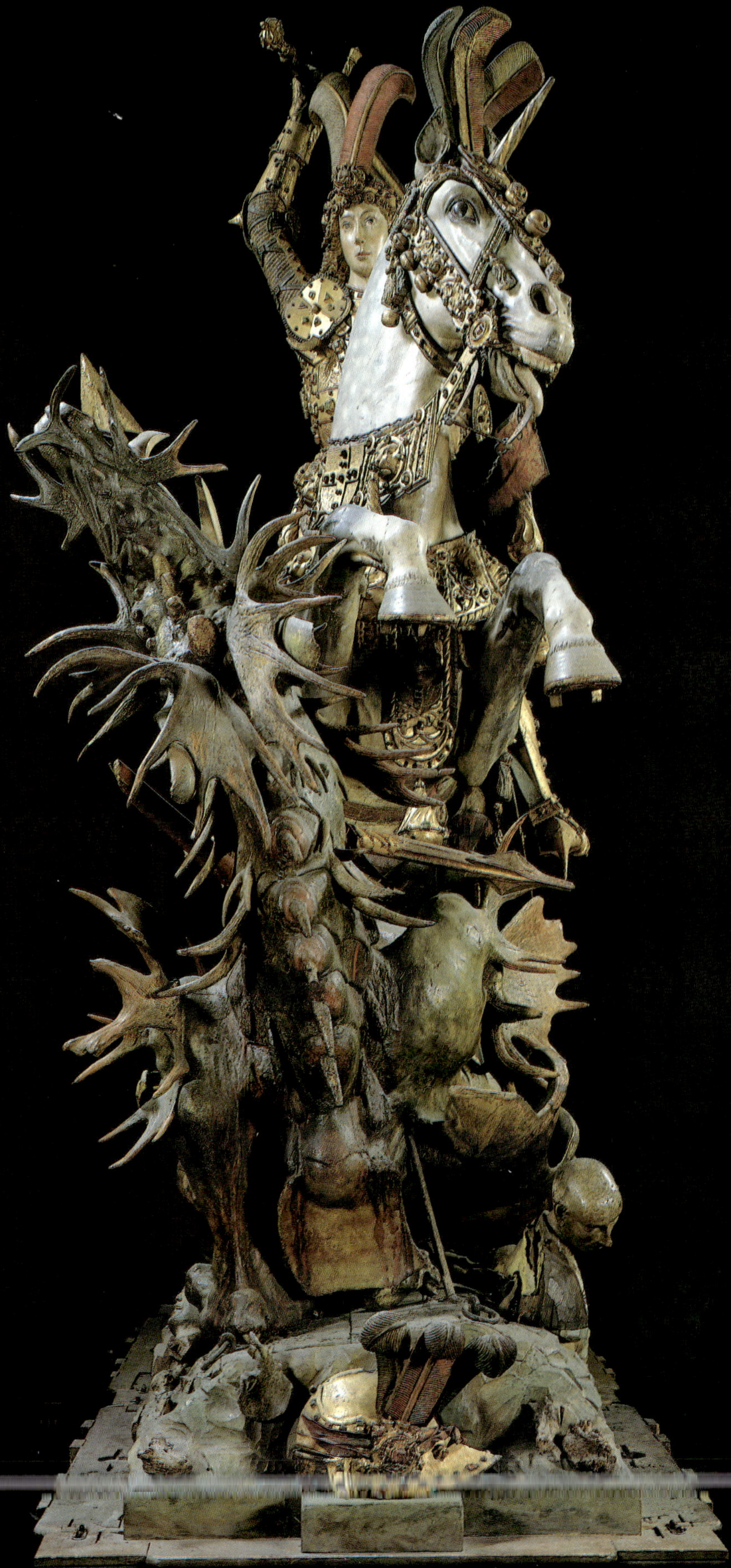

The City of Silene

The coats-of-arms of Lord Sten and his wife, Ingeborg, can be found not only on the plinth of the main group. They are also painted on a smaller scale on both the front and back of the castle. One purpose was to ensure that the identity of the founders of this enormous altar should be visible on each element of the composition and from every direction. But at the same time it could also have been a means of recalling political events.

In 1471, the city threatened by the dragon in the legend could stand for Stockholm, which was being besieged by the Danes. At that time the Swedish capital was and was to remain loyal to Sten Sture, and in addition its castle, Three Crowns, was one of the castles whose keys had been passed on to Sten Sture by Karl Knutsson on his death-bed. In the real battle, therefore, the city had belonged to him and the Sture bearings on the castle could therefore have had the twofold function of marking this fact as well as his role in the endowment.

Under the crenellation an additional ten coats-of-arms were painted, distributed somewhat irregularly between the four walls. It is possible that one or two more once existed but have since been erased. These coats-of-arms are smaller than those of Sten Sture and Ingeborg Tott and represent those who, in addition to the main founders, were involved in providing funds for the great undertaking. The document from 1492 already cited did, after all, state that Sten Sture "with his subordinates" had paid for the Saint George group. The coats-of-arms that can now be identified

65. The city gate of Silene on the back of the castle. Above the gate, Sten Sture's coat-of-arms has been painted at one end of the arch and directly above it, beneath the crenellation, the coat of arms of one of his co-founders, whereas the corresponding coat-of-arms of his wife on the other side of the arch no longer remains. Inside the arch, the city gate has been painted with its portcullis raised.

66. One of the sides of the castle – the one on the left seen from the Princess's point of view – with the foremost of the two original relief carvings in place. The castle is 49 inches long, 46 inches broad, and 31 inches in height (126 x 116 x 80 cm.)

with some degree of certainty also turn out to belong to subordinates of Sten Sture, among them many of those in command at the Battle of Brunkeberg. More detailed information about the coats-of-arms can be found in the illustration on page 72, where they are all depicted.

The castle represents the city or fortress of Silene, its walls built of brick painted in varying shades of reddish brown, with white stones inlaid in their towers and corners. The castle has buttresses at the corners and is surmounted by a platform surrounded by pinnacles. An arched opening at the front of the castle provides a view of the town within, where a relief carving depicts the work of building a church, a detail we shall soon return to. The opposite wall has a corresponding vaulted niche in which the city gate has been painted.[29] This wall has been finished with simpler materials, which suggests that originally it formed the back of the statue with a less prominent placing, similar to the position it has today. The sides of the castle are furnished with projecting pentagonal towers with windows painted on them, and in front of them there is a lower, outer wall, also crenellated.

On each side of these towers there used to be four reliefs placed in the space between the inner and the outer walls. Two of these reliefs were preserved until well into this century, but part of one of them has now

67. The dragon approaching Saint George and the princess. This is the relief that can still be seen on the left wall of the castle (see illustration 66). The dragon's muzzle is a modern reconstruction.

68—69. Saint George escorting the princess who is using her belt to lead the defeated dragon into the city. This relief was still intact in a photograph taken in the 1930s. Later, half was stolen, and the remainder then removed (see illustration 31) although it was later replaced at the front of the right-hand wall of the castle in 1988.

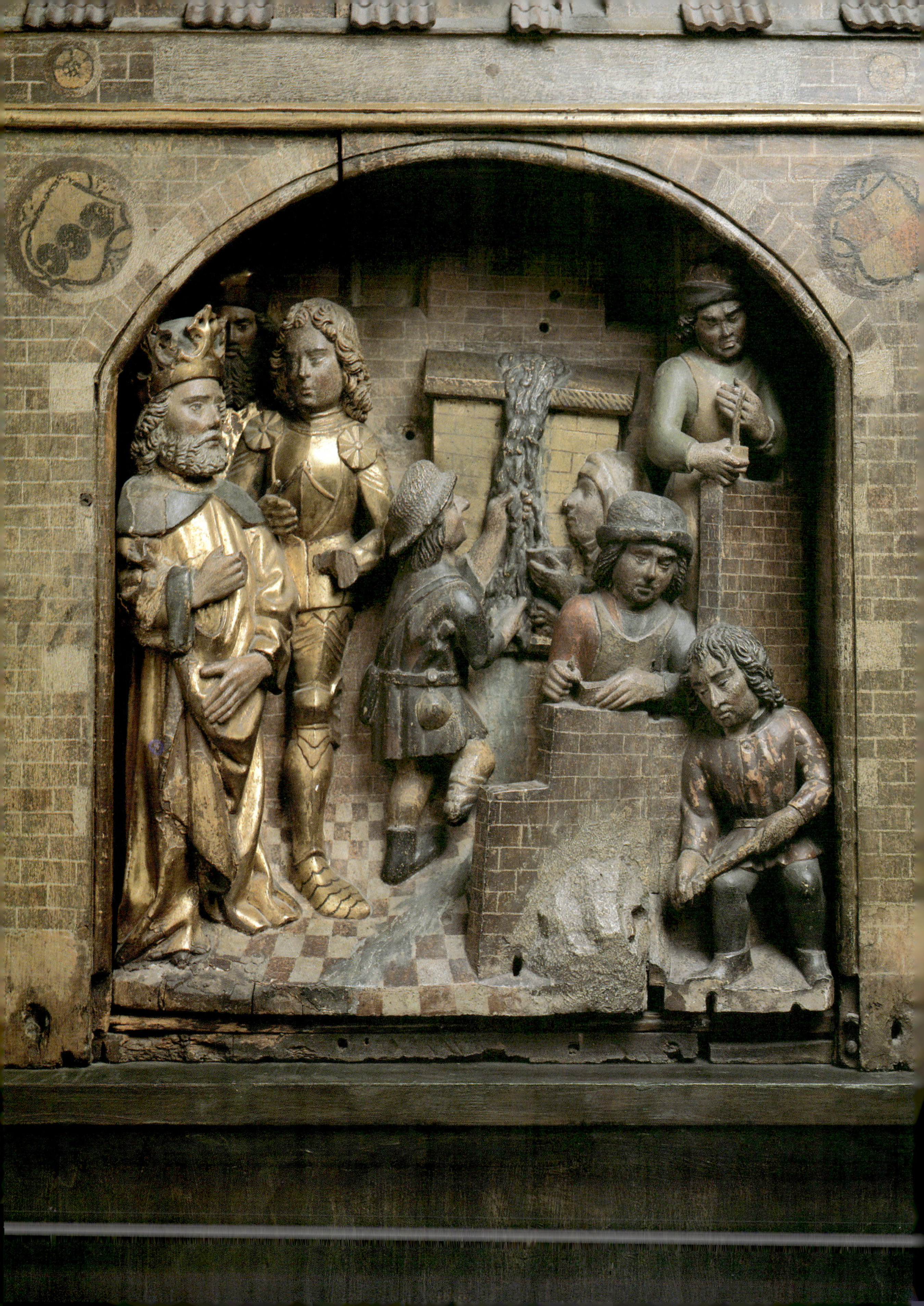

70. Saint George and the King of Silene inspecting the workers who have already started building a church. Two lepers are seeking a cure for their illness in the spring which miraculously gushes from its altar. A relief on the front of the castle. The coats-of-arms of Sten Sture and Ingeborg Tott are positioned on each side of the arch.

disappeared. One of these reliefs, which in execution can almost be likened to small free-standing sculptures, depicts the dragon approaching Saint George and the princess. The saint is on horse-back, and she is standing close to him urging him to flee, which he has no intention of doing, intending on the contrary to stay and defend her. "While they spoke thus, the dragon raised its head from the lake and appeared." It is this point in the legend that the surviving relief depicts.

The other relief showed Saint George after his victory, escorting the princess on horseback, as she is leading the dragon, secured by her belt, into the city (only the princess and rear half of the dragon have survived).

In both these reliefs the figures are depicted from the knees up, as their lower extremities are concealed by the wall and the pinnacles on the sides of the castle. Saint George is not only wearing his helmet, but also has a throat protector projecting from his suit of armour, a detail not found in the large sculpture. These images too are painted realistically.

The somewhat larger relief (almost 24 inches – about 60 cm.– in height) on the front of the castle reveals a very realistically carved and painted depiction of the building of a church which started in the hitherto pagan Silene after Saint George's victory over the dragon. On the extreme left is the founder of the church, the King of Silene, a member of his council behind him, conferring with Saint George, who has inspired the building. Work has already reached the stage where the walls of the chancel can support the lower sections of the windows, and at its centre the altar is already in place. A miraculous spring gushes from the altar, in which two lepers are seeking a cure. Bottom right, a mortar mixer is stirring mortar on the ground, and immediately above him can be seen a bricklayer adding a row of bricks to the wall. At the top there is another bricklayer, presumably the foreman, using a plummet to check that the wall is straight. He almost completely conceals a fourth builder, standing in the shadow of the arch, emptying the contents of what appears to be a sack into a container standing on the coping of the wall. The sack is almost certainly a skin from which he is pouring water over mortar in the barrel.[30]

The bricklayer has a round cap and a jacket "à la demipartie", i.e. with different colours on each half of the body, like the one worn by the master mason Tord, Alderman of the Stockholm Guild of Masons, in a contemporary picture. This can be found in the Guild's oldest charter, which dates from 1487 – two years before the consecration of the Saint George group in the City Church. At that time it had undergone extensive modernisation, involving the installation of new, decorated stellar vaulting in much of the building. Tord had been one of the men in charge of this work, together with another master mason called Jens. The relief on the castle depicting the building of the church inspired by Saint George, almost certainly, reminded its contemporaries not only of the legend but also of the renovation of the City Church in the 1480s under the leadership of master masons Tord and Jens. The realism of the portrayal would have made such an association inevitable.[31]

This scene, which depicts the consequences of the combat with the dragon in the form of the erection of a church and the miraculous spring, presents the martial saint in another of his roles – as the patron saint of lepers.

The princess's parents, who according to the legend witnessed the combat to decide the fate of their daughter from their city or fortress, should originally have been placed as statuettes on the roof of the castle. The statuette of a king that would in all respects fit in well in this position now forms part of the national collection at Gripsholm. It is the well-known effigy of Karl Knutsson Bonde. This will be dealt with in more detail in a subsequent chapter on Bernt Notke (see the illustrations and text on page 126 ff.).

71–80. The small coats-of-arms on the castle belong to some of Sten Sture's subordinates who helped to pay for the Saint George group. These coats-of-arms are just over an inch (3 cm) high, while those of the principal founders are 3 inches (9 cm). According to a study made by Jan Raneke (a specialist in heraldry) most of them can be identified with more or less certainty and belong to
72. Laurens Axelsson (Tott)
75. Nils Bosson Sture
    (Natt och Dag)
76. Arvid Birgersson (Trolle)
78. Nils Bosson (Grip)
79. Fader Ulfsson or his son Bengt
    (Sparre av Hjulsta/Ängsö)
80. Peder Slatte.

71

72

73

74

75

76

77

78

79

80

The Martyrdom of Saint George on the Reliefs on the Plinth

The plinth of the main statue is a modern reconstruction composed of mediaeval fragments, which, after long and careful consideration, were combined with each other between 1914 – 1932, supplemented by newly constructed sections. Nearly all of the mediaeval sections, three substantial screens with their carved reliefs that had formed part of the walls of the chantry and the great carved coats-of-arms on each end had been found in the City Church in the early years of this century. For centuries they had been fastened to the walls but during the neo-Classical period they had been painted over with several coats of greyish-white paint to resemble marble, and it was no longer known what the reliefs were meant to represent. In 1901, however, it was discovered that all six reliefs (each

81. Saint George receives his cross and armour from the hands of angels. Detail from the first plinth relief.

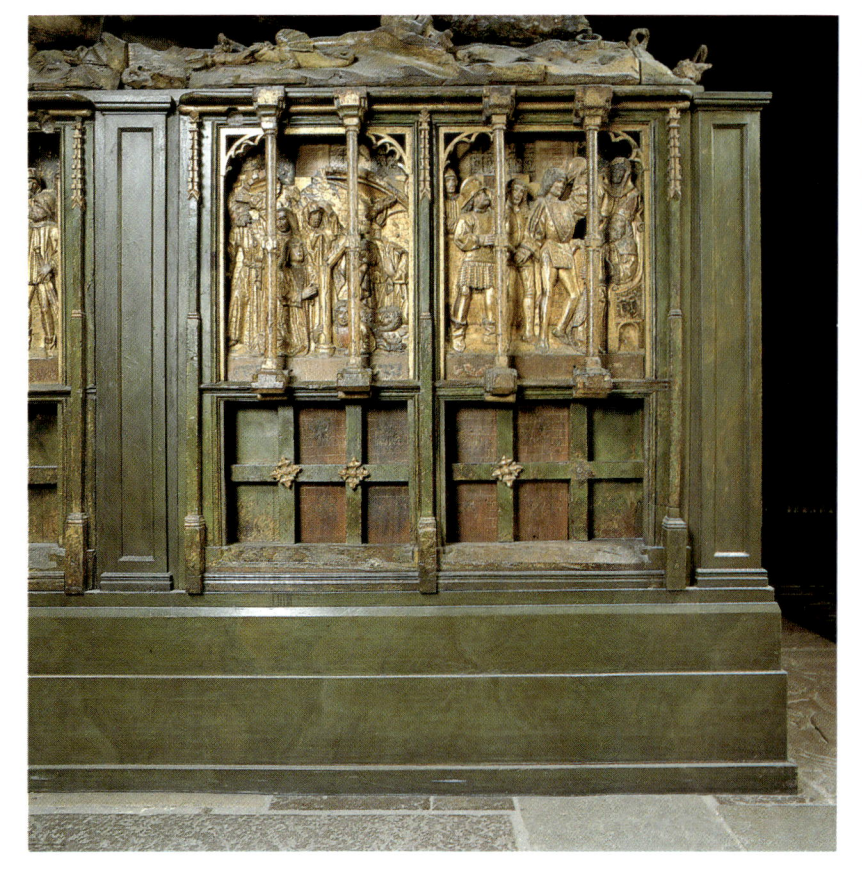

82. A screen – on the front part of the right hand side from the knight's point of view – with its two reliefs, each behind two small columns, resting on a grid that was closed up during the mediaeval period. The base and the pillars at each side are recent additions.

screen comprised two) depicted scenes connected with the martyrdom of Saint George. When the original colours had been revealed, it could also be seen how exquisitely the reliefs had been carved and painted. It also became possible to see that the screens had been painted on the reverse side as well – in a uniform green colour with a stencilled pattern of golden flowers and stars. These screens were far too solidly constructed to have been intended for the normal type of reredos in honour of a saint. Instead what had been discovered obviously formed important elements of the structure that had supported the equestrian statue.[32]

Each screen measures just over one and a half metres in height and breadth and two together more or less fill the length of the base-plate under Saint George and the dragon. The northern side of the plinth consists of two of these screens and three recently constructed pillars, one in each corner and one in the centre between the two screens, resting on a deep base running the length of the plinth which is also of recent construction. The corresponding parts of the southern side are equally recent, but here as well the eastern screen is a modern reconstruction, as only two insignificant fragments of the original remain. The screen itself was easy to copy from those that had been preserved. But where were its two re-

83. The interior of one of the screens. A frame strewn with stars surrounds the backs of the reliefs with their patterns of flowers. The darker square in the top right-hand corner shows their condition before restoration. The planks above and below were nailed up during the Middle Ages to close up the original apertures.

liefs to come from? It turned out, however, to be possible to find two late-Gothic reliefs with suitable motifs from the martyrdom of Saint George that matched those of the monument in both dimensions and style and could therefore be assumed to have belonged to it originally. Each end of the plinth was embellished with the coats-of-arms of the founders (about 49 inches high by 27 inches broad – 123 x 70 cm), which, as already mentioned, were still to be found in the City church.[33]

The eight reliefs on the plinth of the main statue, therefore, all point to the original identification of the saint as a major martyr. In this way, the images on the multi-faceted altar to Saint George in the City Church satisfied the many different aspects and cults associated with the saint. But it was the chivalrous element alone that was emblazoned on a monumental scale to fit in with the special purposes for which this foundation had been endowed. Five of the eight reliefs on the plinth of the main statue take their motifs from the description of Saint George's martyrdom in *Legenda aurea*. Three of the episodes depicted, however, cannot be found in that account. They can be read instead in the German version of the George legend that was most widely known at the time when the monument was created. This version was widespread in Germany during the last three decades of 15th century, both in manuscripts and in a number of printed editions, among them two from publishers in Lübeck. It lacks, on the other hand, a couple of the episodes portrayed on the plinth that come from *Legenda aurea*. It is this text, therefore, which had then long been available in both German and Swedish translations, which seems to have been the main source for the reliefs, apparently supplemented by material from a late-mediaeval German version – unless a now unknown version of the legend with all of these episodes was available when the reliefs were composed. In the following description, the text on which each relief is based will be referred to; in addition the whole of the Saint George text from *Legenda aurea* is printed in the documentation at the end of this volume (page 176–182).[34]

In the oldest Greek legend, Saint George's adversary and executioner was the ahistorical King of Persia, Dacianus. In the Byzantine Empire this was corrected and Dacianus became instead a Roman Governor during the reign of Diocletian , who instigated the most extensive persecution of the Christians in 303, the year in which Saint George is said to have lost

84. The current placing of the reliefs on the plinth.

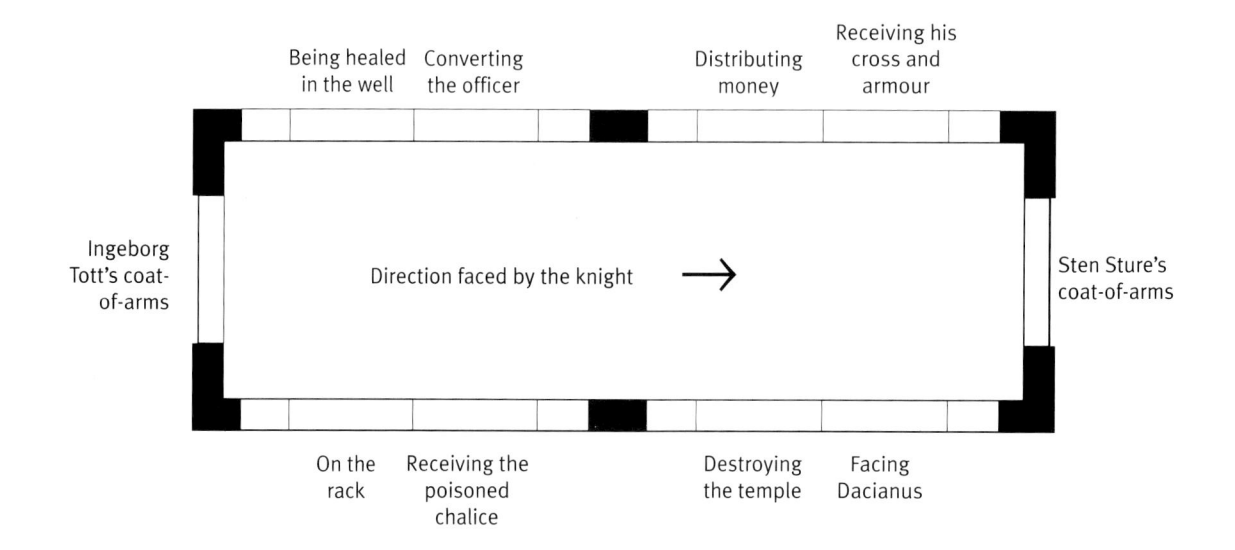

his life. In the series of reliefs, Dacianus is furnished with what in the late Middle Ages were seen to be the insignia of Roman Imperial authority, so that he looks like Caesar himself, even though he is only intended to represent one of his Governors.

Most of the figures on the reliefs have had their noses cut off and some have had their eyes damaged. This probably took place during one of the rare periods of iconoclasm during the relatively peaceful Swedish Reformation. Both Peder Swart and Messenius have described how such destruction was carried out in Stockholm in the 1520s. Messenius writes[35]

– The furious mob rage through the streets
fighting to bring the idols down
their screams and shouts drown out the sound
of axes hewing at their plinths
and ears and noses crudely severed –

85. The presumed placing of the reliefs on the plinth (if two that have since disappeared can be incorporated into a hypothetical reconstruction of the chantry in the plinth).

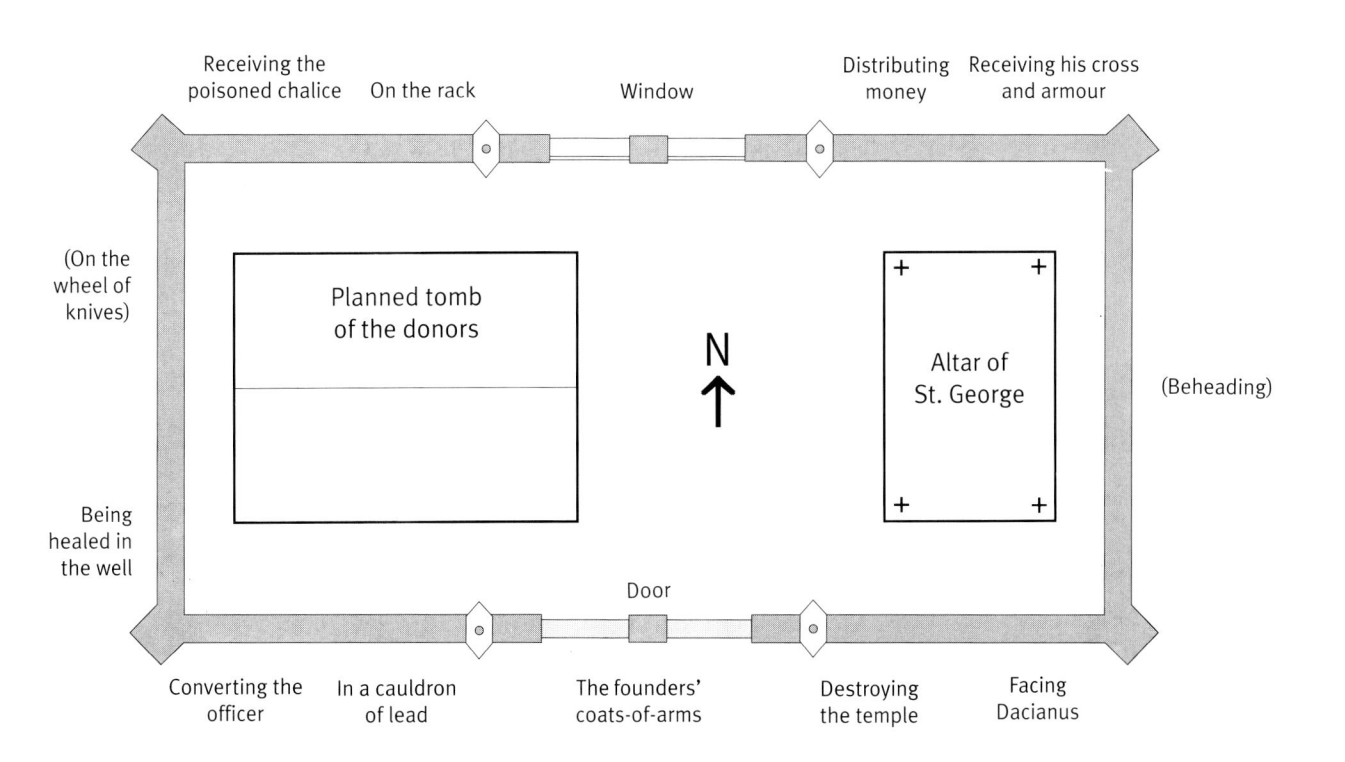

The iconoclasts were probably driven by the age-old belief that the simplest way of "killing" an image, of depriving it of the breath of life, was to destroy its nose. This can be compared with the destruction of Classical statues by the early Christians, which have often had their noses destroyed even if they are otherwise well preserved. The reliefs on the plinth, therefore, show traces of this kind of systematic vandalism. The noses of the princess and the knight, however, are undamaged – they were obviously too high to reach, whereas the reliefs on the plinth were easily accessible.[36]

Originally, below each relief a text in low German had been painted which described the content of the motif above. This we know, because one of these texts (the one below the last relief but one) was recorded by the Royal Antiquarian Johan Peringskiöld at the end of the 17th century, before it was obliterated entirely by later coats of paint. It has proved impossible to uncover them, but as has been seen above, the texts of the legend have enabled identification of the motifs of the reliefs.[37]

Above the reliefs there is a crenellated wall, separated from the screen by a horizontal aperture which originally admitted light and air to the burial chapel in the plinth. During the Middle Ages, and probably as a result of its founder's decision to be buried elsewhere, these apertures were obstructed with planks of wood, and on them windows and intervening sections of wall have been painted to provide an appropriate background above each relief. At the same time, the grids of solid timber below the reliefs, through which it was possible to view the interior illuminated by the light entering above, were filled in. The planks of wood inserted behind the grid also have their outer surfaces painted to resemble brickwork. These are, however – like the planks nailed in place above the reliefs – unpainted on the inner side, unlike the rest of the interior of the plinth which is painted green with a pattern of gold (see also illustration 83).[38]

In front of each relief there are two small wooden columns, which have profiled bosses in the centre and elaborately faceted bases and capitals. These protective columns, which also obscure the reliefs, were removed temporarily while the photographs illustrating this book were being taken.

The reliefs should be viewed from left to right, beginning with the four on the southern side and then the four northern ones (in other words they should be viewed anti-clockwise, starting from the south-west side). If, however, this viewing is to correspond with the legend, in one's imagination the north-eastern screen with its two reliefs should change places with the two reliefs on the recently constructed south-eastern screen. This order is the one that will be followed here, while at the same time pointing out where exactly on the plinth each relief can be found today.[39]

The narrative of Saint George's martyrdom recounted by the reliefs that still exist lacks certain important episodes. If these were included, which one must assume they were, their place would have been at each end of the plinth, where the coats-of-arms are today. Instead one could envisage the coats-of-arms either on or above the doors in the middle of each wall. Precisely which motif would then have been placed where on the plinth is indicated in more detail in the following description and is also shown in the diagram 85.

Finally, it must be pointed out that we do not know with complete certainty how the different items in the Saint George group were originally arranged or where in the church the work was sited.

The scholarly debate on these two closely linked topics and the new arguments that I wish to adduce are described more closely in the documentation at the end of this volume. What follows is merely a brief summary of my conclusions.

Several written sources and a number of circumstances suggest that the monument stood in the centre of the church until 1528, when Olaus Petri had the whole group moved to a side entrance because it "takes too much room in the church". It most probably stood in the chancel arch, i.e. the broad arch at the northern end of which the pulpit stands today. There a triumphal crucifix was probably suspended over Saint George and the dragon, who were placed on a high plinth which, in all probability, was composed at least partially of the screens with their reliefs that have been preserved (see illustration 139). These, with apertures above and below, originally formed the walls which surrounded the altar of Saint George and the burial places of the founders to form a chantry abutting on to the chancel screen.

The original extent, shape and the number of reliefs cannot therefore be determined accurately. In the more detailed presentation of the six preserved and two added reliefs that follows, we shall, however, assume that it looked very much like the plinth does today.[40]

PLINTH RELIEF I
Saint George receiving weapons from the angels

The first relief (to the extreme left of the southern side of the plinth) depicts a version of the legend current in Germany and Sweden in the later Middle Ages, which contains the following episode:[41]

When Saint George had determined to seek martyrdom and eternal life, he took farewell of his brothers and told them that at a moment of extreme peril during a battle with the heathen an angel had appeared to him and given him a white banner on which a red cross was emblazoned and promised him that in this sign he would gain victory. So it turned out, and he was so successful that only the commander of the opposing army was able to flee from the battlefield.

At the extreme left of the relief we see Saint George's horse, standing still, its saddle empty, its reins held by his squire, still mounted on his own horse. Behind him two men can be seen riding away. They are Saint George's two brothers – the one with the long beard probably Theodor, and behind him, now headless, Demetrius. What Saint George has told them is depicted in the relief's central scene, where the dismounted knight is kneeling, his hat reverently placed on the ground, his hands clasped in prayer. From a descending angel he is receiving a lance and a shield with a red cross on it, while another angel has already landed with his helmet.

In comparison with the narrative of the legend, the scene has been embellished with a second angel, and the two emissaries of heaven are giving the saint weapons in addition to the red cross as a sign of victory, here on a shield rather than a banner. These additions may have been the concrete products of the artist's imagination, perhaps influenced by the enactment in mystery plays of the legend of the saint and the features added there – in this case relating to the equipment of a knight. The helmet here is of a different type from the one worn by Saint George in the reliefs on the castle or the one lying on the base-plate of the main group. Here, too, his horse is more simply harnessed and he is not himself in knight's armour.

The weapons which the angels are bringing play no role in the coming martyrdom. Saint George's description to his brothers prior to the martyrdom of how he had previously been given a cross as a sign of victory against the heathen has only symbolic content at this stage of the legend and the series of reliefs. It is a way of manifesting the heavenly aid which will assist Saint George to gain martyrdom and eternal life. Christ attained this through his sufferings on the cross, and now it becomes a sign that George also is to triumph in his long suffering. This meaning becomes particularly clear in a 15th century Swedish manuscript in which the angel proffers the banner with its cross to the saint immediately before his final execution. In a number of German manuscripts and printed editions, as in the series of reliefs, this episode marks the beginning of the unusually prolonged martyrdom.

86

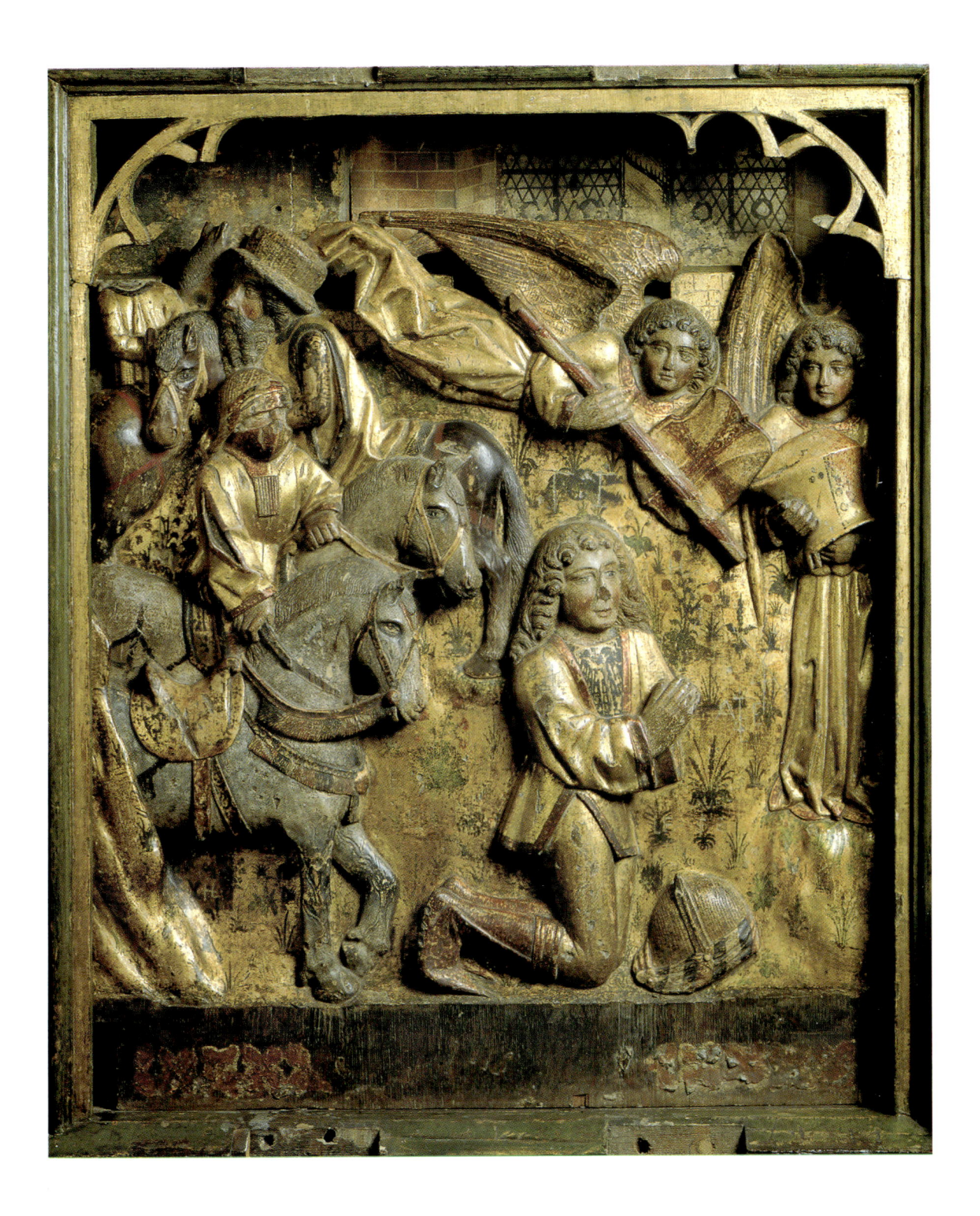

PLINTH RELIEF 11
Saint George giving away his possessions to the poor

The second relief is in the same screen as the previous one (and is therefore the second from the left on the southern side of the plinth). It depicts the account in *Legenda aurea* of the beginning of the martyrdom. When Saint George saw the extent of the persecution of the Christians that Dacianus had started, with 17,000 executions and numerous apostasies "deep was his sorrow and he gave away all that he owned". He appeared before the people and proclaimed his faith as a Christian.

In this relief Saint George appears in the same costume as in the previous one, but he has fastened his short jacket with a braid over his chest and has of course removed his riding boots. The possessions he is in the process of giving away are represented as a well-filled sack in his right hand and a pile of coins, of which some are scattered across the table. The once silver but now black pile shows numerous traces of the impressions of real coins.[42] These have added to the illusion of reality in the same way as the use of different materials from the real world that will be described later. With his left hand, Saint George is handing a coin to an old man who is limping up to the table supported by a crutch and receiving the alms with gratitude. He has a travelling hat slung on his back and a large purse hanging from his belt. Behind, an old woman is standing, perhaps his wife, as she has a matron's veil over her hair, and is smiling with pleasure at this overwhelming generosity.

This seems to be attracting a multitude of people judging from the last person arriving, who can be seen above the crest of the hills, much reduced in size because of the distance.

A contrast to the poor people in the right foreground is provided by the four eminent men surrounding the saint, who are portrayed on a larger scale, with better clothes and faces not marked by hardship and straitened circumstances. They witness how the saint is giving away his possessions and proclaiming his Christian faith to all. The man on the extreme left is pointing at him and wears a tall, pleated hat, which, like his collar, is decorated with letters of the alphabet – ERVX-EVC and WHAO – meaningless, as far as is known, but used purely for decorative purposes, as letters often were by artists at that time. Like his neighbour, whose hat has a wide turned-up brim, his head is cocked a little to one side in unconscious expression of the impact of this remarkable event, enabling the artist to endow the image with rhythm. The next man has fastened his gown at the throat and drawn the hood over his head, while the fourth, in a richly patterned costume with a broad collar of expensive fur is bare-headed. This openness, together with his noble features, suggests that he is a Christian, while the other three are probably pagans keeping their distance from what is happening. This is true, at any rate, of the man on the extreme left, who later reappears as the saint's antagonist.

87

PLINTH RELIEF III
Saint George on the rack

What, according to the account in *Legenda aurea,* is the next scene is depicted on the extreme left of the northern side of the plinth. The saint declared in front of the enraged Dacianus that "I have given up all that I own in order to serve the God of heaven more freely. But when the Governor could not overcome him, he gave orders that Saint George should be placed on the rack and that his body should be torn apart, piece by piece … and he ordered that salt should be strewn in his wounds."

Like the other reliefs, this is also a study of brutal violence executed with great realism. This is true both of the portrayal of the victim's body with its veins and sinews and of the executioners with their varying and in some cases complex expression of feelings.

The relief shows how Saint George is secured to the rack, a plank placed on two trestles. Behind it, in the middle there is a man with a broad knife cutting bloody slits all over the victim's body and limbs. Another is holding up a box of salt, and a third executioner is rubbing salt on to the victim's legs. Under the rack a small pig is licking up the blood dripping to the ground. To the extreme left, the governor can be seen in splendid clothes with fur trimmings on his hat, collar and sleeves. One hand holds a sceptre, the other is raised in command, in front of a courtier, who, with a glance at his ruler, is pointing at the face of the saint, which is remarkably unmoved by this torture, but seems rather to be smiling.

It may seem surprising that in the middle of this dreadful torture Saint George does not display an agonised but a smiling face. It would be anachronistic to interpret this in today's psychological terms as an expression of masochism. This is the smile that Gothic sculptors had begun two centuries earlier to portray on martyrs. It is intended to signify that thanks to their martyrdom they were able to go directly to eternal bliss, which was seen as a state of unceasing joy.

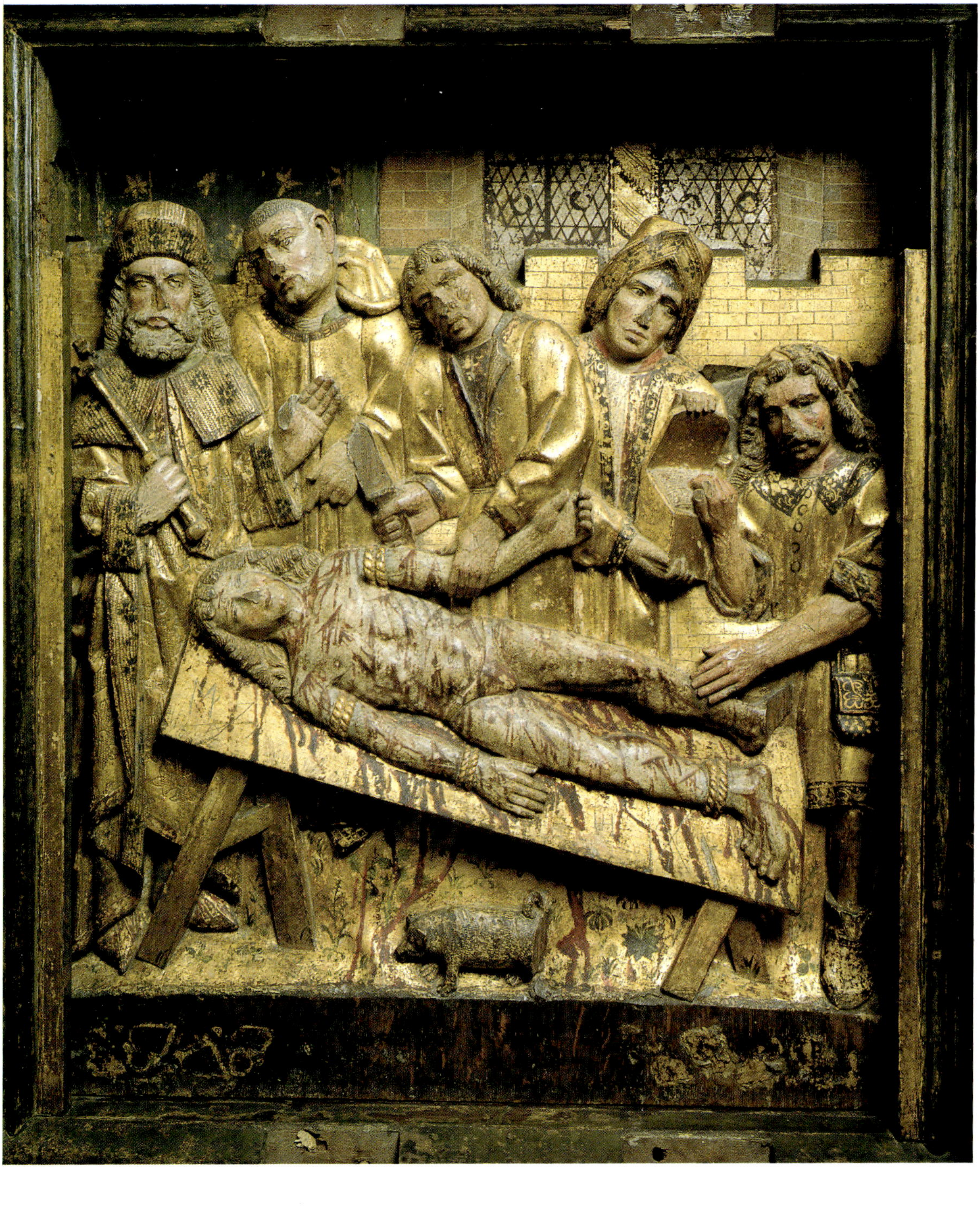

PLINTH RELIEF IV
Saint George receives the poisoned chalice

This relief is placed in the same screen as the previous one (and is therefore the second from the left on the northern side) and depicts the episode that follows in *Legenda aurea's* narrative. In it, Dacianus, seeing that he could not torment Saint George into submission, summoned a sorcerer (the Latin term is *magus,* which also means "wise man" and is the term used in the Vulgate about the three wise men who followed the star to Bethlehem). "When he had called upon his gods, he mixed wine with poison and gave it to Saint George to drink. This man of God made the sign of the cross and emptied the chalice unharmed." When the addition of a stronger poison had no effect, the sorcerer threw himself at Saint George's feet, sought his forgiveness and became a Christian, but was beheaded immediately.

In the relief, the sorcerer is portrayed as a man of authority in the clothes of a scholar. Both his costume and his face closely resemble those of the man on the extreme left in the preceding relief watching Saint George give away his possessions, so this is probably meant to be the same person. Now the sorcerer is standing using a rod to mix poison and wine in the chalice in his hand. Next to him stands Saint George, now dressed in a foot-length gown, his right hand raised with two fingers extended, in other words already making the sign of the cross that is to render the poison harmless. He is being restrained by two soldiers, the one closest to us with a sword at his side, and in the same corner, behind a wall, there are two spectators in the distance. On the other side stands the Governor, Dacianus, with the same costume and sceptre as in the previous relief, but now that he is indoors he has exchanged his hat for a crown.

Unlike the previous relief, which takes place in the open air, as is indicated by the irregular surface of the ground painted with grass and herbs, this relief depicts an interior with a flat chequered floor.

89

PLINTH RELIEF V
Saint George comes back to life in the well, healed by Christ and His angels

This relief, the third from the left on the southern side of the plinth, is one of the two reliefs forming the newly constructed screen that were not found in the City Church. It comes from the church at Ed, just north of Stockholm, and had ended up in the Nordic Museum when, in connection with the restoration of the Saint George group around 1930, the link with the plinth reliefs was perceived and it was included among them. For both the subject and the style linked the relief from Ed with the others, and conservation work revealed that it also matched them with regard to the original polychromy and the way in which this had subsequently been painted over.

This is nearly 3 inches (7 cm.) lower than the other reliefs, a difference in height, however, which would have been made up for by the projecting wings of the angels, which have since been broken off (there are traces of notches and fastenings for them on the back of the relief). But as the Ed relief was considerably narrower – it measures only 18 inches (47 cm.) in breadth compared with the others which range from 25 to 26 inches (63 – 67 cm.) – the restorers added new sections of landscape on both sides so that it would fit into its current position. Many scholars have, however, proposed that the narrower dimensions of this relief indicate that originally it was intended for one of the ends of the plinth, like another equally narrow relief, now lost. We also know what the motif of this lost relief should have been. Immediately after the poisoned chalice scene (which was probably placed at the end of the southern side originally) in the legend there follows the episode in which Saint George's body is cut into many pieces by a wheel with knives – as portrayed for instance on the console relief under the statue at Chartres (illustration 9B).

The version of the Saint George legend most widespread in Germany in the last decades of the 15th century then says that his body, divided now into ten sections, was cast into a well. But Christ revealed Himself in an earthquake together with his Archangels. The angels gathered together the sections of the body and Christ reunited them, causing Saint George to rise again. This late mediaeval version of the legend reflects the early Christian account of the saint of indestructible life, who was repeatedly tortured to death, only to revive again and again.

In the rocky landscape of this relief, there is a round well-house with a conical roof, which one can imagine to have housed the winding wheel. In the opening, where normally a pail would be hanging, Saint George can be seen peering out. He has the same long curly hair and the jacket, open at the front with narrow lapels, that he was wearing in previous reliefs on the plinth. The bleeding stumps of the arms he is holding out show that his hands have been cut off. In front of the well stands Christ, in a crown of thorns and a robe, together with two angels, dressed as deacons, as was the custom in contemporary art, but with their wings now broken off. The angels are holding Saint George's severed hands and feet, which Christ is about to replace so that the saint can be healed.[43]

90

PLINTH RELIEF VI
Saint George converts an officer at the court of Dacianus

This relief, on the extreme right of the southern side of the plinth, is the other relief now in the newly constructed screen, which was not found in the City Church. It belongs to the church at Danderyd where the original can still be seen. None of its paint work has been preserved, however, so that only the carefully cleaned oak is visible, enabling on the other hand the fine wood carving to be admired. When it was realised that the motif, style and dimensions matched those of the Saint George reliefs (compared with them, it is just over an inch higher and nearly three inches – 7 cm.– narrower), a plaster cast was made and painted to match the colours preserved on the other reliefs. It is this painted plaster cast which is now situated behind the small columns in the plinth and which is reproduced here in colour, while the original relief in Danderyd is illustrated later (Illustration 103). The format of this relief shows that it originally formed part of one of the sides, and its motif, which was only identified correctly a few decades ago, is the episode following the one in the previous narrow relief, probably made for one of the ends. The narrative now continues, in other words, round the corner on to the next side of the plinth.[44]

In the version of the legend current in Germany in the late Middle Ages, we are told that when George had been healed and emerged from the well, he returned to Dacianus's palace, to the amazement of the Governor and his entourage. Here he converted an officer, who was, however, executed immediately at the behest of Dacianus.

In the relief, we see the officer in boots, a short jacket and a hat standing with his hands fastened at different heights to a many sided pillar, to the bottom of which a bare-headed prisoner is bound, with his hands behind his back. In the centre of the relief Saint George is standing, in the same foot-length gown as in the poisoned chalice relief. His left hand rests on his chest, and with his right he is making a rhetorical gesture towards the bound officer. The preaching of Saint George is driving the devil out of this heathen. The demon, with horns and a tail, is emerging from his mouth, grasping at a forelock in a last attempt to prevent ejection. At the same time he is pointing at the idol on the pillar, a small, clothed figure sitting with a sack of money in his right hand, intended, surely, to represent Mammon.

This was the contemporary way of depicting a conversion. The officer is literally bound to an idol, but now the heathen demons are driven out of him. But at Dacianus's command, the convert was executed immediately. On the right the Governor – with the same crown as in the poisoned chalice relief – is raising a hand in command to one of his companions in the same kind of short jacket with slashed sleeves as the eminent prosecutor in the last relief (Illustration 93). In the Danderyd relief this individual already has one hand on the handle of his sword (the blade has gone but the plugs that held it to the relief remain). He is ready to carry out the command to execute the newly converted officer. This relief could well have been followed by one that depicted the account in *Legenda aurea* of Saint George sitting unharmed in a cauldron of molten lead.

91

PLINTH RELIEF VII
Saint George's prayers cause the destruction of the idol and the temple

This relief (the second from the right on the northern side) is the left-hand relief of the two in the remaining original screen and therefore the last but one in the series. It was below this relief that Peringskiöld read the caption in low German that has since disappeared saying that the saint was praying to the idol (*Här schal he de afgot anbeden…*)

The *Legenda aurea* tells us that when Dacianus was unable to vanquish Saint George with threats or torture he attempted to persuade him with honeyed words to sacrifice to his gods. The saint pretended to accede to this and a crowd gathered to witness his sacrifice in the temple. "George knelt down and prayed that God to His greater glory and to convert the populace should destroy the temple and its idols so thoroughly that nothing should remain. Immediately a fire descended from Heaven and burned down the temple with all its idols and priests and the earth opened and consumed that which remained."

In the relief, we see Saint George kneeling and praying so that the column breaks and the idol – an ugly little devil – falls and the vaulting of the temple collapses over the people crowded there. They are trying with raised hands to protect themselves from the falling stonework. Dacianus is also doing so, to the extreme left of the relief, his face, like several others, registering terror. The two men closest to the column with the idol have – unlike the others – garments resembling cloaks, with which they have covered their heads. Merely to protect their heads, it used to be believed. But this is exactly how the sacrificial priests of Ancient Rome wore their togas (*toga velata*). In this way the artist, who in the next relief presents even clearer proof of his knowledge of the Classical period – which has not been noticed earlier either – obviously wants to identify them as the priests serving the idol (*"sacerdotes"*) who according to the legend were destroyed with their temple. We see that one of them has been struck in the head by the falling pillar and collapses bleeding to the floor. On the floor lies a man whose head has almost been severed. Another is being swallowed by the earth – he is already buried up to the waist, even though he is desperately clinging to the pillar.

The divine power which Saint George is invoking and which is destroying the temple – fire from heaven in the words of the legend – is embodied in the relief by a shower of wedges and balls falling diagonally westwards from above. They are making holes in the vaulting and inside the temple they act as projectiles that strike the heathens and the throat of the idol. As he falls, the idol is holding his own tail, like the demon in the previous relief.

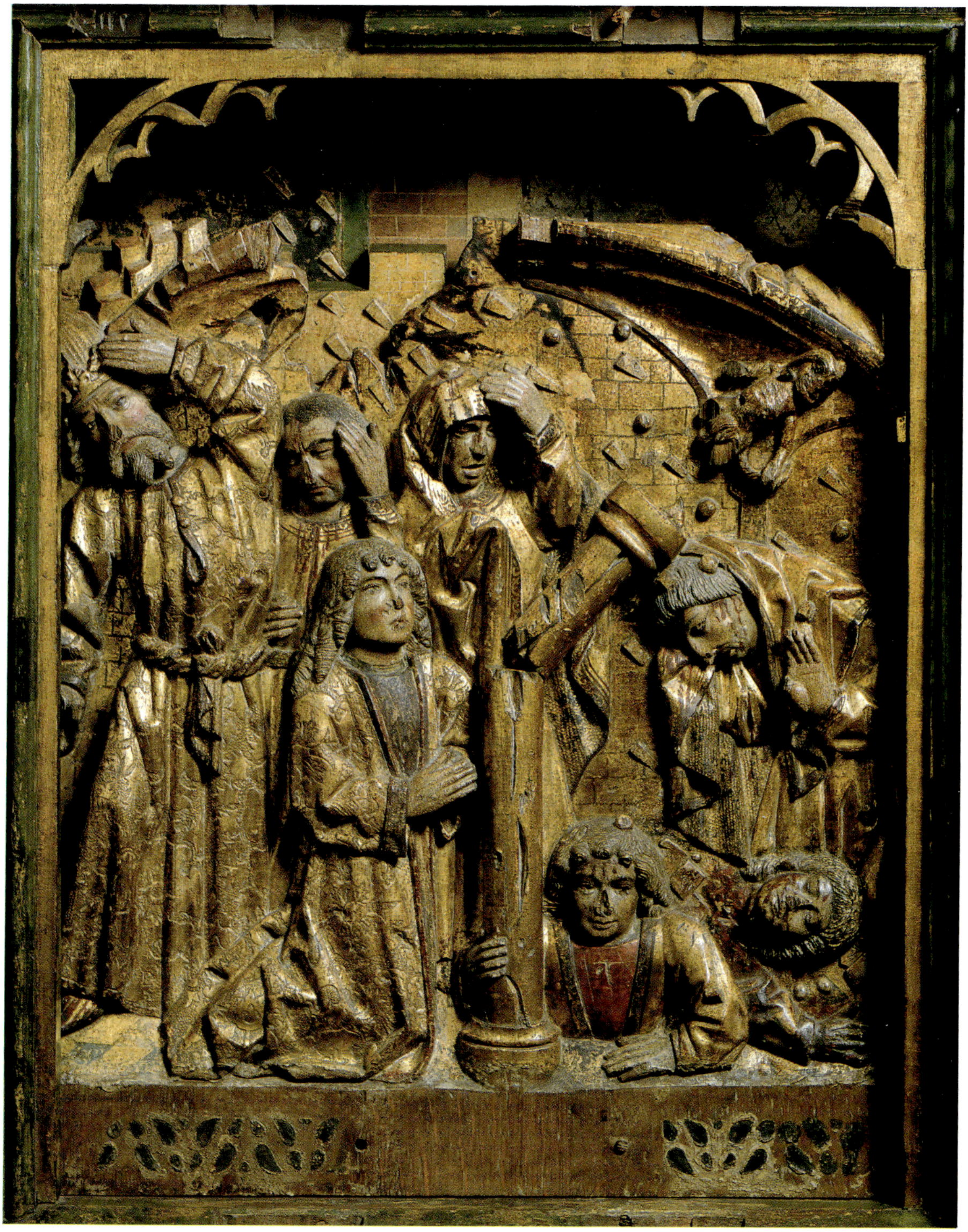

PLINTH RELIEF VIII
Saint George faces his judges

This relief (furthest right on the northern side) forms part of the same screen, discovered in the City church, as the previous one, and is the last in the series that has been preserved. *Legenda aurea* recounts that after the destruction of the idol's temple, Saint George was again brought before Dacianus, converting his wife before being finally condemned.

To the extreme left, behind a wall, a spectator is standing watching the events in the foreground. There Saint George, in golden armour, is being led forwards by a soldier and a captain or a prosecutor dressed elegantly with slashed sleeves and a pleated shirt in the latest fashion. He raises his hat respectfully to Dacianus, who is enthroned wearing his crown and carrying his sceptre.

Behind the Governor stands Alexandria, his wife, as indicated by the matron's veil she is wearing covering her head and throat. The colour of her face is darker because later over-painting has been preserved here for the purpose of documentation. She is pointing sternly at Dacianus, her face expressing repudiation, as if she is uttering the first words given to her in the legend: "Cruel tyrant and executioner ... now let me tell you I want to be a Christian." Here she plays the same role as the wife of another Roman Governor – who urged Pilate to release Christ as a righteous man according to St Matthews Gospel, a narrative which has often been depicted similarly.

Even if Dacianus is referred to as a king in some places in *Legenda aurea*, he is described there explicitly as the Roman Governor and on the whole that is how he is addressed. Therefore he is depicted with the Roman Empire's emblems of rank, which in the Middle Ages were the same as those of the Holy Roman Empire. Consequently, the crown that Dacianus is wearing is the Imperial Crown with its enclosed hoops, not the open circlet worn by contemporary kings. The double-headed Imperial eagle is painted on his throne.

As we have seen in the other reliefs, here as well, as was customary in the Middle Ages, the artist has depicted the clothes and attributes of his contemporaries in scenes which were enacted nearly 12 centuries earlier in the late-Classical period. But in this relief there is one interesting exception. While Saint George once again appears in golden 15th century armour, the soldier holding him from behind with a rope around his arm is equipped like a Roman soldier would have been in the Classical period. His chest is protected by armour, he has a short kilt of strips of pleated leather with vertical metal facings (*pteruges*) and short leather boots (*caligae*). Here in the north, this is an early harbinger of the approach of the Renaissance from Italy, and its rediscovery of the Classical period.

After this episode, in which Dacianus finally gives the order for Saint George to be executed, the series of reliefs on the plinth should properly have concluded with the depiction of his head being removed by the executioner's sword, or in other words the consummation of the martyrdom through which he became a saint. This important image should have been placed on the front end. What it might have looked like is shown by Illustration 157.

93

94. Saint George's squire and his brothers in the first relief. The squire has the same type of throat protection and helmet as his master in the reliefs on the castle. His brother Theodor has a long, dark beard and a travelling hat, with a textile texture that has been produced using a tool similar to a pastry-wheel which has been rolled across the surface leaving grooves in the gesso. Above his horse, the now headless body of his brother can be seen.

95 – 96. The cripple and the coins in the second relief. The money bag and the pile of coins have been made to look realistic by covering the gesso with the impressions of real coins. It has been possible to identify a couple of different coins minted in Stockholm in the 1470s from these impressions – among them the örtug reproduced on the right. The enlarged picture bottom right shows the print of both its face with the head of St. Erik and its tail stamped with the three crowns. The silver paint which covered the surface has blackened with age.[45]

97–100. Four details from the third relief showing Saint George on the rack. Compare the faces of Dacianus and the executioner both with each other and with the smiling face of the saint. Attached to the belt of one of the executioners is a bag with the head of a lion painted on its flap as if embroidered there.

101. The sorcerer with his chalice of poison in the fourth relief is depicted in the garments of a scholar. His pleated hat is an early version of a doctor of philosophy's bonnet, and the little cape over his shoulders still forms part of academic gowns in some countries. The veins on the hand stirring the poison are finely carved in the wood, while the texture and pattern of his clothes have been reproduced in the gesso by using a tool like the one described in the caption to illustration 94 or by giving it a smooth surface to create different types of reflections in the gold. In this relief, as in most of the others, the noses have since been cut off.

102. In the fifth relief Christ comes with his angels to heal Saint George. Christ's raised hands clearly displays the mark of the nails of the cross. The angel closest to the well is holding the victim's right hand and both of his severed feet. The crackled surface of the paint shows that this relief, which for a long time was in the church at Ed, has undergone various vicissitudes. Here, however, as in the other reliefs, the remnants of darker paint used to paint over the relief can be seen – in the face of the foremost angel for instance – as well as damage to the noses.

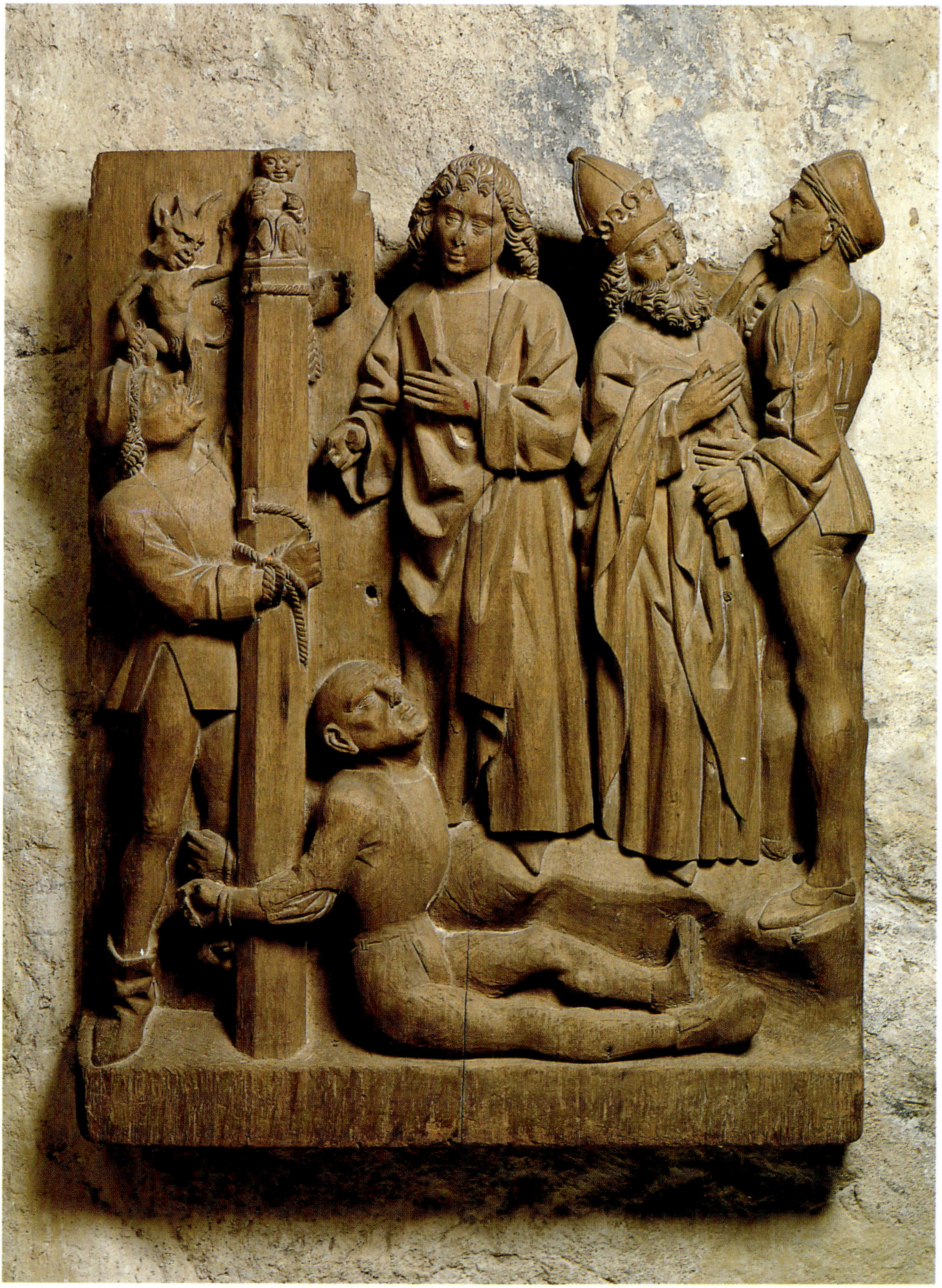

103. The original of the sixth relief, still in the church at Danderyd, has now been completely stripped of paint, so that it is possible to see with what care and excellence the carving has been executed. Here, as well, the saint's nose has been damaged and the blade of the sword, held by the man on the extreme right, is missing, as is the head of the man standing between him and the governor. These details have been replaced on the painted plaster cast on the plinth. The missing head was copied from the head of the man to the right of the sorcerer in the fourth relief with the poisoned chalice episode.

104 – 105. Details from the seventh relief in which Saint George prays for the temple to collapse on to the heathens. The effigy of their idol – holding his tail as he falls – can be compared with the previous picture of the very similar demon being driven out and also of the effigy of Mammon on the pillar.

106 – 107. Details from the eighth relief. The coat-of-arms on the throne of the Roman governor displays the Imperial eagle. This had been inherited from the Western Empire by the Emperors of the Holy Roman Empire. It had recently been adopted from the Eastern Empire by Sten Sture's opponent, Ivan III, to distinguish Moscow, "the third Rome", and thus became the emblem of the Czars of Russia.[46] 107 shows a floor tile decorated with a large A (which has been taken to be the signature of the painter, Albert).[47]

108. There is no known picture portraying Bernt Notke, but this picture and the next show how sculptors and painters worked during his era. A southern German manuscript from around 1475 shows four artists as the children of Mercury in the wilderness; a painter, a smith, a writer, and, at the top, a sculptor. The latter has a wooden carving suspended in a typical contemporary work-bench, so that it can be rotated by using an iron spike at the foot end and a wooden peg in the head while the sculptor is working with his mallet, chisels and files.[1]

Bernt Notke –
The Saint George Master

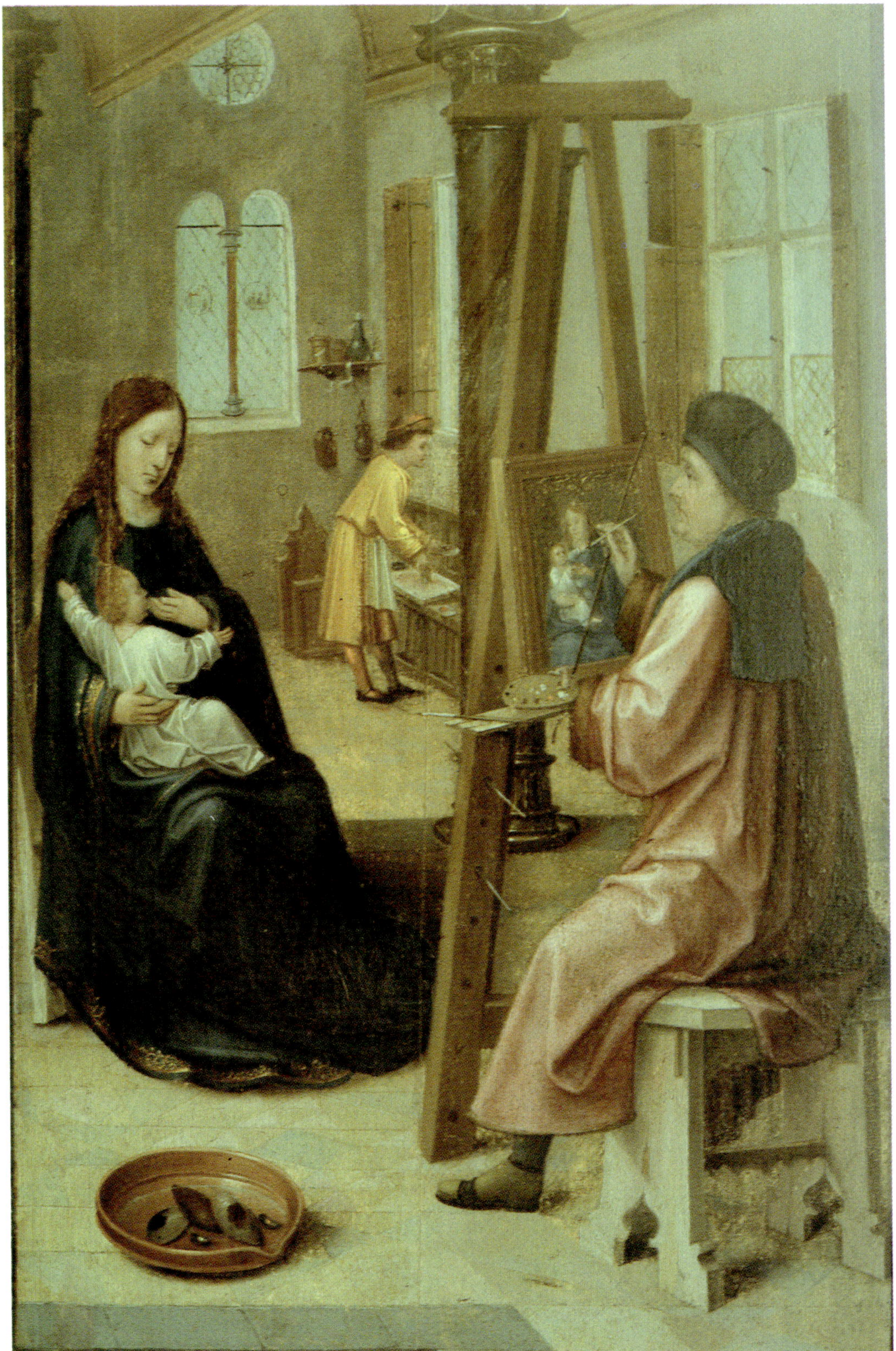

From Antwerp to Lübeck

In documentary sources which have been preserved from the end of the 15th century, there is no information which directly identifies the master painter responsible for this enormous work. A century later, Johannes Messenius, who lived during the era of the Vasa kings, when leading artists were normally summoned from the Netherlands, asserted that it was a sculptor from Antwerp that Sten Sture had summoned to Stockholm to create this major work:

> Lord Sten a letter to Antwerp penned
> To find the artist then most learned
> In sculpture that could be discerned
> Who worked in Stockholm many a year
> To finish on the statue there.
> But when the whole thing was complete
> With such art had it well been wrought
> That in the whole Roman Empire
> To its like could none aspire.[3]

According to Messenius, Sten Sture then had the artist put to death to prevent him from making such a masterpiece for anyone else. This is the kind of legend that is also current about other unique works of art from earlier ages.[4]

The parchment found in the City Church by August Strindberg in 1880, contained the names of both the founders of the monument and of the Papal Nuncio who came with the relics and consecrated it – but not a word about the artist.

Verner von Heidenstam gave him the name of Master Andreas from Andorf in his novel *Saint George and the Dragon,* published in 1900. This fictional account describes him working on his sculpture in a shed in the yard of the Stures' minstrel, Bengt Hake, using the latter's[3] wife as his model for the princess. When the minstrel realises that the artist has fallen in love with his model, he kills Master Andreas.[5]

However not a year had passed before the Swedish art-historian Johnny Roosval in 1901 linked the name of the sculptor for the first time with a real artist – the Lübeck master Bernt Notke.[6] This ascription has since been generally accepted and supported by the findings of a number of Swedish and German scholars. Among the Swedes, Johnny Roosval was a pioneer with a number of articles and two books on the Saint George group (1919 and 1924), while Walter Paatz was one of the first German

109. The evangelist Luke painting Our Lady as depicted on a reredos in Sala parish church created in Brussels at the beginning of the 16th century. This gives us a realistic presentation of a contemporary painter's studio. The master sits at an easel facing his model, working with a palette and brushes, dressed in a painter's smock. So that they will not dry out, some of the paints are kept in mussel shells lying under water on an earthenware plate on the floor. In the background, his apprentice is grinding paint.[2]

scholars in the field with *Bernt Notke und sein Kreis* (1939), a comprehensive study in two volumes. However, in 1970, in his two-volume study of the two reredoses for which there is documentary attribution to Notke, the Danish scholar Erik Moltke expressed doubts about whether he really had been the sculptor who created the enormous works in Lübeck Cathedral and Stockholm City Church attributed to him, or even if he had had anything to do with them at all. In the documents he is referred to merely as a "painter".[7]

However, in the very year that Moltke's book was published, thorough restoration of the Triumphal Crucifix at Lübeck disclosed Bernt Notke's signature in two of the major sculptures. Since then, several more of his most important works have undergone restoration and his signature has been discovered on three more major works (at Århus). These examinations – which have not, however, included the Saint George group – have increased the intensity of research about Notke and his work, yielding a clearer picture which has been summarised in a new study of the artist in German by Gerhard Eimer (1985). In the light of these new findings about his other major works, Notke emerges even more clearly as the master responsible for the Saint George group, as will be shown below.[8]

What then is known about Bernt Notke and his work according to the most recent findings?

In all probability he was the son of Michel Notke, a leading shipowner and merchant in the Hanseatic city of Tallinn (Reval), who traded with Flanders, and his second wife, Gertraut Saffenbergh from Visby. We do not know when Bernt was born – but it was probably around 1440 – but we do know with absolute certainty that his birthplace was Lassan. This was a small community at the mouth of the river Peene in Pomerania. It is possible that the trader's wife had been left at this staging point on the trade route to Flanders to safeguard his interests, as was so often the case with the families of Hanseatic merchants involved in foreign trade.[10]

110. Bernt Notke's trade-mark – a pair of compasses and a hammer – from his seal.[9]

It was hardly possible to receive any training as an artist in a little place like Lassan. Notke's later work shows that he was trained in Flanders, with which his father had trading connections, at that time the artistic metropolis of northern Europe. Here the great painters of the preceding generation, Robert Campin and the Van Eyck brothers, had laid the groundwork for a revolutionary new realism. This was developed further during the period in which Notke was being trained there around 1460 by the elderly Rogier van der Weyden, by Dirc Bouts and a number of other masters. Notke has adopted certain groupings of figures from the two last-mentioned painters and in general his work – not least the Saint George group – testifies to how strongly he was inspired by this new realism in the Low Countries.

It is not known, however, in which studios he was trained as a painter and sculptor. On the other hand, after a thorough basic training in both these skills, he obviously served important years of apprenticeship with Pasquier Grenier, who supervised a large studio for the production of tapestries in the city of Tournai. One of the works produced there shortly after 1460 was a magnificent suite of large woven tapestries for the Duke of Burgundy which portrayed the feats of Julius Caesar. On the tapestry which shows Caesar crossing the Rubicon, the harnesses of his and his squire's horses are decorated with round lion masks, a singular detail which Notke adopted and used on Saint George's horse in the Stockholm. Notke's specific task in Pasquier's studio seems to have been to prepare life-sized weaving patterns, which were erected behind the looms. As a rule, he worked from a small painting, which had to be magnified to monumental dimensions.[11]

What he learned from this work could well have helped make him a master of wooden sculptures of monumental dimensions as well. Because this is what he produced in a couple of works which were unusually large for that period. One example of this is the Saint George group. Notke could also have learned from Pasquier Grenier how to run a large artistic undertaking successfully by allocating specific tasks to a number of different specialists. For Bernt Notke was also to prove a go-ahead entrepreneur, the able manager of a commercial studio on an unusually large scale for the Baltic countries. At some time in the 1460s Notke established himself in Lübeck. The guild regulations there demanded legitimate birth and two years' residence in the city before acceptance as a master. According to its oldest existing document, in 1467 "Bernt Notke the painter" displayed his birth certificate from Lassan to the council in Lübeck, which then undertook to protect him and his journeymen from being harassed by the Guild of Painters as a newly arrived competitor. The Guild also required a master to be married and to have his own household, a rule introduced to enable journeymen and apprentices to live in their master's establishment. No information has survived about Notke's wife, but in his will from 1501 a daughter Anneke is named and, in somewhat obscure terms, another mentally handicapped daughter as well.

111. Bernt Notke's signature on a letter from Stockholm dated May 24th 1484.

112. Julius Caesar – with his name and the imperial eagle on his costume – crossing the Rubicon. The position of his hand shows that the die is cast. Note the lion masks on the harness of his and his squire's horses. Detail from a tapestry, woven in Pasquier Grenier's studio in Tournai in the 1460s, now in Berne Museum.

113. Lion masks on Saint George's horse in Stockholm City Church. Between them can be seen the three water-lily leaves of Sten Sture.

During his first ten years in Lübeck, Notke lived in a street in one of the meaner quarters, but in 1479 he was able to purchase a stone house on the elegant Breite Strasse. There are records of journeys to a number of cities around the Baltic, including several to Stockholm at the beginning of the 1480s. These will be dealt with in more detail later, as will the years he spent in Stockholm. In 1497, however, he had returned to Lübeck and lived there until his death in 1509. During his final years he was the supervisor of the works at St. Peter's Church, which involved managing a large brick works with extensive exports to the whole of the Hanseatic area, a task involving considerable administrative responsibilities in other words. He himself was responsible for keeping the books. At the same time he was in the process of extending his studio with an additional building, but this was forbidden by the City Council.

The brief entries in the documents provide no basis for the far-reaching conclusions that have previously been drawn about Notke's character (that he was gloomy, proud, violent, ruthless, obstinate, etc.). His will evinces concern for his daughters, his two maids and his two apprentices. On the other hand he refused to redeem a previously promised lavish surety of 35 marks for a fellow-artist, Henrik Wilsing. In his letter on this subject – which also mentions work on the Saint George statue and which we will therefore return to later - the latter describes Notke as "en selsen man" (a strange, remarkable, peculiar person), who he would still like, however, to have as a good friend. The other written sources present a picture of an energetic manager of a workshop and a successful business-minded entrepreneur.

114. Death dancing with the Empress. A detail from the Dance Macabre wall-hanging in the Church of St. Nicholas in Tallinn.

From Dance Macabre Wall-hangings to a Large Signed Group of Sculptures

The two earliest works that can be confidently attributed to Bernt Notke were two painted wall-hangings, each around 100 feet (30 metres) in length, whose subject was the Dance Macabre. They were created in the 1460s after Notke's return to the Baltic area, one for Lübeck and the other for Tallinn. Both were painted on woven linen and therefore used the same technique as the weaving patterns for Pasquier Grenier's studio. The Dance Macabre wall-hanging at Lübeck, which was about 100 feet (30 metres) long and nearly 6 feet (2 metres) broad, was dated 1463 and hung in the confessional chapel of the Church of St. Mary. The original was lost in 1701 and replaced with a copy, which was in its turn destroyed during a bombing raid in 1942.

Only the first quarter of the original Dance Macabre wall-hanging in the City Church of Tallinn (St. Nicholas's) remains, a length of almost seven metres. In content, it differs only in detail from the Dance Macabre in Lübeck. When the Tallinn wall-hanging was cleaned in the 1960s, its great expressiveness and very finely painted details became visible. A decisive role in arranging this commission was probably played by Diderik Notke, the priest in Tallinn. In 1468, the artist persuaded the council in Lübeck to urge its counterpart in Tallinn to enable his relative to dispose of his financial resources freely and without restriction. [12]

The composition is the customary one for late mediaeval representations of the Dance Macabre. Skeleton figures lead reluctant human beings, pair after pair, to form a macabre row of dancers. The people are portrayed in hierarchical order – the Pope first, then the Emperor and the Empress, Cardinal and King. These are all that remain in the fragment in Tallinn, but the copy in Lübeck portrayed 24 pairs of dancers with a peasant and a couple of young people bringing up the rear. Beneath each figure we are told who they are and there is also a verse. In the Lübeck rendering, these were written in straight lines, but in Tallinn they are inscribed on a curved scroll which emphasises the rhythm of the dance. One of Notke's innovations was to paint the view of a city in the background, thus providing us with the earliest known portrayal of Lübeck with its many towers.

The Dance Macabre motif probably gained currency from the epidemic of the Plague which swept over Western Europe in the first half of the 1460s and afflicted both Lübeck and Tallinn. These wall-hangings left Notke with a taste for portraying skulls and mummified parts of the body which he indulged in several of his later works, none more richly than beneath the dragon in Stockholm.

Notke's next major work was a sculpture – the enormous Triumphal Crucifix in Lübeck Cathedral. This merits more detailed presentation here as – especially in the light of recent findings – in several respects it appears to be the closest parallel to the Saint George group in the artist's oeuvre. The Crucifix group was created between 1470-1477 and commissioned by the Bishop of Lübeck, Albert Krummedik, who, after spending many years involved in political intrigues in the Curia in Rome, had returned to be enthroned in his diocese only a few years before commissioning the work. This expensive *magnum opus* was paid for by the Bishop himself, using his own funds according to the Latin inscription on the front of the massive beam that supports it, indeed from his inheritance according to the inscription in low Ger-

115. Part of the Dance Macabre wall-hanging in the Church of St. Mary in Lübeck. This is a copy made in 1701, which has also now been destroyed. Here we can see death dancing with an abbot, a knight, a monk, a lord-mayor, a canon, a noble, a physician and a usurer, the silhouette of Lübeck with its many characteristic towers behind them.

116. The skull of one of the skeleton figures in the Dance Macabre in Tallinn

man on the back of the same beam. When funds were low the work was discontinued for a few years and in 1474 the Bishop had to acquire more capital by pledging five of the properties pertaining to the see. Bishop Albert had other reasons for plunging more and more heavily into debt, but it is clear that the Triumphal Crucifix was his major investment. He had a special altar consecrated beneath it, and there his burial place was arranged.[13]

The group is positioned on a substantial transverse beam decorated with two graceful pointed arches reaching across the broad nave of the brick cathedral just before the transept. There, the group soars into the vaulting to rise well over 50 feet (17 metres) above floor level. In the centre is the Crucified Christ, 12 feet tall (3 metres), surrounded by the chief mourners, Mary and John. Their figures are also almost 10 feet tall (3 metres). Kneeling between them and the cross are Mary Magdalene and Bishop Albert. If they were standing, their figures would also be as tall as the previous ones, so that all four figures are sculpted one and a half times larger than life. High pedestals against each wall of the nave support Adam and Eve, both life-size figures. They are holding the fruit of knowledge and concealing their nakedness with fig-leaves to show that the Fall has taken place – from which man was not redeemed until Christ's death on the cross. Their faces reveal conflicting feelings ranging from presumption to shame and the mourners in their posture, gestures and features embody different expressions of sorrow, all characterised by rather restrained

117. The Triumphal Crucifix in Lübeck Cathedral and behind it the chancel screen decorated with sculptures, also from Notke's workshop.

but exceptionally effective means. This is great art which finds its climax in the crucifix and the poignant face of the dying Redeemer.

Foliage is growing out of the horizontal beam of the cross, and from its tendrils emerge over thirty small figures. They represent God the Father and prophets, apostles and evangelists, depicted here because in some way they prophesied or bore witness to Christ's act of redemption. Below, around the upright, there are ten or so small figures, among them an angel with the Bishop's coat-of-arms and two small founder figures. In all probability they depict the Lord Mayor, Andreas Geverdes and his brother Georg, who belonged to one of the leading patrician families in Lü-

118. The head of Christ on the Triumphal Crucifix.

119. One of the dead about to be resurrected thanks to Christ's Act of Redemption on the Cross. Detail from the Triumphal Crucifix.

beck. They had mainly contributed to the finance for the large wooden chancel-screen across an adjoining bay of the nave. This is decorated with about a dozen statuettes of saints, the four largest representing the cathedral's patron saints.[14]

Bishop Albert Krummedik himself celebrated the ceremonial consecration of the Triumphal Crucifix group on August 15th 1477. Those among the congregation were able to compare the bishop himself standing in the church to his sculpted portrait, kneeling larger than life up on the transverse beam supporting the cross. Relics had been enclosed in the skull of the Crucified Christ, but in the following year, to increase the drawing power of the crucifix, Bishop Albert had yet another relic added, a piece of the True Cross itself. This was enclosed in a valuable gold cross attached to a necklace hanging around the neck of the Crucified Christ, which disappeared after the Reformation. This second ceremony took place on September 11th 1478 and was attended by no fewer than eight bishops from northern Germany and Denmark, led by the Archbishop of Lund. As each bishop was empowered to offer forty days indulgence, the benefits of visiting the crucifix were multiplied eight times. Letters of indulgence embodying these benefits were issued on this occasion. However, no more than anywhere else was it enough merely to visit the statue to pray before it to win this indulgence – the letter of indulgence had to be paid for. Even if this was an unusually extensive and costly indulgence, the income it produced would hardly have sufficed to defray the vast sums that the increasingly indebted Bishop Albert had invested in the enormous Triumphal Crucifix. These amounted to 2,000 Lübeck marks, in other words about half of what Sten Sture claimed were the total costs for the Stockholm Saint George.

The exceptionally thorough examination using the most up-to-date methods which was undertaken during conservation work in the 1970s has made it possible to study in detail how the sculptures were constructed. Dendrochronological analysis reveals that while the chancel-screen was constructed of older, matured timber, the oaks from which the large sculptures were carved, were felled during the winter of 1470. They were in other words carved from green timber, as there is evidence that a pair of them had been completed during the two following years. Mary and John were each sculpted from a substantial tree-trunk, turned so that root-ends form the broader shoulder sections, the slimmer upper-half of the trunk being used for the feet. As was customary at the time, the figures were then hollowed out from behind, both to make them lighter and to prevent cracking when the timber dried. The hollow interior was then scorched to dry the timber more quickly and to protect it from attack by insects. As they were both free-standing sculptures which would also be seen from behind, the hollowed areas were then covered with planks of timber.[15]

It was then the job of the craftsmen entrusted with finishing the work to cover any cracks or joints in the timber with pieces of linen and to coat the whole figure with a thin layer of gesso, a mixture of chalk and glue resembling plaster of Paris, in which very fine details like veins could be shaped. Finally the painter applied the paints and gilt, often in several layers and with the gold-leaf finished in different ways to produce matte, shiny or variously patterned effects.

One of the specialities of Notke's studio was the extent and the inventiveness of the use of different additional materials both to save labour and to increase the illusion of reality. The large swollen veins on the nailed feet of the crucified Christ are shaped from strips of leather which have been fastened to the timber and then covered with the gesso and painted. Mary Magdalen's previous worldliness has been characterised by her extravagant hat, its wide brim edged with thin strips of material, which have been created from parchment.[16]

The clothes worn by the founder are so true to life that one can almost believe that Bishop Albert loaned his most magnificent vestments to Notke's studio. The thongs that edge the broad trimmings of his cope are made of plaited string and the miniature reliefs that decorate his mitre have been made of papier-maché using a mould, a much simpler process than carving them from wood.

The official inscription on the beam supporting the crucifixion group names only the founder, and, as is usual in this context, contains no mention of the artist. The work has generally been attributed to Notke, however, on stylistic grounds, although as previously mentioned, in 1970 a Danish scholar wanted to contest this and for the Saint George group as well, raising doubts as to whether Notke had ever even been a sculptor at all. In the same year, in the course of the conservation work the large statues in the crucifixion group were opened so that the interiors could be sprayed to protect them from attack by vermin. When these hollow spaces were exposed for the first time for five centuries, the artist's signature was found in two of them. On the inside of the plank used to seal the statue of John was a sheet of parchment with a text in low German which read in translation "In this year of grace 1472 Bernt Notke then made this work with the help of his journeymen, the first Eggert Svarte by name, carver, Lucas Meer, finisher, Bernt Scharpeselle, finisher, Ilges, finisher [and] Hartich Stender, painter. Pray [to] God for their souls that they may find grace before God." On the inside of the corresponding plank in the statue of Mary was a similar inscription in low German, this time in chalk. Bits of it are missing, but it lists after "Master Bernt Notke" the journeymen also involved and their trades (three names can still be read and they appear to be the same as in the other inscription). It concludes with the following words: "In 1471 this work was done. God grant them all eter-

120 – 121. Mary Magdalen and Bishop Albert Krummedik in the Triumphal Crucifix group in Lübeck Cathedral. Her face is like a tragic mask.

nal life." In addition, in the actual hollow of the statue of Mary there is another inscription in chalk, this time in Latin "Bernt Notke made me" (with the unusual word order *"fecit me"*).[17]

These inscriptions tell us therefore who the specialists were in Bernt Notke's studio involved under his direction in fashioning the statue of Mary in 1471 and the statue of John the following year. These signatures are not intended for mortal view but testify covertly to God who had created and painted these cult figures made to His greater glory.

According to the by-laws of the Lübeck guild of painters, a master was allowed only two journeymen or apprentices at any one time. Notke had got round this regulation by employing in addition to these craftsmen a number of finishers (*beredare*) with no special training. Only in this way was it possible for Notke to complete his enormous works in so short a space of time. The statue of Mary was after all signed only one year and the statue of John two years after the timber had been felled.

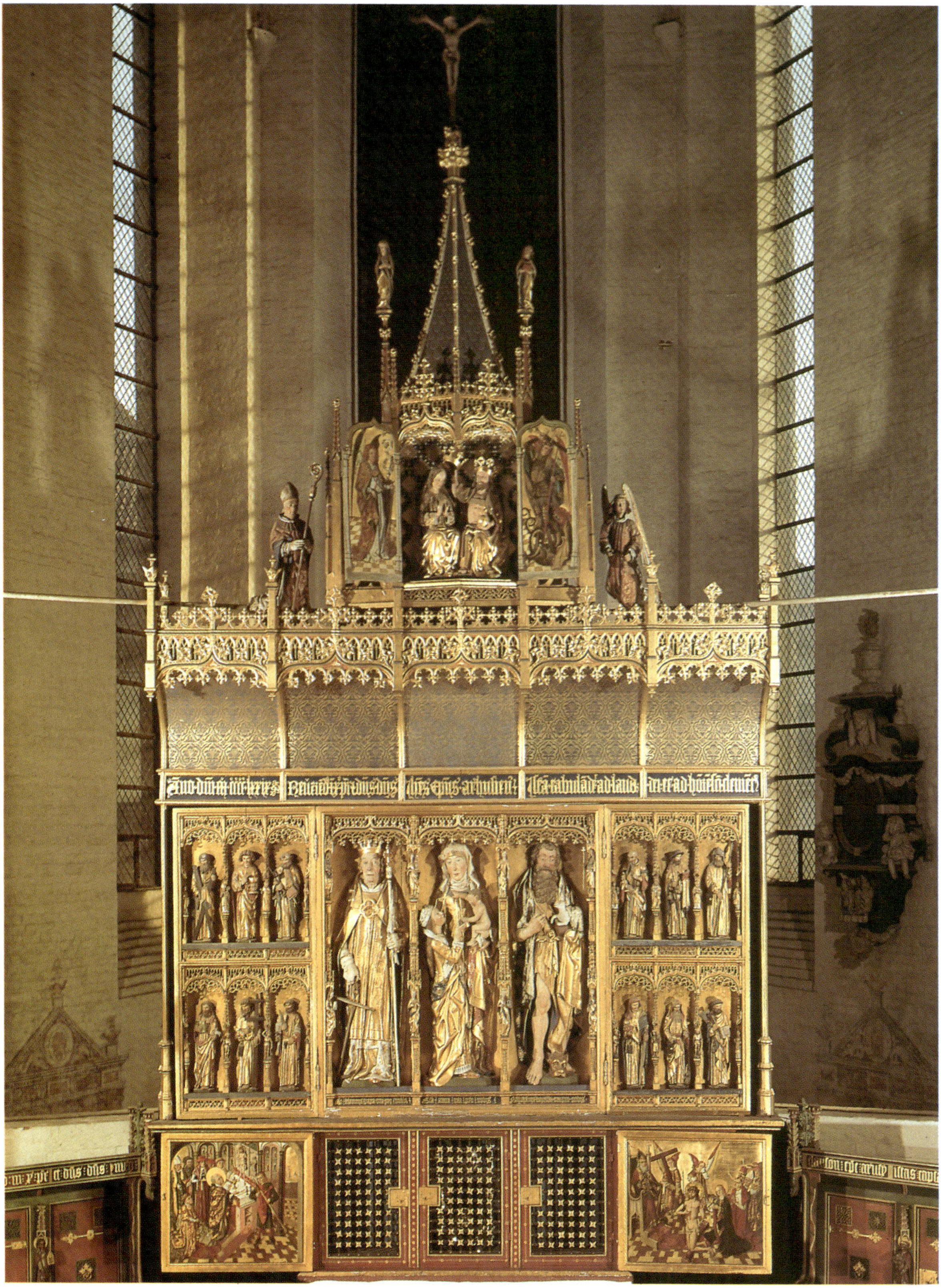

The Reredoses at Århus, Tallinn and Uppsala

The next works that can be attributed on documentary grounds to Notke are two reredoses. The first is of a traditionally Scandinavian type with a row of statues, while the second is a new departure, following examples from the Netherlands with a dramatic scene at its centre.

The reredos behind the high altar at Århus was, when consecrated in 1479, with its height of almost forty feet (12 metres), the largest in Scandinavia. At its centre it contains three life-size figures representing St. Anne flanked by John the Baptist and St. Clement, the pope who was the cathedral's patron saint. The inner wings house a host of carved saints in varying sizes (from 26 to 8 inches – 65-20 cm.). Above them there is a large projecting canopy, surmounted in its turn by a smaller reredos with a sculptured representation of the coronation of the Virgin Mary, and above this soars a crucifix. The remainder of the reredos is dominated by no fewer than 24 painted panels, placed mainly in the two upper and lower rows of movable wings, depicting various scenes from the life of Jesus and the lives and martyrdoms of different saints. This reredos has undergone thorough conservation during the 1970s in which successive layers of over painting have been removed to expose the original colours. The skin surfaces of the statues have a cool, almost enamel-like lustre with clear bright colours on their garments.[18]

During conservation Bernt Notke's signature was discovered here as well. In this case it is not concealed but is clearly visible in the text beneath the feet of the three main statues: *Bernardus .... fecit me* (Bernt .... made me).[19] As was his practice, he has used parchment on all three large statues to create the illusion of certain thin materials, for instance in Anne's neckerchief, the Infant's swaddling clothes and John the Baptist's original scarf. The trimmings of the clothes on the statue of the Pope are formed of string beneath the gesso. The faces are varied and characterised effectively. In the statues of the apostles, the broad but varying physiognomies afford interpretations of different types of personality.

This reredos was endowed by Jens Iversen Lange, the Bishop of Århus. We are given this information in the large dedication inscription in the reredos. In addition, his portrait appears twice: a statuette depicts him in a kneeling position on the canopy and a painting below shows him being presented by his patron John the Evangelist to the Man of Sorrows. The painting in particular is an unusually individualised portrait. Infra-red photography reveals that the artist has made corrections while painting the

122. The reredos of the high altar in Århus Cathedral opened for a festival with all its statues visible. In the wings stand the twelve apostles with small statuettes of saints on the pillars between them. At the top of the reredos the coronation of the Virgin Mary is depicted and she is flanked by the founder on the left and by an angel who once held his coat-of-arms on the right.

portrait, raising the ears for instance from their original position, which was too low. Even the most critical scholars accept that it was painted from life.

Notke had an opportunity to paint the portrait of Bishop Jens when he was in Lübeck in September 1478 to take part in the second dedication of the Triumphal Crucifix, when the gold cross was installed. The commission was, however, probably placed earlier. In December of the same year, Jens Iversen was already complaining that the reredos had not yet been delivered as agreed. The Lord Mayor of Lübeck responded by asking the bishop for an additional advance payment for Bernt Notke for the "valuable picture" on which he was working. He had already been paid 100 gulden by the bishop and spent 200 gulden himself but now more cash was needed, in which case delivery was guaranteed in April 1479. During a visit to Århus three years later, Notke signed a receipt for the total cost of the reredos and also received a honorarium of 20 gulden and a valuable horse from the bishop, who died one month later. It appears, however, that Notke did not receive the whole sum for which he wrote the receipt, as there was later a dispute about a substantial part of it. Notke demanded 800 gulden from a rich Danish merchant in Århus. When he refused to pay, Lübeck seized a consignment of linen belonging to him worth the same amount, and Notke then declared himself satisfied. Violent protests were made in the Danish council of state, but without result as far as is known.

123. Bishop Jens Iversen Lange, who endowed the altar at Århus, in a portrait painted on one of the lower wings.

After these monumental works for two cathedrals, Notke produced a considerably smaller reredos for the Church of the Holy Ghost in his native city of Tallinn, where his relative Diderik Notke was a priest. This church served two functions, being both the chapel of the City council and of the neighbouring hospital. The inscription on the 12 foot (3.5 metres) high reredos bears the date 1483. In the following year the artist sent a reminder about the outstanding payment of 50 Lübeck marks for this work. This too was later over-painted but after the latest cleaning its well preserved colours have emerged with a bright, rich lustre. No signature has been found on this work. Like most reredoses, its two pairs of movable wings display only paintings both when it is closed and in its normal open position. In all a total of ten with motifs from the Passion and the legend of St. Elisabeth, which is particularly suitable for a hospital chapel.[20]

But like the reredos at Århus and many others, when the Tallinn reredos is opened fully for festivals only sculptures are visible, of which the largest is 3 feet (90 cm.) high. In the wings are four standing figures of saints and its centre shows the miracle of Pentecost. It depicts Mary and the twelve apostles standing in rapture with upturned faces watching the outpourings of the Holy Ghost, a suitable motive for a church with such

124. Pope Clement in the Altar at Århus. The golden edgings of his cope are made of string and the warts on his face of wooden plugs, over which the gesso and paint or gilt has been applied.

a dedication. The effect of perspective has been sought by making the reredos unusually deep, the architectural details in the background are on the slant and the rearmost figures are somewhat smaller than those in the foreground. Whereas the apostles at Århus had widely varying faces, in Tallinn they are stereotypes, almost all with curly hair and beards and Notke's typical long, narrow, upturned nose. This may be because the master was less involved in the production of this cheaper reredos, or because it was entrusted to other assistants.[21]

Two of the figures, however, stand out as different. On Mary's immediate left stands John the Evangelist, with a clean-shaven face, blond hair and in his hand the poisoned chalice that he rendered harmless with the sign of the cross. He resembles the Stockholm Saint George, especially in the relief in which Saint George is dealing with his poisoned chalice in a similar way. The man farthest left, kneeling with his hands clasped in prayer pointing downwards, also differs from the others. Everything suggests that this clean-shaven figure with its richly coloured brocade garments and more individualised features represents the founder. Different opinions have been expressed as to whether it depicts the then warden of the church – and therefore the person who commissioned the reredos – Didrik Hagenbeke, the Lord Mayor – or the priest Diderik Notke, which is less probable.[22]

The large reredos for the high altar in Uppsala Cathedral has also been

125. St. Anne herself in the reredos at Århus. Her neckerchief, Mary's turban and the Infant's swaddling-clothes are made of parchment.

126. The Miracle of Pentecost in the reredos in the Church of the Holy Ghost, Tallinn.

attributed to Bernt Notke. This burned down in 1702 but about half of its extensive pictorial decoration is known to us through the copies made before the fire and afterwards published in 13 copperplates by Johan Peringskiöld's, then Royal Antiquarian, in his book about Uppsala. In addition to a picture of St. Erik's reliquary from one of the outer wings, the copperplates provide us with all the pictures on the inner wings. The interiors of these wings displayed the legend of St. Erik in eight sculpted scenes. They showed Erik being crowned, how this idealised King of Sweden refused to tax his subjects, how he arranged for churches to be built, four scenes depicted his crusade in Finland, the last one his final mass. The exteriors of the wings comprised four painted panels which portrayed his martyrdom. The two panels on the left wing together form the presentation of a cavalry battle between Swedes and Danes that has already been reproduced in a previous chapter (see illustration 29). Among

123

the Swedish knights, Sten Sture could be seen riding in the foreground. His horse was adorned with the same small bells as those on Saint George's horse in Stockholm. And just as in Stockholm, severed heads, arms and skulls are lying on the ground beneath his horse in the Uppsala painting. The paintings reveal in many details and in their dramatic composition

127. John the Evangelist with the poisoned chalice and other apostles in the central panel of the reredos in Tallinn.

obvious influence from Flemish art.[23]

Where the reredos in Uppsala is concerned, there are no documents with either the name of the artist or any date. Stylistic analysis, admittedly on the basis of the copies, attributes it to Notke. The coat-of-arms of Archbishop Jacob Ulfsson indicate that it was commissioned at some time during his long occupancy of the see (1469-1515). In addition the coats-of-arms of Sten Sture, his mother, his maternal uncle (Karl Knutson Bonde) and his son-in-law can be found. It is possible that the reredos was commissioned shortly after the Battle of Brunkeberg, which seems to have provided the inspiration for the painting of the cavalry battle led by Sten Sture. His presence there also suggests that he contributed money to the large and expensive reredos in honour of the traditional patron saint of the realm, St. Erik, who was also said to have aided him in achieving victory at Brunkeberg (see p. 38). What is known, at any rate, is that in 1472 Sten Sture endowed an eternal lamp before the high altar of Uppsala Cathedral. This may have some link with the date when the reredos was commissioned. There are a number of reasons for assuming, however, that it can hardly have been completed before the middle of the decade, not least the dates of the Flemish painting which provided Notke with inspiration.

A number of smaller reredoses have also been attributed to Notke together with statues of saints, and examples of both can be found in Sweden. There is no reason to study these in more detail here, however, especially as several of these attributions are questionable and have been challenged by certain scholars.[24]

Kon. CARL VIII Knutson...

A Portrait of a Swedish King

There is a statuette of a king in the national portrait collection at Gripsholm Castle, of exceptionally great artistic value and unanimously and convincingly attributed by scholars to Notke, which is highly interesting in connection with the Saint George group. This is the well-known effigy of Karl Knutsson Bonde kneeling behind a coat-of-arms surmounted by a crown. Two of the fields of the coat-of-arms contain the three crowns of Sweden, the other two the lion of Norway with St. Olof's axe, while the small shield in the centre displays the emblem of the Bonde family, a boat. Karl Knutsson had not only been king of Sweden on three occasions (1448-57, 1464-65 and 1467-70) but also King of Norway 1449-50 after his coronation in Trondheim. [25]

This 26-inch high (6 cm.) statuette is carved from oak and its well-preserved polychromy has never been painted over. Where the sculpture was originally found is unknown. It can be traced back to the 18th century. The first time it is mentioned is at the beginning of the 1780s when the Ambassador of Spain, Count de Guemez, bought it for a trifle "during a journey down in the country". He bought it from a Swede who later, because of dubious business dealings, left the country, but where this individual acquired the statuette is unknown. Shortly afterwards, the Spanish Ambassador courteously handed the statuette of the king over to one of his descendants, Baron Carl Göran Bonde, who kept it at his manor at Fituna. In 1827, the Baron donated the statuette to Gripsholm, where a national portrait collection was in the process of being established. At that time the statuette still had its hands, which have since disappeared, as can be seen from a description of the new acquisition published in the same year. The describes the king as praying, "his hands together". The exact position of his hands can, however, still be seen in a painted plaster cast of the statuette which has adorned the burial vault of the Bonde family at the church in Spånga since 1744.[26]

The only other damage visible on the original is to some of the points of the royal crown, on one side of the nose (where some of the paint has flaked off) and on smaller areas of the face (the eyebrows and lower lips). The king is wearing a cuirass which can be seen through slashes in his gown at the throat, over the chest and in the sleeves. This heavy brocade garment cloaks the rest of his body, falling in substantial pleats which bend to lie on flat on the ground. The face is exceptionally life-like and painted so that it is even possible to see the stubble of a greyish beard on the powerful jaws and the double chin. Only the portrait of its founder painted by Notke on the reredos in Århus displays the same detailed life-like

128. King Karl Knutsson Bonde. A painted wooden statuette. Donated to the National Portrait Collection at Gripsholm Castle in 1827.

effect, although this can hardly be said of the sculptures of the two kneeling figures of the episcopal founders on the same reredos or the Triumphal Crucifix in Lübeck. Nevertheless, these too testify to his skill in portraying individuals and are moreover of the same type as the statuette of the king.

However, in many respects the statuette resembles even more the statuette of the princess in the Saint George group. Both the posture and the shape of the abundant spiralling curls match each other and details in the treatment of the garments are similar, both in the styling of the pleats and the way in which the effect of gold brocade is produced. In both cases the pomegranate pattern is the same. Unlike the kneeling figures of the bishops, the princess is holding her hands in more or less the same positions as the statuette of the king once did, according the plaster cast. Both are holding out their hands in prayer stretched parallel to but some distance from each other. But while the tips of her fingers meet, the king's do not. Like the princess, the king is wearing several rings, two of them on different joints of the same finger.

We do not know where the statuette of the king originally stood. Scholars have put forward a number of alternative proposals. One suggests that it originally stood in the Abbey Church at Vadstena, where Karl Knutsson's first wife is buried. Another is that it once formed part of the funeral monument above the king's own grave in the Church on Riddarholmen in Stockholm, where he was buried after his death in 1470. A third suggestion is that the statuette once belonged to the reredos behind the high altar in Uppsala Cathedral, where the painting of the battle referred to above also portrays Karl Knutsson. But if this were the case, this statuette would have been destroyed by the fire which consumed the rest of the reredos.[27]

In our opinion the hypothesis which is most tenable and based on the strongest arguments in this matter suggests that the statuette of the king was originally placed on the castle of the Saint George group where the princess is now erroneously sited. This would allow Karl Knutsson to appear in the role of the King of Silene, regarding the fate of his daughter and praying for her to be saved from the dragon. In representations of the Saint George legend the king (sometimes the queen as well) is depicted looking down from the city, as can be seen both in foreign bas-reliefs and Swedish wall-paintings from the late-Gothic period. And there was every reason for Sten Sture to place his uncle and political predecessor in the role of the legendary king, praying for his victory in the battle for national independence. As the last native monarch, he proclaimed the legitimacy of Sten Sture's struggle, thus completing the political symbolism of the group.[28]

In the process of writing this book, measurements have been made

129. Karl Knutsson's hands on the plaster cast made of the wooden statuette which has been standing since 1744 on the burial vault of the Bonde family at the church in Spånga.

130. The hands of the princess in Stockholm City Church. Note the numerous rings on both hands.

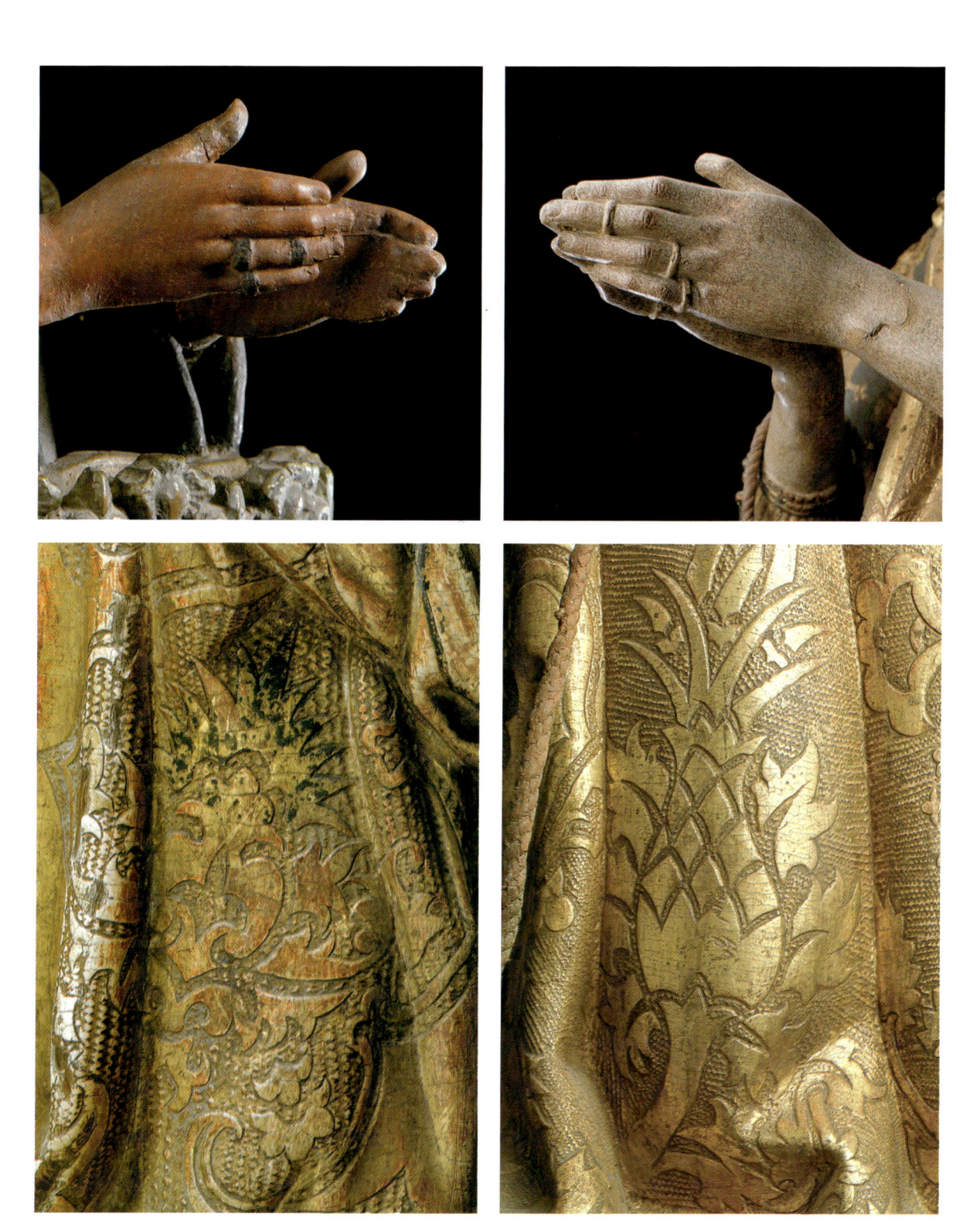

131-132. Detail of the brocade with its pattern of pomegranates from the statuette of the king at Gripsholm on the left, and the statue of the princess in Stockholm on the right. In reality the figures and the patterns are of different sizes but here they are reproduced at roughly the same size to make it easier to compare them.

129

which confirm that the statuette of the king would fit easily on to the roof of the castle, even leaving room for a possible representation of the queen and an extra tower.²⁹ It should also be noted that the king's coat-of-arms does not rest on the ground but that it is raised 3 inches (8 cm.) above it. If the statuette is placed on the roof of the castle, the coat-of-arms would therefore be fully visible above the surrounding crenellation which is 3 inches (8 cm.) high. It should be added that there is yet another reason for depicting Karl Knutsson on the Saint George group. As has already been pointed out, it was he who introduced the cult of Saint George as saint and knight to Sweden. It would seem from every point of view suitable to depict Karl Knutsson, who had himself invoked Saint George in his battle against the Danes and the Swedish nobles supporting the Union, kneeling here and praying to the saint to grant his successor victory in his battle against the same adversary.

Unlike the youthful, idealised, beautiful faces of the knight and the princess, this king has chiselled, clearly individual features. It must have been the ageing monarch who was called to mind when the effigy was carved more than a decade after his demise in 1470 at the age of 62. The head of the statue also matches the reconstruction of Karl Knutsson's profile created by an osteological expert on the basis of the form of his skull

133-134. Ivar Axelsson Tott and Magdalena Karlsdotter Bonde. Their names can be read on the pennants next to their coats-of-arms. Behind the woman there is a representation of the crucifixion, and behind the man the risen Lord. Painted in tempera on panels owned by the Tott family, now at Gavnö Castle in Denmark.

when his grave in the church at Riddarholmen was opened. This confirms that we are dealing with a portrait in the proper meaning of the word and one that was definitely based on pictures created during the king's lifetime.[30]

The same features can be seen in Karl Knutsson's daughter Magdalena Bonde, who is portrayed together with her husband, Ivar Axelsson Tott, in two portraits painted by an unknown artist some time after their marriage in 1466. The originals are today at Gavnö Castle in Denmark. Her portrait reveals the characteristic upturned nose, the small mouth, and the narrow chin surrounded by folds of fat, features that differ from those of her husband but resemble her father's. Another detail that distinguishes her portrait from that of her husband is that she is wearing several rings on her left hand. Like her father, she is wearing two on different segments of the same finger. At that time rings were regarded as important means of identification. This is made clear, for instance, by the description of how attempts were made to keep the death of Sten Sture secret by making one of his men wear his master's garments, knight's chain and rings (see above p. 48).

Both the statuette and these paintings confirm that here we are dealing with portraits from life, a genre which reached Scandinavia during the latter half of the 15th century from the Netherlands, and of which Bernt Notke is the leading representative.

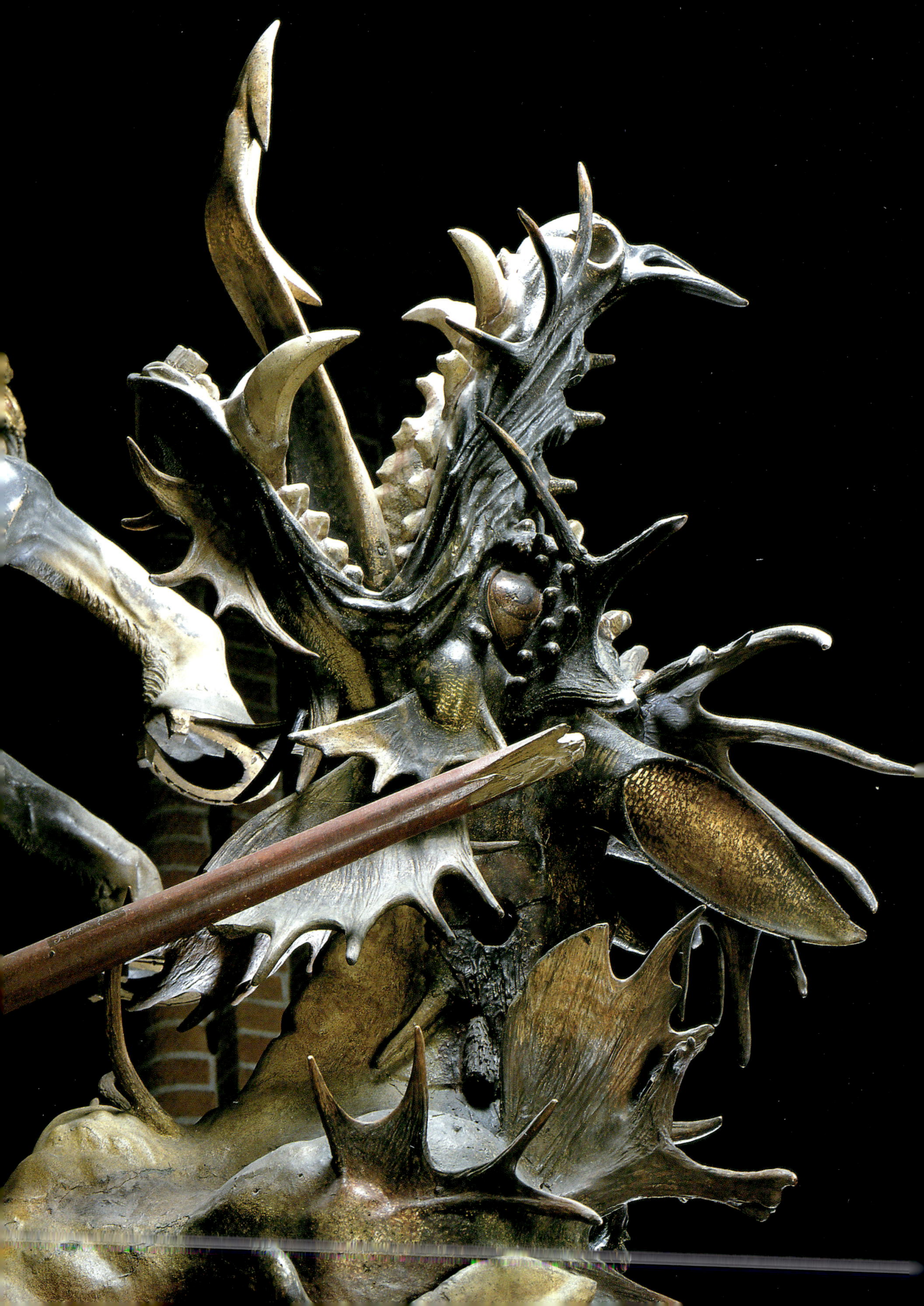

The Saint George Statue in Stockholm

The time has come to return to the Saint George group in Stockholm. After many years, in the 1480s Sten Sture found that the time was ripe to fulfil the promise he had made at the Battle of Brunkeberg to erect an altar to the glory of Saint George. Ten years were needed to prepare for the work of erecting new vaulting and not until the middle of the decade could the plans to erect a monumental and expensive sculpture in the enlarged church be put into effect. During the whole of the 15th century, it was to Lübeck that such commissions were customarily addressed from Sweden. Bernt Notke's massive achievements in the cathedrals of Lübeck and Århus were consecrated in 1477 and 1479, as is confirmed by reliable written evidence, making him the first person to turn to in Lübeck or indeed in the whole Baltic region for works of a size and quality beyond the ordinary.[31]

The reputation of such works could spread throughout Scandinavia in a number of different ways. The complex and extensive kinship connections provided one of them. The Bishop who commissioned the Triumphal Crucifix in Lübeck, Albert Krummedik, had a kinswoman in Uppland, north of Stockholm, Lady Agneta Krummedik at Örbyhus Castle, who had previously commissioned an extensive series of paintings for the church of which she was patron at Vendel (see illustration 25). Bishops were in touch with their fellow-bishops in other Scandinavian sees, and they also belonged to the councils of the realm in the respective countries, together with the most prominent secular lords. There is evidence that the dispute about payment for the Århus reredos was discussed in the Danish council. These councils of the realm also met each other when negotiations took place between the Scandinavian countries.[32]

We also know that in the 1480s Sten Sture sent several of his closest men – a Councillor of the Realm and his private chaplain – to Lübeck directly to negotiate a treaty with the Hanseatic League and that there they met Bernt Notke, who acted as a witness for the head of the Swedish delegation and as their representative.[33]

Notke had visited Sweden previously. During the 1480s there is evidence placing him in Stockholm on two occasions (in 1483 and 1484) and in Lübeck on three (1484, 1486 and 1487). As far as the other years are concerned, and in particular for the important period in which the Stockholm monument was created 1488-1490, there is no information at all about him. From 1491 to 1494 there are continuous references to his be-

135. The head of the dragon in Stockholm. The spiny growths are made of the elk's antlers.

ing in Stockholm, and also in 1496. In documents from Stockholm he is most often linked with resident German merchants and tradesmen as a witness in various disputes. He was held in high regard, since in 1493 he was chosen along with noble Swedish supporters of the Stures to swear an oath when the castle bailiff was replaced. In the same year he appeared as a witness in the Council Chamber when he was cross-examined by Sten Sture himself. From 1491 to 1493 Notke held the office of Master of the National Mint in Stockholm. This appointment was made by Sten Sture and was definitely anything but an honorary post, as its occupant could have great impact on the national exchequer. The fact that Notke was entrusted with this office was almost certainly due to his commercial flair, of which there is a great deal of evidence in other contexts. It was also, of course, mainly to pay him for the enormous work he was creating. On the fall of Sten Sture in 1497, Notke returned to Lübeck.[34]

Bernt Notke is indirectly linked to the Saint George group in one document that has been preserved, which is the letter referred to above when he is described as "en selsen man" (a strange, remarkable, peculiar person) by his fellow-artist Henrik Wilsing, who, however, would once again like to be a good friend of his. This letter was addressed to one of the burghers of Stockholm in 1506, and is signed with the words "Henrik Wilsing, who helped to make George in Stockholm" ("henrick Wylssynck, de den Joryen help maken toe dem holm"). This has led to the conclusion that Wilsing was one of Notke's assistants, as the letter concerns a transaction between them – although admittedly much later.[35]

Bernt Notke obviously took his workforce with him to Stockholm, or parts of it, and that is where the enormous work was probably created.

136-137. The veins on the feet of the Crucified Christ in Lübeck (on the left) and on the stomach of Saint George's horse in Stockholm (on the right) are made in the first case of strips of leather and in the second of string under the gesso.

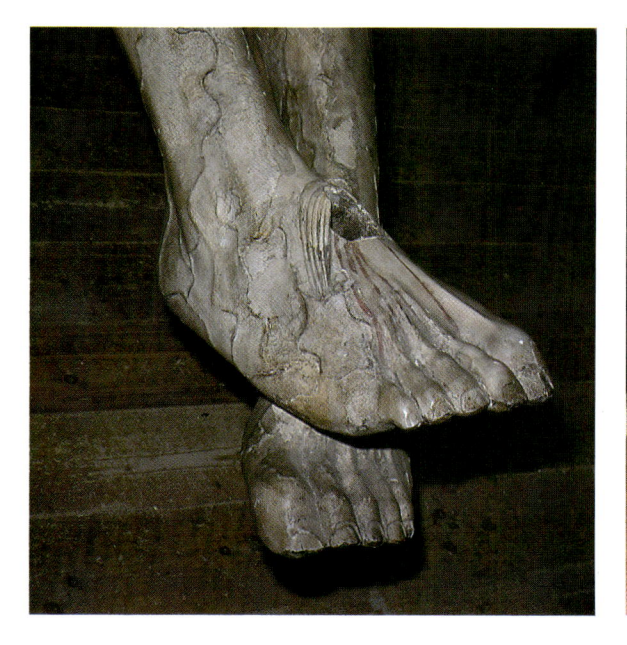

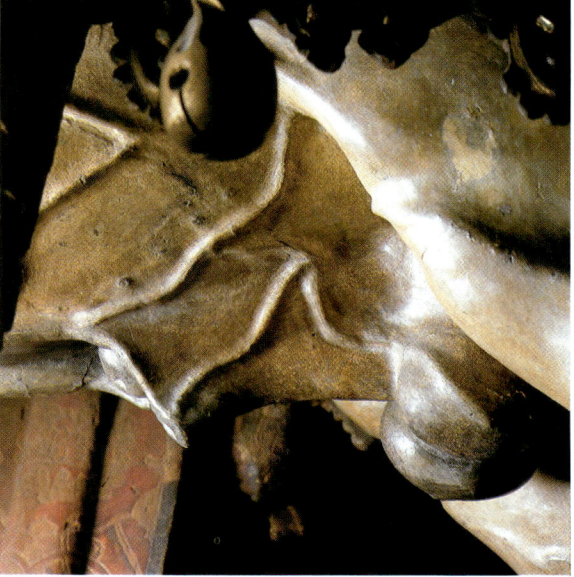

138. A sculptor's mallet, found in the stomach of the horse.

Evidence for this can be found for instance in the imprint mentioned above of coins minted in Stockholm in the 1470s which can be seen on the reliefs on the plinth (illustrations 96-96).³⁶ Previous generations of scholars have devoted a great deal of energy to attempting to distinguish and identify the contributions made by the individuals involved in the project. But the only one whose name is known with certainty is Wilsing, and according to Paatz he did the simpler work on the large sculptures and the reliefs on the castle. On the other hand, in Paatz's opinion, all but two of the reliefs on the plinth of the main group were carved by Master Bernt's journeyman, Thönnies Hermensson. All that is known with any certainty about this individual, however, is that he visited Stockholm on Notke's behalf in 1484. The Master himself carved the relief now in Danderyd, perhaps to set the pattern for the style of the rest of the work, and of course the fine detail of the large sculptures.³⁷

Roosval and several other scholars have been of a different opinion about how the work was divided up. Later, Sten Karling put forward the idea that the A found on a tile in the final plinth relief (see illustration 107) can mean that it was Albertus Pictor who painted the reliefs and signed them with his initial. All of this is, however, guesswork that cannot be confirmed.³⁸ We must imagine that the work proceeded in the same way as on the Lübeck crucifix. Notke assumed overall responsibility for the whole undertaking, submitting a sketch of the proposed work which his client approved. He then allocated the various tasks to his different specialists and supervised their work, offering advice and providing examples.

From a technical point of view the Saint George group matches Notke's other work, particularly the Lübeck crucifix, which it most resembles. Both the large sculptures and the reliefs in each group are carved from oak, the timber specified for the workshops manufacturing reredoses in Lübeck. This was covered, as was customary, with a layer of gesso on which the paint and gilt could be applied.³⁹ The horse and its rider are hollow, as they would otherwise have been too heavy. A sculptor's mallet was forgotten inside the stomach of the horse, and a playing card inside one of the relief screens (a two of clubs). They were found during the restoration work, and exhibited in a display case until they disappeared in 1978 after a break-in.

139. How the Saint George statues may have been placed in the City Church originally. The reasons for proposing this reconstruction are presented in more detail in the documentation section at the end of the book.

The Saint George group also displays Notke's inventiveness and his predilection for extraneous materials. To reproduce the effect of the bulging veins on the horse he has placed string below the gesso – in exactly the same way as on the feet of the crucified Christ in Lübeck. The roan's hide is painted naturalistically and in certain places real hide has been used to reproduce the longer hair in the ears and under the jaw – and bristles mixed with linen for the knotted tail and for the mane which lies in small curls. Even the horse's equipment is formed of real materials to some extent. The stirrup leathers are made of real leather, while the pommel and the bit are made of iron, and the guiding reins of metal chain, an important detail in reality to ensure that the enemy could not render a war-horse ungovernable by severing the reins.[40]

Most of the horse's equipment and all of the rider's armour have, however, been carved from wood. Here paint and gilt have been used to create the illusion of metal plates and the precious stones set into them. To reproduce the effect of fabric, parchment has been used in certain places, as it has in other works by Notke. This can be seen in the lapel of the bust of the dead man on the base-plate, which also has traces of real hair adhering to the skull. One of the stones on the base-plate is covered with a layer of fine splinters of glass, glued there to produce the effect of an exotic, glittering and fearful terrain. Among these extraneous materials, however, the many elk antlers used to create the spiny growths on the dragon are the most remarkable.

From a stylistic point of view, certain details on the Saint George group and the reliefs that belong to it match peculiarities to be found on Notke's other works. Attention has already been drawn to the similarity between John the Evangelist on the reredos in Tallinn and Saint George, especially in the poison chalice scene. Skulls which are very similar in appearance to the ones on the base-plate under the dragon in Stockholm can be found painted on the Dance Macabre wall-hanging in Tallinn and sculpted in the Triumphal Crucifix group in Lübeck (cf. illustrations 45 & 46 with 116 & 119).

In addition to similarities in both style and techniques the Saint George group displays resemblances with Notke's signed Triumphal Crucifix in other respects as well. This is true in particular of the overwhelming size with which the main protagonists in both groups have been portrayed. In both cases they are considerably larger than life, which is extremely unusual where wooden sculptures are concerned.[41] The closest parallel can be found in the famous reredos of the high altar of St Mary's Church in Cracow by Veit Stoss. It was created by this great Southern German master between 1477-89 in what was then the capital of Poland and commissioned by the German congregation there. The polychrome sculptures are carved on the same scale as Notke's but, unlike his, they reveal an almost mannered agitation.[42]

The Saint George group in Stockholm and the Triumphal Crucifix in Lübeck were also positioned in much the same way in both churches. The fact is that everything suggests that the group in Stockholm was also placed below the triumphal arch in the transept. Both rose to a great height. Saint George was probably galloping towards the east. The princess was probably kneeling in front of the knight and the dragon on the same elevated plane, her back turned to the combat, her hands and eyes raised in prayerful petition to the high altar. The city of Silene, in the form of the castle, may have stood behind the horse. Below this main group the screens with their reliefs enclosed a chapel. This perhaps abutted on to the choir screen, as was customary in the late-Gothic period (many such examples can still be seen in England). In some ways this arrangement corresponds to the chancel screen with the Triumphal Crucifix in the adjoining bay in Lübeck Cathedral.[43]

A crucifix in the City Church has also been attributed to Bernt Notke. Here the figure of Christ measures only 51 inches (128 cm.) but in style and anatomical detail it resembles the enormous figure on the crucifix in Lübeck. The crucifix in Stockholm now lacks all of its paint and has been hung on one of the southern pillars in the chancel. Originally, it may well

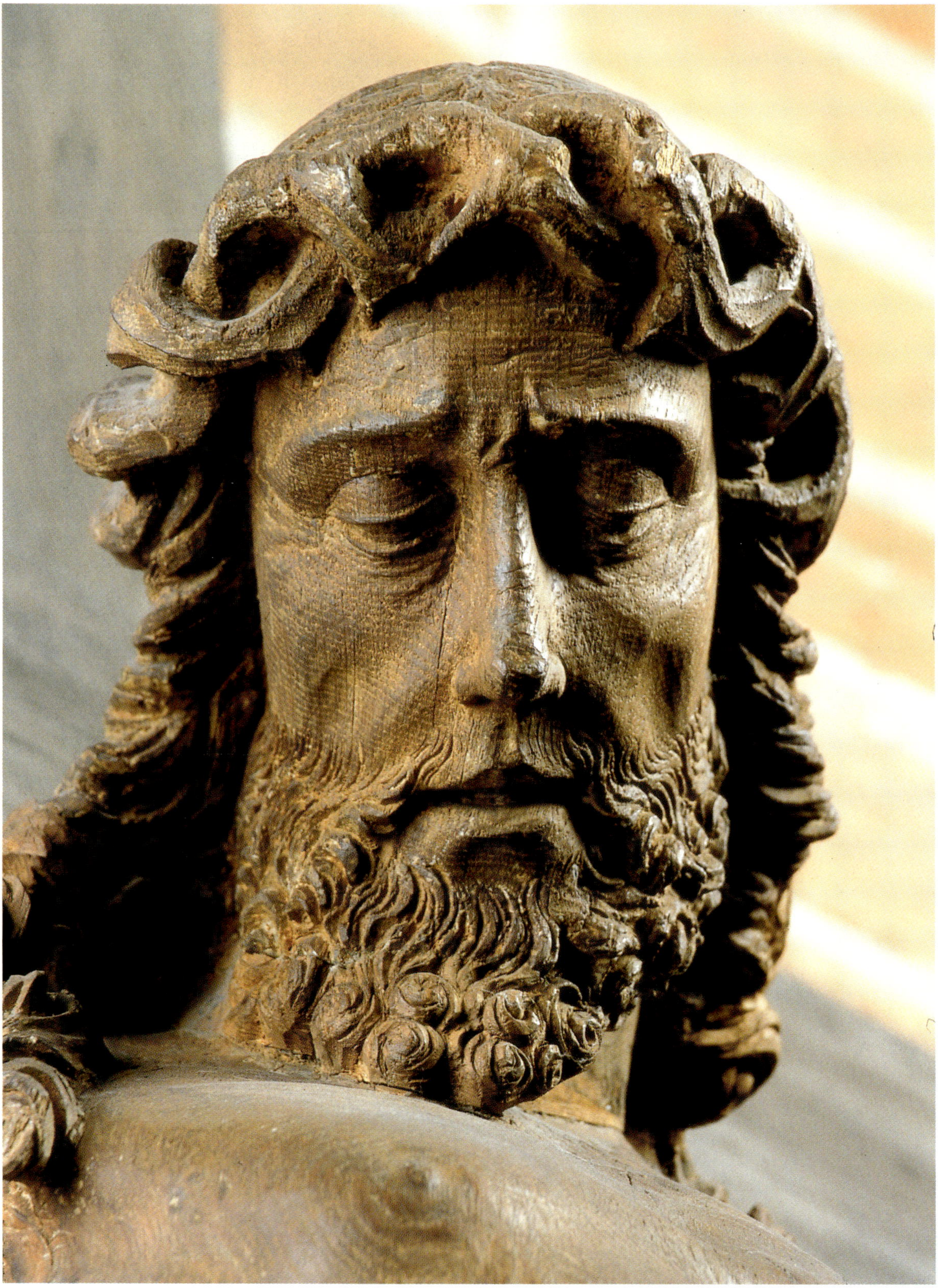

140. The head of the Crucified Christ in Stockholm. The angle of the head was altered in 1934 when the beard was also given a pointed finish.

141. The Crucifix in the City Church attributed to Bernt Notke.

have hung in front of the Saint George group. In this position in the City Church it would have been its triumphal crucifix and shown whence Saint George, his eyes raised, derives his strength in his combat with the dragon.⁴⁴

Both Saint George and Lübeck's Crucified Christ bore relics in the chains around their necks. In Lübeck the relics were enclosed in a golden cross hanging from a real chain. On Saint George the chain is carved and in the large pendant on his chest there were four compartments in which the relics were originally laid. Older descriptions tell us that they were covered only by a transparent pane of glass so that the relics would be visible. In 1700 both the relics and the pane of glass were removed and a lid resembling a cuirass was carved of wood to replace it: this gilt lid still conceals the reliquary. ⁴⁵

In both Lübeck and Stockholm a special altar as well as the founder's grave were placed under the sculptures. The two gigantic altar groups in Lübeck Cathedral and Stockholm City Church are therefore similar in many respects. We can also compare the expenses incurred by the founders of the two enormous sculptural groups. As has already been mentioned, we can establish that the Saint George group cost Sten Sture and his subordinates twice as much as Bishop Albert Krummedik paid for the crucifix in Lübeck – 4,000 mark as opposed to 2,000. In both cases these are sums that correspond to millions in today's terms. The Saint George group also represents an artistic climax in Notke's oeuvre as it does in the history of European sculpture.

It was to be his last major work. His first had been the Dance Macabre wall-hangings with their harrowing depiction of the power of death. In the Triumphal Crucifix in Lübeck he has portrayed with poignant effect the death of Christ and the sorrow of His mourners but also demonstrated that it created the possibility of the resurrection of the dead. In Stockholm, too, Notke makes great play with death both in his depiction of its many victims on the base-plate and of death itself in the figure of the enormous dragon. Here, however, victory over terror of death is not a secondary motif as it was in the Lübeck group, but is instead the optimistic main theme of this work of art. It is, nevertheless, the enormous and terrifying reality of the threat of death that gives Notke's representation of Saint George its uniqueness and its extraordinary power. This makes Saint George's struggle and victory over death and evil all the more arduous and admirable. This is also the real theme of the depiction of the saint's martyrdom in the reliefs on the plinth.

A Perennial Motif

142. A relief carving on a reredos from the 1490s in the church at Lillkyrka, Östergötland, which imitates the plinth relief in Stockholm City Church depicting Saint George undergoing torture on the rack (Illustration 88). Here too Dacianus has a beard and a hat, one of the torturers is cutting the saint with a knife while another rubs salt in the wounds. Compare his cropped hair and cauliflower ears and the third torturer's idiosyncratic headgear with the corresponding details in Stockholm (Illustrations 97 and 99).
Here, however, there are only three torturers not four, and the small animal under the rack has crept out and been transformed into a devil (bottom left). This is the only motif involving Saint George in a reredos in which the reliefs on the centre panel and the other wings represent Our Lady and details from her life.[1]

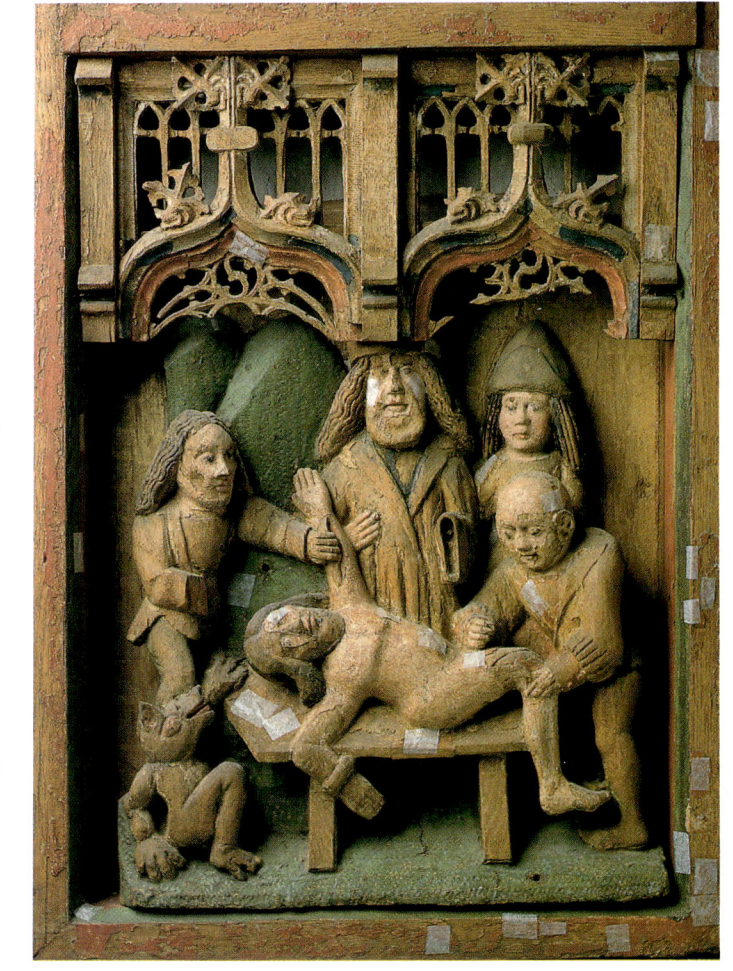

143. The Saint George group by Henning von der Heide in the St. Anne Museum in Lübeck, made in 1504-05 for the city's Chapel of Saint George. As in Notke's group, the original giant dragon was lying on its back piercing the horse's stomach with one of its claws, but in 1619 this was replaced by the small dragon, depriving the work of some of its dramatic effect.

The Saint George group, the result of Sten Sture's unique investment and Bernt Notke's creative genius, was to have an impact that no work of art previously, and few since then, have achieved in Sweden. Innumerable churches all over the realm, from Småland in the south to Norrland in the north and Finland in the east were soon embellished with imitations of the national monument in the form of wooden sculptures of Saint George, sword or lance in hand, in equestrian combat with the dragon to release the princess. Compared to the group in Stockholm City Church, they are all much simpler in design and reduced in size (as a rule they are between 39 to 59 inches high – 100-150 cm.).

In some cases whole groups have been preserved with the knight and his horse, the dragon, the princess and lamb, as is the case in the church at Vika in Dalecarlia and at Hattula in Finland. In several cases only the lamb is missing, in others all that remains is the knight with the horse and the dragon or the princess. In a large number of churches only two or one of the figures have survived, and in some cases only the torso of the knight. Altogether there are around thirty such groups in Sweden and twenty in Finland, counting those in which a more or less complete statue of the knight, the horse or the princess remain.

In addition to those that have been preserved, there are references to many more Saint George groups in ancient records from different churches, made before the groups were to disappear. We also have to take into account that many more disappeared without leaving any trace in documents that happen to have been preserved. "Saint George in the form of a knight on a horse; which in the past was to be found in all our churches" is how Olov Broman, the vicar of Hudiksvall, put it when at the beginning of the 18th century he provided us with a more thorough de-

144. A Saint George group from the 1470's in the church at Vika in Dalecarlia. After the choir screen had been removed in 1727, the figures were placed behind an arch in the chancel, which was later walled up. There was a local tradition that the figures had been immured there, and that they were disinterred at the beginning of the 20th century.

scription of his native Hälsingland than any other province had hitherto been blessed with. In Broman's day, many of these statues still existed, but today there are only two such groups left in Hälsingland, which will be dealt with in more detail below.[2]

Broman also describes where these Saint George groups were normally sited in the churches, the position that in many cases they still occupied at the time he was writing – standing on the northern side of the choir screen, next to the triumphal crucifix.[3] Examples of this elevated position dominating the nave can also be cited from other provinces. For example, the groups that have now disappeared in the churches at Adelsö (which was dedicated to Saint George) and Hammarby were placed on their choir screens. This position was clearly frequent, and approximates to the position that Notke's group was in all probability given on its plinth under the triumphal crucifix in Stockholm City Church, as has been described above.[4]

There is no room here to present all the Saint George groups from the last half century before the Reformation that have been preserved in Swedish and Finnish churches (they are listed in the Swedish edition of this work). As has already been mentioned, they number about fifty altogether, ranging from Falsterbo in the south (if we are to include the three that survive from what were then Danish provinces) up to Övertorneå in the north and in deepest Tavastland in the east. Here we shall restrict ourselves to illustrative examples.[5]

145. A Saint George group from the end of the 15th century in the church of Övertorneå. Originally the figures stood in the chapel at Särkilax, which was swallowed by the Torne river in the heavy spring flooding of 1516. During haymaking the following summer, they were found on the bank at Matarengi, where a new church was built, later to be Övertorneå. The princess in the group disappeared in the 1950s and was replaced by a newly made copy.

146. A Saint George group dating from around 1500 in the church at Kråksmåla in Småland. The saint was originally raising a sword in his right hand, but this has disappeared and been replaced erroneously by a spear. Note the princess's plaits and the way in which the fabric is draped from her shoulders.

The popularity of the Saint George sculptures during this period cannot, of course, be explained solely as the result of the inspiration provided by Notke's magnificent precedent. Other factors were involved as well, the most important being the intensification of the cult of Saint George during this period, which has already been described and which inspired Sten Sture's choice of motif. Many of those who had formed part of the victorious army at Brunkeberg and joined in singing the Lay of Saint George would have wanted to express their gratitude to their patron saint with an image in their own parish church without waiting for Sten Sture's great statue of the saint finally to be ready. We must not forget, either, that the dramatic motif has its own inherent tension, which could appeal to both artist and patron. And even if Notke was the creator of the most magnificent model, there may have been other powerful sources of inspiration that have now disappeared. Such sources obviously formed the basis of many contemporary wall-paintings of Saint George and the dragon. At times, therefore, it is difficult or even impossible to decide if the inspiration for a Saint George group in a country church comes from Stockholm City Church or somewhere else.

Some of the Saint George groups like those at Vika in Dalecarlia and Färentuna in the Mälar Islands were produced earlier than Notke's and are composed differently.⁶ The horses are standing with all four hooves on the

147. A Saint George group from the beginning of the 16th century in the church at Hattula in Tavastland. The dragon used to be holding the broken shaft of the lance in its front claw, as it does in Stockholm.

ground and the knight is plunging his lance into a dragon that is not lying on its back. A corresponding, but less well-preserved Saint George knight from Sund on Åland is reckoned to be the only "pre-Notke" group in Finland.[7]

Four Swedish Saint George groups have, however, adopted Notke's dramatic grouping with a knight wielding his sword above his head to strike against a dragon who is raising the horse aloft with an outstretched claw. These are the groups in Kråksmåla in Småland, where the dragon is also stretching out its head, and in Hedesunda in Gästrikland, Vätö in Roslagen and Skellefteå in Västerbotten. The Kråksmåla group was probably imported from Lübeck around 1500 while the others were produced in Sweden. The group in Vätö was probably made in Stockholm well into the 16th century.

We must go east to find by far the closest successors to the great group in the Stockholm City Church. They comprise a Saint George raising his sword from the back of a rearing horse held aloft by a dragon lying on its back. Details in these groups reveal, as do the princesses, obvious fidelity to their great model. One of these groups is in the church at Finström on Åland, and is considered to have been made in Stockholm at the end of the 15th century. Others can be found in Sagu, Hattula, and eight more churches on the Finnish mainland. These groups are obviously based on Notke both from the point of view of arrangement and details, but the facial features and style suggest that most of them were made in Finland.[8]

The dramatic grouping of Notke's composition is therefore imitated in many more groups in Finland than in Sweden, and the eleven Finnish specimens are more faithful imitations than any of the Swedish groups of this type. Moreover, the Finnish examples are in a better state of preservation, and will therefore be commented on briefly here.

The eleven Finnish Georges are bare-headed with only a headband in their hair and are raising, or have raised, their right hands to deliver a blow with the sword, although only the one in Finström still retains his sword. In the group that is otherwise in the best state of repair, the one in Hattula, the knight still has even the long empty scabbard at his side, exactly as in Stockholm.

On many of the horses, the fabric of the reins is at least partly rendered in leather. Some have tails made of horse-hair, others of wood. In one or two cases the dragons had four legs, as in Stockholm, but most have only two. Only the largest dragon (over two metres in length in Hollola) retains its reproductive organ – it is a male. Holes suggest that several others once had such organs, which have later disappeared. They seem only to have been males. The dragons have been wounded in the same way as in Stockholm – the tip of the lance has penetrated the throat (sometimes in Finland entering through the jaw) and in some cases still remains in the

148. The head of Saint George. A detail from the Saint George group in Hattula (illustration 147). His horse is galloping so fast that his fringe is being blown upwards.

149. A Saint George group from the beginning of the 16th century in the church at Rusko, Finland, now in the Museum at Åbo Castle. Here as well, all five figures and the base plate have been preserved. The shaft of the lance in the dragon's claw is, however, a replacement dating from 1701.

hole. The dragon has grasped the broken shaft of the lance in one of its claws, although the grip is now empty except in two cases.

It is interesting to note the existence of Sten Sture's coat-of-arms in several of the Finnish churches with these Saint George statues that are such faithful imitations of the one he founded in Stockholm. At Hollola we know that his now expunged coat-of-arms was painted on one of the vaults. In Sagu it still remains: carved in two places on what was once the choir screen, which probably supported the statue of Saint George. This indicates that Sten Sture was in one way or another behind the creation of this statue, and perhaps all the Finnish groups of this type, probably to stiffen spiritual preparedness in Finland in connection with the war on the eastern borders in the 1490s.

Other groups both in Finland and in Sweden may have horses standing four-square with all four hooves on the ground and Georges that sometimes have a lance instead of a sword but reveal nevertheless in details or in general stance that they derive, indirectly at least, from Notke's group.[10] Among them are groups made in the productive workshop of Haaken Gulleson, the great master active in Hälsingland at the beginning of the 16th century. The masterpiece is the group he almost certainly made himself in the church at Bjuråker, where the knight in armour that is gilt in both silver and gold rises erect and confident in his stirrups. He is wearing a knight's chain with the Lamb of God in the pendant on his chest and has a plaited headband in two colours round his golden-blond hair. This chaplet may indicate both here and on its great original a previous victory, for this is what the bays awarded in real tournaments looked like.[11] The regular face has bulging eyebrows and the look of serenity which characterises Gulleson's figures. Saint George's right gauntlet once grasped a lance, the left controlling the reins with which he is holding his grey stallion still, its head lowered. The princess is carved with equally distinct contours and painted as skilfully. She is wearing her plaits arranged in a ring on the top of her head and wears an extremely elegant dress, one half white, the other dark blue, pleated at the front and at each shoulder, with a cape hanging from her shoulders at the back.[12]

Haaken Gulleson did not seek inspiration for the princess from Bernt Notke's princess, although we do not know what provided the impulses that reached his workshop in the village of Fläcka in Hälsingland. The accompanying dragon is now missing as it is in the group in Hälsingtuna, where Saint George is raising his sword and his horse its head. Otherwise there are great similarities with the group at Bjuråker, and also with Saint George and his horse at Lögdö and the torso of Saint George at Stöde, both in Medelpad. But the quality of the execution suggests that the last of these at least was a product of his workshop.[13] A group on the other side of the Baltic has also been attributed to Haaken Gulleson, the one in

150. A Saint George group from the beginning of the 16th century in the church at Tortuna in Västmanland, now in the Museum of National Antiquities, Stockholm. The horse's harness has pendants with the initials of Charles XI and Ulrika Eleonora and the date 168? (the pendant with the last digit is missing), which is when the sculpture was restored and repainted. The dragon's tongue is made of tin plate and the sword is a modern reconstruction.[9]

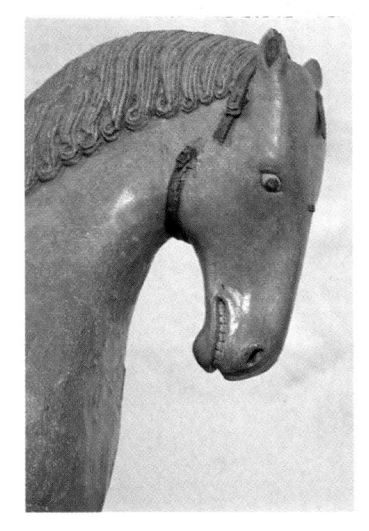

151. In Bjuråker it is only the head of the horse that expresses concern at the approach of the dragon.

152. A Saint George group by Haaken Gulleson from the beginning of the 16th century in the church at Bjuråker in Hälsingland. The princess has the same kind of plaits and cape on the back of her dress as in the group in Kråksmåla (cf. Illustration146) so that one can assume that they were based on the same source.

the church at Laihela in Österbotten, where not only Saint George wielding his sword and a kneeling princess have survived, but with them the dragon – rendered by this master with a rather docile appearance.[14]

Next to the Saint George in Stockholm, the largest and most impressive of the Swedish groups is a life-size statue of a knight in Gotland's Museum of Antiquities (Gotlands Fornsal) in Visby. There the knight is restraining his horse with a tight rein so that it is standing still with all four hooves on the ground as at Vika, Bjuråker, and other smaller Saint George statues. In Visby the bodies of both figures are hollow and they are carved from oak, apart from the knight's right arm which is a clumsier recent replacement in pine. The exact position of the hand that has now disappeared, and what kind of weapon it once held is not known. The

153. Saint George in Gotland's Museum of Antiquities, Visby. Probably carved in the 1480s.

princess and the dragon are missing as well. The Visby knight is wearing armour and an elegant tunic with a carved pattern on the sleeves which is held together by a braid across his chest. The sculpture reveals traces of two coats of paint – the most recent from crude repainting after 1642, probably in connection with the return of Gotland to Sweden. A modern investigation has established what the original colours were: the knight's garments were in gold and red, and the horse was a dapple grey with a small red cross of Saint George on its virtually white brow.[15]

During the years when stylistic features suggest this sculpture was produced, Ivar Axelsson Tott was the Governor of Gotland, a position he held from 1466 – 1487. He was one of several brothers, originally Danish, who controlled a number of the most important Swedish provinces and exerted great influence on Scandinavian politics at the time. Ivar was

154. Ivar Axelsson Tott's coat-of-arms. A water colour by Søren Abildgaard from 1753 based on an original which has since disappeared from Visby Cathedral. National Museum, Copenhagen.

married to the daughter of Karl Knutsson (see Illustrations 133–134 above) and there was an agreement that on the death of the king he was to become Governor of the Realm, although he later had to accept Sten Sture in this position. Sten Sture was married to the daughter of one of his brothers, Åke, and Ivar Axelsson co-operated with him for a long time. In the end, however, Ivar Axelsson and Sten Sture fell out and he was forced to abandon Gotland in 1487 (yielding it to the Danish king). He left the island and died later that year in Scania.

As early as in the 17th century there is mention of the Visby statue of Saint George, whose garments were the Tott family's red and gold, standing in the church of St. Mary, nowadays the city's Cathedral. As recently as 1759, "five large pictures" were preserved there together, and these may have adorned the base of the statue of the knight. Four of them depicted saints, one was a representation of the coat-of-arms of the Tott family surmounted by a helmet above the text "Ywer Acselson ritt" (Ivar Axelsson, Esq.) In design this corresponds exactly with the coat-of-arms in Stockholm for "Sten Sture Esq." (cf. Illustrations 35 and 154).[16]

The two potentates, kinfolk and rivals, seem almost to have been competing with each other in commissioning representative Saint George groups. It has been assumed that Ivar Axelsson was spurred by his kinsman's imposing foundation in Stockholm to procure a similar monument for Visby. In that case, the commission must have been placed before he was forced to leave Gotland in 1487, or in other words a few years before Notke had completed his work. It may therefore be the case that Ivar Axelsson commissioned his monument first, as it is, after all, more dated in expression, reflecting no influence of the later work's dramatic intensity. The material and the quality of the execution of the Visby statue suggest that it was produced in a workshop in Lübeck. The master craftsmen there were aware of the major works their confrères were engaged on, and were inspired by and sought to outdo each other – just as their patrons sometimes did.

It is uncertain where the Visby Saint George group was placed originally, as during the late Middle Ages a large number of the city's churches were still in use. A great deal suggests that it was in the chapel of the castle

155. The head of the Visby knight. Detail of illustration 153.

of Visborg. This was the residence of Ivar Axelsson and an inventory from 1509 mentions that there was an equestrian figure of Saint George in the chapel. The fact that no other equestrian statue of the saint is recorded on Gotland suggests that this is identical with the one that has been preserved, as does the fact that there is evidence that some of the chapel's fittings were later moved to the church of Saint Mary. However, another possible position has also been suggested in the church of Saint Hans, where two of Ivar Axelsson's brothers were buried in 1464 after dying of the plague. Ivar Axelsson may also have intended his grave to be adjacent to theirs, next to the majestic Saint George statue painted in his colours, whose face may also have been an idealised version of his own (cf. his painted portrait, illustration 133, and the face of the statue with its well preserved polychromy, illustration 155).[17]

Although the majestic Saint George group in Stockholm has been imitated repeatedly on a smaller scale, only a few reliefs have been preserved that have been copied from those on the plinth. One of these is a single scene showing the saint being tortured on the rack. This can be found in a reredos from the end of the 15th century in Lillkyrka, Östergötland, which is otherwise devoted to Our Lady (illustration 142). The other is a small suite of reliefs originally part of a reredos but now adorning the pulpit of the church at Tillinge in Uppland, which consists merely of two

156. Saint George in the Temple of Apollo.

157. He is beheaded. Reliefs on the pulpit of the church in Tillinge, Uppland. They come from a reredos from the end of the 15th century in the neighbouring church of Ängsö, Västmanland.

158. Saint George and the dragon from the same reredos in Ängsö church as the reliefs in illustrations 156 & 157. The figure is now positioned on a pier in Tillinge church.

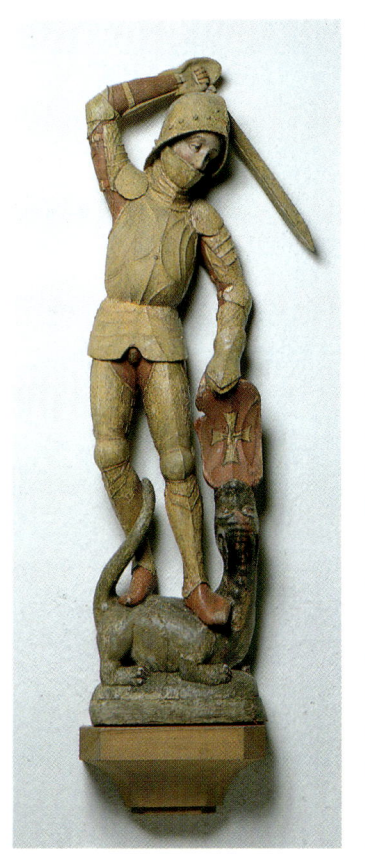

carved scenes. One of them depicts Saint George being urged to worship Apollo, the other how he was finally beheaded. In these reliefs everything is simplified. Each contains eight figures standing in stiff stereotypical postures, albeit with a variety of facial expressions, around the kneeling saint while the bearded Dacianus raises his index finger in a commanding gesture (illustrations 156 and 157).

In the first relief, the column of the temple, to which the image of the idol that has now disappeared was originally attached by a peg in the hole at the top of the capital, and the chequered pattern of the floor are recognisably those of the corresponding relief in the City Church (cf. illustration 92). But its dramatic representation of the collapse of the column and the temple vaults over the heathens who are dead or attempting to protect themselves from the shower of stonework was beyond the capacities of this less gifted sculptor. Instead he has depicted them standing calmly gazing on, in other words at the moment before Saint George's prayer leads to the destruction of the temple. The saint is kneeling in a long golden mantle as he is in the corresponding scene in the City Church. There is another kneeling figure behind him, but it is uncertain whether he is praying to God or to the Governor's deity.

Nothing in Stockholm corresponds to the other relief at Tillinge, which depicts the execution of the saint (illustration 157). But this scene must originally have been represented there as the conclusion of the reliefs depicting the martyrdom. This relief at Tillinge is interesting because it probably refers to its original in more or less the same way as the previous one. It therefore gives us some indication of the probable appearance of the final representation of the consummation of the martyrdom in the City Church. Saint George is kneeling on the ground with his hands tied together – the execution naturally took place out of doors. He is now wearing his armour as he is in Stockholm as he is finally brought before Dacianus to be sentenced to death. In the relief at Tillinge the executioner is raising his sword with both hands. The sculptor has, however, mistakenly reversed his tunic, so that we can see its lapels and the buttons that fasten it across the chest even though otherwise he is standing with his back to us. Behind him two men with bound hands are waiting their turn to be executed – probably because they have been converted by Saint George.[18]

Both these reliefs once formed the right wing of a reredos, and the remaining sections also adorn the pulpit at Tillinge, apart from one for which there was no room so that it was erected on one of the piers instead. The left wing of the reredos depicted two corresponding scenes from the legend of Catherine of Alexandria – her disputation and beheading. In the fixed central section of the reredos there were two statues of the saints, almost a metre in height, on each side of a representation of

Our Lady. There was no room here to depict Saint George on horseback, but for the small niche available here, as in other reredoses, a standing effigy of the dragon-slayer had to suffice. A corresponding figure could also be found in the City Church in the form of a statuette in the reredos of the high altar from 1468 (cf. illustrations 24 and 158) which is now in the National Museul of Antiquities. In the Tillinge statue we can also see the dragon winding its tail round the saint's right leg.[19]

When the pulpit at Tillinge was being constructed in 1753, "an old gilt altarpiece" was purchased from Ängsö, and it was broken up and the pieces used to embellish the new addition. The reredos came in other words from the neighbouring church of Ängsö in Västmanland. Conditions there were still absolutely feudal. The church and its furnishing came into existence at the behest and expense of the lord of the manor, living in nearby Ängsö Castle, who also appointed the priest and provided his living. At the end of the 15th century, when the reredos was created, the manor was owned by Bengt Fadersson, a Councillor of the Realm, who belonged to the Sparre of Hjulsta and Ängsö family and who died in 1494. He was the son of Fader Ulfsson, who died in 1488, a knight and Councillor of the Realm, and his wife Elin, who bequeathed the manor to their son. Her father had been Nils Bosson Sture, of the Natt och Dag family. He and Fader Ulfsson were among Sten Sture's supporters in the Battle of Brunkeberg and subsequently. Both contributed to the cost of the Saint George group in the City Church, as the coats-of-arms of both the Sparres and the Natt och Dags are among those of Sten Sture's supporters on the castle there (see illustration 79).[20]

Not only Fader Ulfsson and his wife but also his son Bengt should therefore have been eager to acquire a reredos for their own manor church in honour of the nation's patron saint. For them it was probably also an advantage that its smaller and simpler reliefs recalled the ones on the great monument in Stockholm that they had helped to pay for. It was not finished until 1489, when Fader Ulfsson had been dead for some time, and it was probably his son Bengt that commissioned the reredos. Judging from its style, it is likely that it was carved in Stockholm, where the sculptor was close to the inspiration provided by the models in the City Church.[21]

Bernt Notke's realistic and expressive style in the monument in Stockholm also provided impulses for sculptors and other artists working with completely different motifs during subsequent decades. This more general influence lies, however, outside the scope of our subject here.

As far as Saint George and the Dragon is concerned, however, it was in the Lübeck region that Notke's group inspired its two most significant successors. These are more or less life-size and the artists have both learnt from and reacted against their great predecessor.

The first was created only fifteen years after the dedication of Notke's work and was carved by his most prominent pupil, Henning von der Heide, in Lübeck (illustration 143). Today this Saint George group is displayed in the city's Saint Anne Museum but it was originally created for Lübeck's Chapel of Saint George in 1504–05 (that at least is when the artist was paid for the work, a total of 230 silver marks). The group is regarded as being the most important work created by this successful master at the height of his powers. Originally the rearing steed was borne aloft by

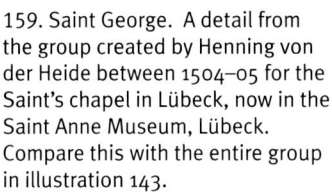

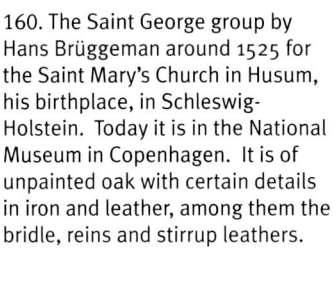

159. Saint George. A detail from the group created by Henning von der Heide between 1504–05 for the Saint's chapel in Lübeck, now in the Saint Anne Museum, Lübeck. Compare this with the entire group in illustration 143.

160. The Saint George group by Hans Brüggeman around 1525 for the Saint Mary's Church in Husum, his birthplace, in Schleswig-Holstein. Today it is in the National Museum in Copenhagen. It is of unpainted oak with certain details in iron and leather, among them the bridle, reins and stirrup leathers.

an enormous dragon, lying like the one in Stockholm on its back with one claw in the charger's stomach. In the second decade of the 17th century, however, this dragon was replaced by the current dragon, which is far too small, which seems to be running away on all fours with its tail between its legs. As a result, the group has lost a great deal of its original impact. As in Stockholm, this group also includes a helmet carved in wood which is not intended for Saint George's head, and a kneeling princess. She is wringing her hands with anxiety, her eyes imploring Saint George to assist her, whereas the hands of Notke's princess clasped in prayer, her posture and her gaze express dignified calm.[22]

There are corresponding differences in the figure of the knight in the two works. Henning von der Heide gives us a Saint George who does not seek assistance from above but who relies entirely on his own powers and leans forward in the saddle to strike at the dragon with furious exertion. Here the individualism and condottiere spirit of the Renaissance has begun to affect the motif. This is the decisive difference from the equestrian saint in the Stockholm, whose gaze is not directed at the dragon to decide where best to strike but upwards towards a higher power, probably directly towards the church's triumphal crucifix. The image of the Christian knight, who in combat derives strength from above, has probably found its ultimate artistic expression here in Stockholm City Church at the end of the Middle Ages.

Around 1525, in other words after another twenty years, another great northern-German sculptor, Hans Brüggeman, created a notable Saint George group in wood for the Church of Saint Mary in Husum in Schleswig-Holstein. This almost life-size group was erected in the north aisle about three metres above the floor so that it stood out as a silhouette against the east window. The church was demolished at the beginning of the 19th century and the statue is now in the National Museum in Copenhagen. Brüggeman has also used Notke's expedient of having the dragon lie on its back stretching out a leg, its claw gripping the horse's body, so making it possible to depict the horse in full gallop. And exactly as in Stockholm, the tip of the lance has penetrated the dragon's throat while the broken shaft is held tightly by the dragon's right front claw. Whereas, however, the enormous dragon in the City Church still has enough strength to raise its head in a threatening counter-attack, its sexless successor has already been vanquished, writhing on the ground, its rear legs splayed, its head downcast in the paroxysm of death. No wonder then that this horse does not seem frightened as its two predecessors did. Unlike the two other groups, here the knight is wearing his helmet. His mouth half-open, as if from exertion, his gaze weary under the heavy eyebrows, he looks down at his vanquished foe and raises his sword for the coup-de-grâce. His face, with its long pointed nose and prominent lower lip and jaw, more closely resembles the Emperor Charles V than the Duke of Schleswig, later to be King Fredrik I of Denmark, who at the same time commissioned an enormous reredos from Brüggeman (now in Schleswig Cathedral).[23]

Brüggeman's Saint George, despite the elegance of its design and the many finely carved details, is somewhat bloodless. Unlike its predecessors, it was never intended to be painted. It is the first example in the Baltic area of an innovation that originated in Renaissance Italy: unpainted sculptures.

The Reformation abolished the cult of saints and thus put an end to their raison d'être in the art of the Reformed countries. The Swedish reformers were, admittedly, more tolerant than most others and did not demand the destruction of existing Catholic effigies, but allowed them to remain in ecclesiastical interiors. As has already been mentioned, this was true of many Saint George groups which survived until the beginning of the 18th century in their accustomed places.

On the other hand, no new pictures of the saints were produced after the Reformation. The only major exception to this rule was Saint George, who obviously had a much firmer grounding in popular piety than any other saint. One comment to Johan III's Ecclesiastical Ordinance of 1575 contains explicit permission to depict Saint George (together with Saint Christopher, of whom only one or two paintings are recorded). The reason given is that he embodies the office of "authority" – obviously because Saint George did not carry his sword in vain. At the beginning of the 18th century a priest called Broman could still offer a Lutheran interpretation of Saint George as the emblem of "the Candid Teachers among the Congregation, who with the Sword of the Spirit contend with false Teachers and Heretics and vanquish them."[24]

Thorough examination of Swedish ecclesiastical painting during the first century after the Reformation reveals that Saint George and the Dragon were depicted in six churches.[25] In Finland as well there are several post-Reformation paintings of Saint George. The most impressive of them is the one painted in 1668 on the Triumphal Arch of the church at Pyhämaa, in other words in the position that corresponded to the one often occupied by mediaeval Saint George groups.[26]

The oldest of the Swedish post-Reformation representations of Saint George is to be found in Veta Church in Östergötland. It was painted in 1588 and contains all the features made familiar by Notke's work: in it the richly harnessed grey horse, a large plume and a unicorn's horn on its brow, is rearing while Saint George, crowned with a tall plume of feathers, is raising his sword. The tip of the lance has penetrated the dragon's throat but its jaw is still agape revealing rows of fearsome teeth and a barbed tongue. The princess is kneeling before the city of Silene, where her father is anxiously following the development of events. Saint George and his dapple-grey are similarly depicted in Vårdsberg in Östergötland (painted in 1615), where, moreover, the dragon is lying on its back with its legs in the air.[27]

These paintings imitate, therefore, more or less faithfully the massive sculpture in Stockholm, which Gustav II Adolf described as the most eminent work of art in Sweden.[28] What could happen when it was to be copied in a remote country church can be seen from Åland in the 1650s'. There a picture of Saint George was commissioned for Saltvik church from a Master Mårten in Nääs, to enable him to atone for his profligate

161. Saint George and the Dragon. Wall-painting from 1588 in Veta Church, Östergötland.

162. Saint George and the Dragon. Painting in Saltvik church on Åland, painted by Master Mårten in Nääs in the 1650s from a sketch made in situ by Master Christian of the sculpture in the City Church of Stockholm.

163. The statue of Saint George and the Dragon in the City Church in Stockholm. Water colour by Olof Rehn, 1755. Royal Library, Stockholm.

wife's extra-marital affairs. The painting was to be executed "as a counterfeit" of the sculpture in Stockholm. For safety's sake, another painter, Master Christian, was sent to Stockholm to make a sketch of the model, for which he was paid four riksdaler. Mårten's painting of Saint George has survived in Saltvik Church – albeit in a dilapidated state with some of the paint gone – and testifies to the care lavished on the oldest documented copy of the Stockholm sculpture.[29]

It should be observed that the base plate seems then to have been considerably longer than it is now, and that the princess can be seen kneeling at the front of it, her back turned to the dragon. The older account books in the City Church also record that she was "in front of" the knight. In

164. Saint George and the Dragon. Carved and painted funeral monument from the middle of the 17th century in Hovby church, Västergötland.

the next copy that has been preserved, however, in the form of a little artless water-colour by the archivist Olof Rehn from 1775 (now in the Royal Library, illustration 163) an uneven fracture can be seen on the base plate just in front of the dragon and the princess has been placed on the castle. During the intervening years, therefore, she has been given her current erroneous position. In both these pictures, one a century later than the other, the knight is wearing his helmet on his head.[30]

During the 17th century Saint George could also be portrayed in three-dimensional relief carvings, as in the previously overlooked carved and painted funeral monument in Hovby church in Västergötland (illustration 164). In the armour and tall boots of the Thirty Years War he guides his dapple-grey ambler across the dragon, jabbing his spear into the dragon's jaw. High up on a cliff, the princess is kneeling with the lamb next to her, while opposite her parents are each peering from a window in the castle of Silene, provided with both towers and chimneys. Immediately above the saint an angel is hovering with a medallion in its hands. Unfortunately the inscription on the epitaph has been painted over. It is said to have come originally from a neighbouring church at Norra Härene, but it is not known in whose memory it was created. It may have been an officer

165. "On the knight Santiöra and the dragon". A Dalecarlian painting dated 1807 and signed by Skiött Per Persson, Tällberg, parish of Leksand. Now in the Dalecarlia Museum, Falun.

166. A relief on an iron hob from around 1700. From Huseby bruk, Småland, now in Kristianstad Museum.

who had distinguished himself during the wars of the period and who wanted to identify himself and his exploits with the martial saint who customarily granted victory in battle to the Swedes. Saint George and the dragon were also represented in cut and painted steel plate on a funeral monument from the 17th century in Bälinge church in Sörmland.[31]

Saint George was not only depicted in churches, however, but also, for instance, in Dalecarlian paintings (picture 165) and on hobs cast in several ironworks in Småland until well into the 19th century. The oldest hob is in a Baroque style, dating from around 1700 (illustration 166). As his mount rears, the knight raises his sword against the dragon, which grasps the broken shaft of the lance in its claw, the tip of the lance piercing its throat. A later hob is similar, the only difference being that the dragon is lying on its back. Both depict the city of Silene with the princess kneeling on a raised platform and the lamb beneath her. The positions of the figures and their postures are so reminiscent of the grouping in the City Church after the princess had been placed on the top of the castle that this must have served as the model. But on the hob reliefs, a circular tower also rises from the platform and the saint is in touch with cosmic powers, as a sun, moon and stars are depicted in the heavens. And a naked putto with a bassoon and a victor's wreath is hovering above his head. This is an archaising baroque motif based on Roman reliefs of Victoria, the winged goddess of victory who hovers with the victor's bays above the head of the conqueror.[32]

Saint George was, in other words, adopted by popular art. A good example can be found in the carved and painted reliefs that embellish the backs of a series of three-legged rustic chairs from western Blekinge (illustration 167). These contain all the elements of the hob reliefs, but in simplified form, apart from the omission of the city of Silene. The sun and the star are there, however, as is the putto who is flying up with a wreath for the victor, the bassoon proclaiming his triumph to all and sundry.

Stockholm's potent Saint George was used as a familiar image in the most significant political controversy in Sweden in the 19th century. The struggle for Parliamentary reform was visualised in December 1865 in a much discussed woodcut in a contemporary periodical. In a faithful rendering of the monument in the City Church, Louis de Geer, the advocate of reform, was depicted in the guise of the knight raising his sword against a dragon consisting of the four estates. Two of these estates, the Peasants and the Burghers were already headless, and all that remained was to ensure that the other two, the Aristocrats and the Clergy, joined them on the ground, so that the Assembly of Four Estates could be replaced by a parliament with an upper and a lower house.

Saint George was to be important to two leading artists at the turn of the century. In his autobiography, Carl Larsson describes the amazing

167. The carved and painted back of a chair with initials and the date 1842 on the reverse. From the parish of Jämshög, Blekinge, now in Kulturen, Lund.

168. Christian Eriksson's Saint George and the dragon on the tower of the City Hall in Stockholm. Executed in beaten copper by Ragnar Myrsmeden.

169. A copy in bronze of the Saint George monument in the City Church. Erected 1912 – 13 at Köpmanbrinken in Gamla Stan (the Old Town) through the generosity of Consul Hjalmar Wikander.

impression made on him by Notke's monument. It was for him a poor boy's experience of "the consummate work or art". He was later to use it as the cover illustration on the first exhibition catalogue of the newly founded Artists' Association in 1886 "where I light-heartedly turned Saint George and the dragon into an allegory of opposition to the Academy of Arts" (the dragon is of course the Academy with ossified teachings).[33] Anders Zorn found in Saint George a significant personal symbol. A representation of the saint's combat with the dragon is carved in the gable-head of his house in Mora together with the artist's coat-of-arms. Zorn acquired from the chapel at Sollerö a late mediaeval wooden sculpture of Saint George (in which the horse looks like a Dalecarlian horse). In addition, Saint George and the dragon are carved in relief on his gravestone (based on Christian Eriksson's original). In none of these versions did Zorn include the princess.[34]

During our own century, Stockholm has acquired two successors to the Saint George monument in the City Church. One of them is the full-scale bronze casting, which was erected in 1913 at Köpmanbrinken in Gamla Stan (the Old Town). Here it is possible to see how different the monument appears as a free-standing monochrome sculpture without the context provided by the gothic church interior and when the knight is wearing a helmet on his head.[35] The other adorns Stockholm City Hall, which was inaugurated in 1923. Three large sculptures around its tower portray three figures considered decisive in the creation and well-being of the city and the realm. While Birger Jarl is commemorated with a burial monument and Engelbrekt with a statue on a pillar, Saint George is given the place of honour high up on the tower. The enormous gilt sculpture of his combat with the dragon to liberate the princess was created by Christian Eriksson as a free imitation of the monument in the City Church.[36]

This visible reminder of Saint George's reputed intervention to save both the capital and the kingdom is augmented each noon by an audible memento: as the clock strikes twelve, the chimes of the carillon in the City Hall play the Lay of Saint George. At the same time puppets representing figures in the Saint George legend emerge from an opening below. They are led by Saint George, after him comes the princess, naked on a white horse, and finally a squire leading the dragon, vanquished but still alive, by the tail. The procession then disappears into another opening in the tower. The colourful naïve figures were made by Gustaf Nilsson, an artist working with metal.[37]

Even today Saint George is a powerful symbol in Sweden. His battle with the dragon is used time and time again, especially in cartoons in newspapers, adverts and posters as the emblem of the struggle by different people, groups or ideas against what they perceive as a threat or an injustice. In Stockholm in particular, there is obviously a widespread belief that the familiar silhouette of the champion in the City Church is the most striking symbol of effective opposition to current threats. He was conscripted for instance in 1983 by a number of trade unions to provide an eye-catching focus for the poster illustrated here. As he hews the head off the "monster of cut-backs in public spending ", for safety's sake, like the bronze in Köpmanbrinken, he is wearing his helmet. In 1987 Stockholm's Saint George could also be seen raising his sword against the venomous breath of the dragon of air pollution on a poster created by Peter Tillberg for the acclaimed exhibition "Luftangrepp" (Attack from the air) at the Museum of National Antiquities in Stockholm.

More than 450 years after the Reformation Saint George is still a living symbol in Sweden, and can still be invoked to serve current political ends. He is also familiar as the emblem of the Scout movement in Sweden, as he is in other countries. With the exception of Santa Lucia, he is probably the only mediaeval saint who still lives in public consciousness and is recognisable to all and sundry.

During the First World War Saint George was enlisted by both sides. He was depicted in combat with the dragon on both British and Austrian war posters. A number of posters from the Russian Revolution represen-

170. A trade union poster from 1983.

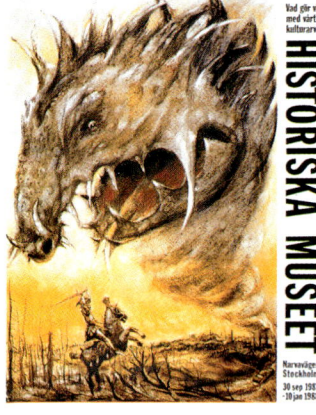

171. A poster by Peter Tillberg for the exhibition "Luftangrepp" (Attack from the air) at the Museum of National Antiquities in Stockholm, 1987.

172. The patron saint of Moscow on a badge from the 840th anniversary of the foundation of the city in 1987. Cf. illustration 2.

173. Saint George vanquishes the dragon of nuclear warfare. A bronze by the Russian sculptor Zurab Tsereti. Erected in 1990 at the United Nations skyscraper in New York.

ted Trotsky in the likeness of the Saint George familiar from the icons. One of them shows him driving his spear into a snake-like dragon with a top hat, bearing the device "counter-revolution". And Saint George is still depicted as the patron saint of Moscow. Even during the Soviet period Moscow used his image while celebrating its anniversaries, as it still does (see illustration 172).[38]

The most terrible peril that threatened the post-war period was the nuclear arsenal that the two super-powers developed so that they could destroy each other if attacked, imperilling humanity as a whole. Almost half a century was to elapse before Russian initiatives in negotiations between the two powers enabled détente and disarmament. The great monument to nuclear disarmament is the enormous Saint George statue in bronze that was erected in 1990 outside the United Nations headquarters in New York. This was created by the Russian artist Zurab Tsereti and was a gift of what was then the Soviet Union to the United Nations. The inscription on the base of the statue tells us that it depicts "Saint George vanquishing the dragon of nuclear warfare symbolised by genuine parts of a Soviet and an American nuclear missile, an SS 20 and a US Pershing".

The equestrian statue also represents both east and west. The figure of Saint George with his flowing robe and the way in which he thrusts his spear down into the dragon from his rearing horse derive from the venerable traditions of the Russian icon (cf. illustration 2). But the idea of portraying this motif as a free-standing sculpture, and on such a large scale as well, comes from a western tradition. Where the size is concerned, Tsereti's work surpasses even Bernt Notke's. This is also true of the way in which the even larger horse, which is rearing more steeply, still remains in balance. Almost all of the weight is borne by the rear legs, with the narrow weapon providing some degree of support. In actual fact, the weapon is a cross, not a spear. This is intended to signify that it was not force but peaceful negotiation that conquered the threat of the nuclear missiles. There are two missiles, one Russian and one American, each forming the body of a dragon, so that only the heads have been sculpted. One of the dragons is already dead, its head behind the horse's tail, while the saint is in the process of thrusting the cross into the chest of the other, forward facing, dragon. There is no princess in this group. It is not for her survival that this knight is killing the twofold dragon formed by the missiles, but for the survival of humanity.

Modern artists, too, have been fascinated in different ways by Saint George's combat with the dragon. One international example can be found in Wassily Kandinsky, the great pioneer of abstract painting. From 1910 up until his death, he depicted Saint George in many of his works,

174. Wassily Kandinsky "Tempered élan". Oil on cardboard, 1944. Musée National d'Art Moderne, Paris. The large diagonal shape, which principally represents restrained power, is reminiscent of the equestrian motifs beloved by the artist. Below its centre Saint George can be seen on an escutcheon. Cf. Moscow's crest in illustration 172.

painted to begin with in a naïve or expressionist style. Kandinsky developed one of them into "Der blaue Reiter", the celebrated coloured woodcut that formed the front cover of the journal founded in 1912 with the same name. This was also the name given to the group of artists who gathered around Kandinsky in Munich, numbered among the pioneers of modernism. In the abstract painting that Kandinsky later developed Saint George sometimes appears in highly stylised form, but always recognisable from his earlier works.[39]

The saint represented two central values for Kandinsky that were linked to each other. One was spirituality – his knight is usually interpreted as the "spiritual" artist in conflict with the evil of materialism. Saint George also represented his native country and above all the beloved city of his childhood. An image of the dragon-slayer shields the chest of the Tsar's double eagle in the Russian coat-of-arms, and Saint George was also, as we have already seen, the patron saint and emblem of Moscow. Patriots and mystics such as Kandinsky regarded Russia and its capital as spirituality's prime abode in this world. In the Slavic tradition, Moscow is the third Rome – the first Rome had been the Father's city, the second, Constantinople had been the Son's, and the third was now the city of the Holy Spirit in the apocalyptic thousand-year empire. This was an idea that was first presented in a visionary letter addressed by Philotheus, a monk in Pskov, to the Grand Duke of Moscow in the 16th century and which has been revived time and again, most recently during the period which gave rise to Kandinsky's Saint George pictures.[40]

It is against this complex background that Kandinksy's last painting should be seen. It was created a few months before his death as a biomorphic composition in an abstract style. He painted it in France, where he had taken refuge, in March 1944, immediately after the Russians had recaptured Pskov, where Philotheus had seen his influential vision of the unique greatness of the Muscovite empire. In the centre of the painting a stylised shape represents the coat-of-arms of Moscow and the double headed Imperial eagle's escutcheon surmounted by a crown. In it Saint George can be seen on horseback with his banner and its cross, his shield and flowing gown.[41] Above the escutcheon, three round shapes symbolise the Tsar's crown, and it is suspended by the ribbons with which it is usually hung from the neck of the double headed eagle. Here, in other words, Saint George represents the same values as in the sculpture in Stockholm – protection, liberation and victory for a city and for a nation – even though they could hardly differ more in style.

In order to finish with a modern Swedish work, we have chosen Torsten Renqvist, the most celebrated sculptor working with wood in recent decades. In a series of articles published in 1984, in which various writers described an encounter with a picture of particular personal significance,

175. George and the dragon. A sculpture by Torsten Renqvist, 1973, in painted aspen. Atheneum, Helsinki. The base is four metres long.

Renqvist gave the following account. In the summer of 1955 in the church at Övertorneå he caught sight of the wooden sculptures of Saint George and the dragon from the 15th century (reproduced here as illustration 145). "At that time I was a painter, but faced with this work, I had a premonition that I would go in for something else." Which turned out to be carving wooden sculptures in which philosophical issues are epitomised in a personal and distinctive style. Today these form the basis of Renqvist's reputation as an artist.[42]

One of his most important works is the group of sculptures called "Saint George and the Dragon". A small scale sketch of this work was produced in plane in 1972, and in the following year Renqvist created the large version in painted aspen – nearly 13 feet long (4 metres). After having been displayed at various exhibitions the work was acquired for Atheneum in Helsinki for a price of 400,000 Swedish crowns – an artistically significant Saint George sculpture commands a high price even today.[43]

The unequivocal heroes of earlier periods representing good in combat with evil have been called into question by the upheavals experienced in the 20th century. For instance, Ulysses has become a complicated modern human being in the novels of James Joyce and Eyvind Johnson, "Ulysses" published after the First World War and "Strändernas svall" (The Surge of the Waves) after the Second. The Second World War and modern psychology have also influenced Renqvist causing him to question Saint George's encounter with the dragon. In his sculpture Saint George has thrust his lance into the earth and left his horse to graze peacefully beside it. Alone, one-armed and almost blind, with neither weapons nor armour, an uplifted enquiring gaze on his sensitive face, he encounters the enormous dragon. This too is standing quite still, slowly raising its head, jaw closed, towards George's lowered hand. The dragon's spiky contours include not only wings and legs but also dugs, scrotum and a powerful phallus about to penetrate a vagina. In other words the creature is a hermaphrodite copulating with itself.[44]

The artist has revealed that the dragon's body – apart from the sexual organs – is based on a drawing done by his daughter Anne-Li when she was a child, while the head is a reference, as he only realised later, to a small picture of a dead bird which he himself painted during the 40s. And the sway-backed figure of George is based on a newspaper photograph of a Nazi executioner facing a firing squad in 1945.[45] From these formal models, Renqvist has created a George and the dragon for our age. In a text accompanying the sculpture, he gives us clues with which to interpret it.[46]

"There is a gap between the laws we consider to apply to nature and those we claim apply or should apply to human beings. It has been said that man is by nature perverse; our moral and ethical beliefs distance us from the nature from which we undeniably spring.

There is therefore a division, and it looks messy. If we take a leap over it, we become strong, fair and terrible in the way fascist ideology would like its elite to be. On the other side, the saint rushes by talking to himself.

I envisage Saint George descending into the crevice. There he is admittedly only George. There he can touch both sides of the gap.

Because! Those who can see what he is supposed to defend in what he is intended to destroy find themselves in a difficult predicament. This hardly ever occurs in myths. But in reality all the time.

It must be possible to follow a belief in a "righteous" life. Saint George cannot help us here. He too became a dragon. But a white one."

176. George and the Dragon. Detail from the sculpture by Renqvist in the previous illustration.

The sculpture is painted in only two colours. The horse and the dragon are as black as earth, representing nature, one tame, the other wild. The vertical white effigy of George is in contrast to their horizontal forms, parallel with the ground. He is not a saint, but a human being, seeking to reconcile his ethos as cultural product with nature, his own origin with the chaotic and vigorous origin of all that is created or creates, beyond good and evil. This is a human being who is also not least an artist who has relinquished his tools – Renqvist used a paintbrush as the lance in the 1972 sketch – to seek contact with the primary sources of creativity.

This recalls Renqvist's encounter with Saint George and the dragon at Övertorneå which resulted in the artist abandoning his brush for ever. The princess was missing then – she had been stolen. She has been omitted from Renqvist's work, however, for more profound reasons. There is no place for her in his questioning analysis of George.

Significant artistic innovations have created for our age its own version of the ancient motif. Bernt Notke provided us with the most consummate embodiment of the divinely inspired mediaeval martial saint in combat with the dragon of evil. Shortly afterwards, Henning von der Heide gave expression to the changing ideals of the Renaissance – a Saint George relying on his own powers in his duel. After all the violent changes in value systems and understanding of the individual that the 20th century has entailed, an even greater shift of perspective has taken place in Renqvist's interpretation of the theme. Belatedly, his human George tentatively attempts to make peace with the dragon, now perceived as the force of nature, both within and around him.

But in every age great art, especially when it deals with themes which are central and therefore continually reworked, often encompasses more than its intended message and its studied forms. Seen from the point of view of the long development of the figure of Saint George, Renqvist's work gives rise to many associations that the artist can hardly have intended but which are interesting in this wider context. His mangled, one-armed, almost blind George recalls the great martyr with his severed limbs. And the gesture he is making to the dragon recalls a version of the legend that predates the description of his feats of arms – the one in which Saint George meets the dragon on foot and vanquishes it merely by making the sign of the cross over it.

Finally, Renqvist's dragon has only one counterpart among all the dragons that Saint George can be seen subjugating in this volume, and that is Notke's. However different the demeanour of the two dragons may be, they still share many similarities. Both are unusually large in relation to human beings, both have unusually spiny shapes and both are hermaphrodite. Renqvist says that he was not aware that this was the case with Notke's dragon – its sexual organs cannot be seen from the floor of the church and they are reproduced for the first time in illustrations 39 and 40 in this book. But both works of art, despite the five centuries that separate them, are based on ancient beliefs about self-generating dragons, progenitors of the whole natural order for good or ill. Different cultures were soon to embrace different aspects of this. In the east dragons became symbols of the positive forces of procreation. The dominant tradition in the west saw them instead as monsters spawning evil that could only be defeated by gods, heroes and saints like Saint George.

The saint of indestructible life and the vanquisher of dragons has revealed, therefore, a remarkable power to survive both ideological and artistic revolutions. This is fundamentally due to the archetypal force with which the figure is endowed. Five hundred years ago Sten Sture and Bernt Notke had the ability to exploit this and make of it something sublime. Sten

Sture did so as part of his political battle and the enormous undertaking of founding the altar dedicated to the saint. The artist mustered these powerful impulses and transmuted them into enormous tension. After five centuries this still resonates in his masterpiece, his matchless embodiment of Saint George's combat with the dragon.

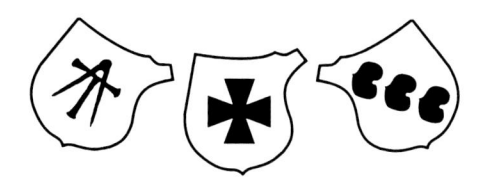

Documentation

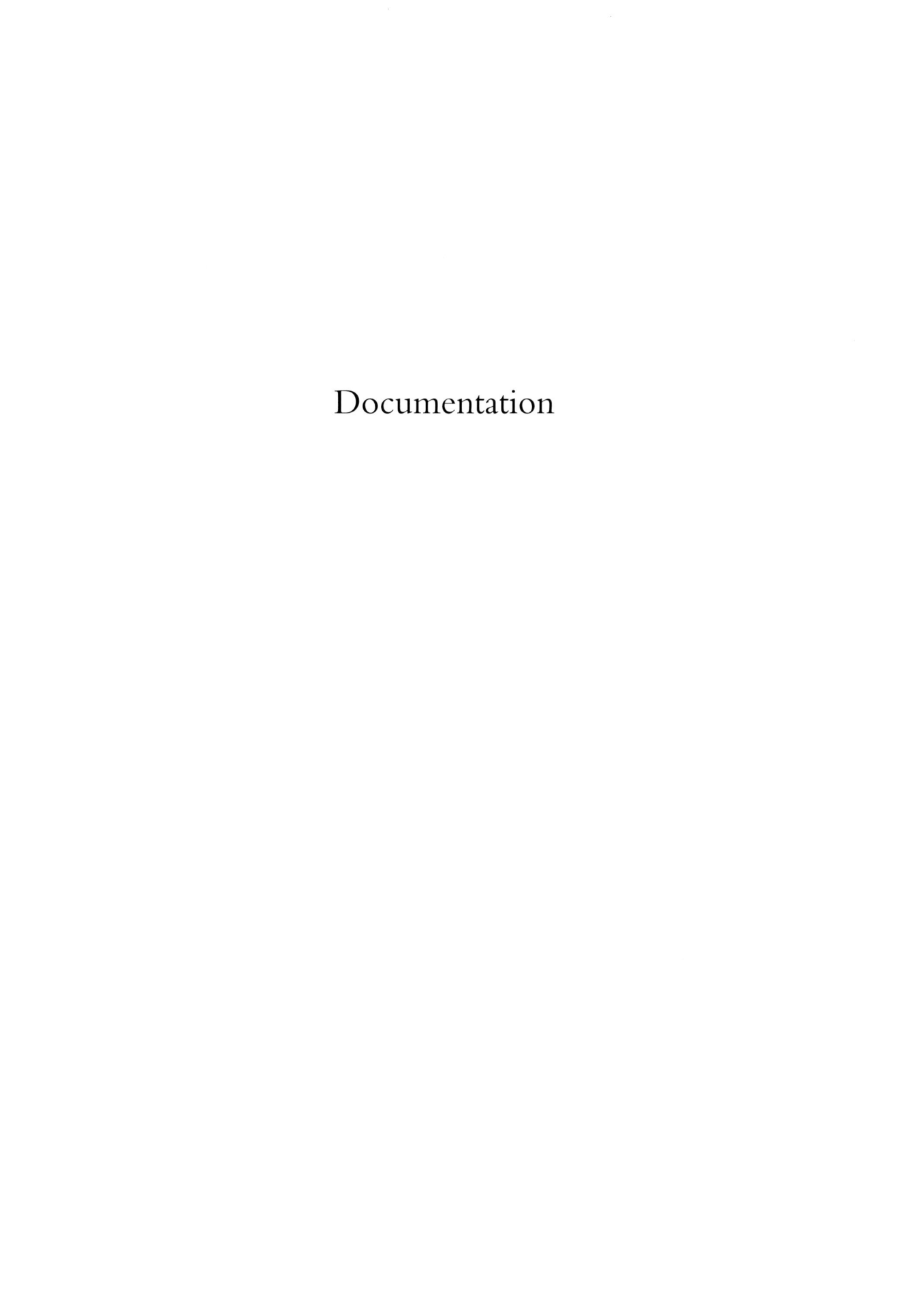

The Legend of St George According to Jacobus de Voragine

The legend of Saint George was one of almost 150 legends of saints that the learned Dominican Jacobus de Voragine, who later became Archbishop of Genoa, compiled during the third quarter of the 13th century to form *Legenda aurea,* the Golden Legend. This is the name it was given when it became the most popular and most widely circulated collection of legends in the Middle Ages, and a liturgical handbook and a book of homilies as well. To begin with, it was circulated in hand-written manuscripts in Latin – of which the oldest dates from 1282.[1] Translations to the vernacular languages soon followed. The Swedish translation is one of the earliest, made around 1300. During the 15th century, three more Swedish versions of the legend of St. George were produced. The ways in which they deviate from each other will be examined after the basic text has been presented below.

From the middle of the 15th century, publication of the Golden Legend began in printed form both on the continent and in England. During the five decades up until 1500 no fewer than 97 Latin editions were published and 76 translations.[2] These translations often involved major and minor alterations in the narrative and in the subject matter, as we shall discover when we turn to the Swedish versions below. Some of them were written in verse, among them the oldest German translation, "Das grosse Passional" and two of the Swedish versions.

However, Jacobus de Voragine begins his chapter with a long etymological discussion of the name George, for which several alternative derivations from Greek words are suggested and provided with elaborate Christian symbolic interpretations. To avoid deterring readers from an otherwise enjoyable narrative, this far-fetched etymological introduction has been printed in smaller type.

At the beginning of the legend we are told that the city of Silene was situated in Libya. This is obviously an erroneous rendering of Lydia which dates back a long way, as it is also found in the versions in early Swedish. Here, however, the Swedish translator knew that the events took place in Asia Minor, as he has added the gloss "where Troy stood of yore" after the erroneous rendering of the name of the province resulting from the confusion of *b* and *d*. Lydia bordered Cappadocia, which is also part of Asia Minor.

---

1 We still lack a complete list of all the mediaeval manuscripts of *Legenda aurea* but there are an estimated 600 European versions (the Bibliothèque Nationale in Paris alone has 60) according to *Złota Legenda,* translated from Latin by Janina Pleziowa, with an introduction and notes by Marian Plezia, Warsaw 1983, p. 45.

2 Ibid.

Legenda aurea:
De sancto Georgio

Georgius dicitur e geos, quod est terra, et orge, quod est colere, quasi colens terram, id est carnem suam. Augustinus autem in libro De Trinitate, quod bona terra est altitudine montium, temperamento collium, planitie camporum. Prima enim est bona ad virentes herbas, secunda ad vineas, tertia ad fruges. Sic beatus Georgius fuit altus despiciendo inferiora et ideo habuit virorem puritatis, temperatus per discretionem et ideo habuit vinum internae jucunditatis, planus per humilitatem et ideo protulit fruges bonae operationis. Vel dicitur a gerar, quod est sacrum, et gyon, quod est arena, quasi sacra arena. Fuit enim arena, quia ponderosus morum gravitate, minutus humilitate, et siccus a carnali voluptate. Vel dicitur a gerar quod est sacrum et gyon, quod est luctatio, quasi sacer luctator quia luctatus est cum dracone et carnifice; vel Georgius dicitur a gero, quod est peregrinus, et gir praecisio et ys consiliator. Ipse enim fuit peregrinus in contemptu mundi, praecisus in corona martyrii et consiliator in praedicatione regni. Ejus legenda inter scripturas apocryphas in Nicaeno concilio cunnumeratur ex eo, quod ejus martirium certam relationem non habet. Nam in Calendario Bedae legitur quod sit passus in Persica civitate Dyaspoli, quae prius Lidda vocabatur, et est juxta Joppen. Alibi, quod passus sit sub Dyocletiano et Maximiano imperatoribus; alibi quod sub Dyocletiano imperatore Persarum praesentibus LXXX regibus imperii sui. Hic, quod sub Daciano praeside imperantibus Dyocletiano et Maximiano.

Georgius tribunus genere Cappadocum pervenit quadam vice in provinciam Libyae in civitatem, quae dicitur Silena. Juxta quam civitatem erat stagnum instar maris, in quo draco pestifer latitabat, qui saepe populum contra se armatum in fugam converterat flatuque suo ad muros civitatis accedens omnes inficiebat. Quapropter compulsi cives duas oves quotidie sibi dabant, ut ejus furorem sedarent, alioquin sic muros civitatis invadebat et aërem inficiebat, quod plurimi interibant. Cum ergo jam oves paene deficerent, maxime cum harum copiam ha-

The Legend:
Saint George

The name George is derived from geos, meaning earth, and orge, meaning to work; hence one who works the earth, namely, his own flesh. Now Augustine writes in his book On the Holy Trinity that good earth is found high on the mountains, in the temperate climate of the hills, and in level ground: the first bears good grass, the second, grapes, and the third, the fruits of the fields. Thus blessed George was on the heights because he disdained base things and so had the fresh green of purity; he was temperate by his prudence and so shared the wine of heavenly joy; he was lowly in his humility and therefore bore the fruits of good works. Or George is derived from gerar, holy, and gyon, sand, therefore, holy sand; for he was like sand, heavy with the weight of his virtues, small by humility, and dry of the lusts of the flesh. Or again, the name comes from gerar, holy, and gyon, struggle; so a holy fighter, because he fought against the dragon and the executioner. Or George comes from gero, pilgrim, gir, cut off and ys, counselor, for he was a pilgrim in his contempt for the world, cut off by gaining the crown of martyrdom, and a counselor in his preaching of the Kingdom. At the council of Nicaea his legend was included among the apocryphal writings becauce there is no sure record of his martyrdom. In Bede's Calendar we read that he was martyred in the Persian city of Dyaspolis, which formerly was called Lidda and is near Joppe. Elsewhere we read that he suffered under the emperors Diocletian and Maximian, or under the Persian emperor Dacian in the presence of seventy kings of his empire. Or we are told that he was put to death by the prefect Dacian during the reign of Diocletian and Maximian.

George, a native of Cappadocia, held the military rank of tribune. It happened that he once traveled to the city of Silena in the province of Lybia. Near this town there was a pond as large as a lake where a plague-bearing dragon lurked; and many times the dragon had put the populace to flight when they came out armed against him, for he used to come up to the city walls and poison everyone who came within reach of his breath. To appease the fury of this monster the townspeople fed him two

---

Translation: William Granger Ryan.

bere non possent, inito consilio ovem cum adjuncto homine tribuebant.

Cum igitur sorte omnium filii et filiae hominum darentur et sors neminem exciperet, et jam paene omnes filii et filiae essent consumpti, quadam vice filia regis unica sorte est deprehensa et draconi adjudicata. Tunc rex contristatus ait: "Tollite aurum et argentum et dimidium regni mei et filiam mihi dimittite, ne taliter moriatur." Cui populus cum furore respondit: "Tu, o rex, hoc edictum fecisti et nunc omnes pueri nostri mortui sunt et tu vis filiam tuam salvare? Nisi in filia tua compleveris, quod in aliis ordinasti, succendemus te et domum tuum."

Quod rex audiens coepit filiam suam flere dicens: "Heu me, filia mea dulcissima, quid de te faciam? aut quid dicam? quando plus videbo nuptias tuas?" Et conversus ad populum dixit: "Oro, ut inducias octo dierum lugendi mihi filiam tribuatis." Quod cum populus admisisset, in fine octo dierum reversus populus est cum furore dicens: "Quare perdis populum tuum propter filiam tuam? En omnes afflatu draconis morimur."

Tunc rex videns, quod non posset filiam liberare, induit eam vestibus regalibus et amplexatus eam cum lacrymis dixit: "Heu me, filia mea dulcissima, de te filios in regali gremio nutrire credebam et nunc vadis, ut a dracone devoreris. Heu me, filia mea dulcissima, sperabam ad tuas nuptias principes invitare, palatium margaritis ornare, tympana et organa audire, et nunc vadis, ut a dracone devoreris." Et deosculans dimisit eam dicens: "Utinam, filia mea, ego ante te mortuus essem, quam te sic amisissem." Tunc illa procidit ad pedes patris petens ab eo benedictionem suam. Quam cum pater cum lacrymis benedixisset, ad lacum processit.

Quam beatus Georgius casu inde transiens ut plorantem vidit, eam, quid haberet, interrogavit. Et

sheep every day; otherwise he would invade their city and a great many would perish. But in time they were running out of sheep and could not get any more, so, having held a council, they paid him tribute of one sheep and one man or woman. The name of a youth or a maiden was drawn by lot, and no one was exempt from the draft; but soon almost all the young people had been eaten up. Then one day the lot fell upon the only daughter of the king, and she was seized and set aside for the dragon. The king, beside himself with grief, said: "Take my gold and my silver and the half of my kingdom, but release my daughter and spare her such a death." But the people were furious and shouted: "You yourself issued this decree, O king, and now that all our children are dead, you want to save your own daughter! Carry out for your daughter what you ordained for the rest, or we will burn you alive with your whole household!" Hearing this, the king began to weep and said to his daughter: "My dearest child, what have I done to you? Or what shall I say? Am I never to see your wedding?" And turning to the people he said: "I pray you, leave me my daughter for one week, so that we may weep together." This was granted, but at the end of the week back they came in a rage, crying: "Why are you letting your people perish to save your daughter? Don't you see that we are all dying from the breath of the dragon?" So the king, seeing that he could not set his daughter free, arrayed her in regal garments, embraced her tearfully, and said: "Woe is me, my darling child, I thought I would see sons nursing at your royal breast, and now you must be devoured by the dragon! Alas, my sweetest child, I hoped to invite princes to your wedding, to adorn the palace with pearls, to hear the music of timbrel and harp, and now you must go and be swallowed up by the beast." He kissed her and sent her off, saying: "O, my daughter, would that I had died before you, rather than lose you this way!" Then she threw herself at his feet and begged his blessing; and when, weeping, he had blessed her, she started towards the lake.

At this moment blessed George happened to be passing by, and seeing the maiden in tears, asked her

illa: "Bone juvenis, velociter equum ascende et fuge, ne mecum pariter moriaris." Cui Georgius: "Noli timere, filia, sed dic mihi, quid hic praestolaris omni plebe spectante." Et illa: "Ut video, bone juvenis, magnifici cordis es tu, sed mecum mori desideras? Fuge velociter!" Cui Georgius: "Hinc ego non discedam, donec mihi, quid habeas, intimabis."

Cum ergo totum sibi exposuisset, ait Georgius: "Filia, noli timere, quia in Christi nomine te juvabo." Et illa: "Bone miles, sed te ipsum salvare festines, mecum non pereas! Sufficit enim, si sola peream, nam me liberare non posses et tu mecum perires."

Dum haec loquerentur, ecce draco veniens caput de lacu levavit. Tunc puella tremefacta dixit: "Fuge, bone domine, fuge velociter!" Tunc Georgius equum ascendens et cruce se muniens draconem contra se advenientem audaciter aggreditur et lanceam fortiter vibrans et se Deo commendans ipsum graviter vulneravit et ad terram dejecit dixitque puellae: "Projice zonam tuam in collum draconis nihil dubitans, filia." Quod cum fecisset, sequebatur eam velut mansuetissima canis.

Cum ergo eum in civitatem duceret, populi hoc videntes per montes et colles fugere coeperunt dicentes: "Vae nobis, quia jam omnes peribimus." Tunc beatus Georgius innuit iis dicens: "Nolite timere, ad hoc enim me misit Dominus ad vos, ut a poenis vos liberarem draconis; tantummodo in Christum credite et unusquisque vestrum baptizetur et draconem istum occidam."

Tunc rex et omnes populi baptizati sunt, beatus autem Georgius evaginato gladio draconem occidit et ipsum extra civitatem efferri praecepit. Tunc quatuor paria boum ipsum in magnum campum foras duxerunt, baptizati autem sunt in illa die XX millia exceptis parvulis et mulieribus, rex autem in honorem beatae Mariae et beati Georgii ecclesiam mirae magnitudinis construxit, de cujus altari fons vivus emanat, cujus potus omnes languidos sanat, rex vero infinitam pecuniam beato Georgio obtulit, quam ille recipere nolens pauperibus eam dari praecepit. Tunc Georgius regem de quatuor breviter instruxit, scilicet ut ecclesiarum Dei curam ha-

why she wept. She answered: "Good youth, mount your horse quickly and flee, or you will die as I am to die." George responded: "Lady, fear not; but tell me, what are all these people waiting to see?" The damsel: "I see, good youth, that you have a great heart, but do you want to die with me? Get away speedily!" George: "I will not leave here until you tell me the reason for this." When she had told him all, he said: "Don't be afraid, child! I am going to help you in the name of Christ!" She spoke: "Brave knight, make haste to save yourself; if not, you will die with me. It is enough that I die alone, for you cannot set me free and you would perish with me."

While they were talking, the dragon reared his head out of the lake. Trembling, the maiden cried: "Away, sweet lord, away with all speed!" But George, mounting his horse and arming himself with the sign of the cross, set bravely upon the approaching dragon and, commending himself to God, brandished his lance, dealt the beast a grievous wound, and forced him to the ground. Then he called to the maiden: "Have no fear, child! Throw your girdle around the dragon's neck! Don't hesitate!" When she had done this, the dragon rose and followed her like a little dog on a leash. She led him toward the city; but the people, seeing this, ran for the mountains and the hills, crying out: "Now we will all be eaten alive!" But blessed George waved them back and said to them: "You have nothing to fear! The Lord has sent me to deliver you from the trouble this dragon has caused you. Believe in Christ and be baptized, every one of you, and I shall slay the dragon!" Then the king and all the people were baptized, and George, drawing his sword, put and end to the beast and ordered him to be moved out of the city, whereupon four yoke of oxen hauled him away into a broad field outside the walls. On that day twenty thousand were baptized, not counting the women and children. The king built a magnificent church there in honor of Blessed Mary and Saint George, and from the altar flowed a spring whose waters cure all diseases. He also offered a huge sum of money to blessed George, who refused to accept it and ordered it to be distributed

beret, sacerdotes honoraret, divinum officium diligenter audiret et semper pauperum memor esset, et osculato rege inde recessit.

In aliquibus tamen libris legitur, quod, dum draco ad devorandum puellam pergeret, Georgius se cruce munivit et draconem aggrediens interfecit.

Eo tempore imperantibus Dyocletiano et Maximiano sub praeside Daciano tanta persecutio christianorum fuit, ut infra unum mensem XVII millia martirio coronarentur, unde inter tot tormentorum genera multi christiani deficiebant et ydolis immolabant.

Quod videns sanctus Georgius tactus dolore cordis intrinsecus omnia, quae habebat, dispersit, militarem habitum abjecit, christianorum habitum induit et in medium prosiliens exclamavit: "Omnes dii gentium daemonia! Dominus autem caelos fecit." Cui praeses iratus dixit: "Qua praesumptione audes deos nostros daemonia appellare? Dic, unde es tu aut quo nomine voceris." Cui Georgius ait: "Georgius vocor, ex nobili Cappadocum prosapia ortus Palestinam Christo favente devici, sed omnia deserui, ut servire possem liberius Deo coeli." Cum autem praeses eum ad se inclinare non posset, jussit eum in equuleum levari et membratim corpus ejus ungulis laniari, appositis insuper ad latera facibus patentibus viscerum rimis sale plagas ejus fricari jussit.

Eadem nocte Dominus cum ingenti lumine ei apparuit et ipsum dulciter confortavit, cujus melliflua visione et allocutione sic confortatus est, ut pro nihilo duceret cruciatus. Videns Dacianus, quod eum poenis superare non posset, quendam magum accersivit eique dixit: "Christiani suis magicis artibus tormenta ludificant et deorum nostrorum sacrificia parvi pendunt." Cui magus: "Si artes ejus superare

to the poor. Then he gave the king four brief instructions: to have good care for the church of God, to honor the priests, to assist with devotion at the divine office, and to have the poor always in mind. Finally, he embraced the king and took his leave. Some books however, tell us that at the very moment when the dragon was about to swallow the girl alive, George, making the sign of the cross, rode upon him and killed him.

At this time, in the reign of Diocletian and Maximian, the prefect Dacian launched against the Christians a persecution so violent that in one month seventeen thousand won the crown of martyrdom, while many others, being threatened with torture, gave in and offered sacrifice to the idols. Seeing this, Saint George, overcome with grief, gave away all his possessions, laid aside his military trappings, and put on the garb of the Christians. He then pushed into the middle of the crowd and cried out: "All your gods are demons, and our God alone is the Creator of the heavens!" This angered the prefect, who retorted: "By what rashness do you dare to call our gods demons? Where do you come from and what is your name?" George answered him: "My name is George, I come of noble forebears in Cappadocia. With the help of Christ I have conquered Palestine; but now I have left all that to serve the God of heaven more freely." The prefect, seeing that he could not win him over, commanded that he be stretched on the rack and had him torn limb from limb with hooks. His body was burned with flaming torches, and salt was rubbed into his gaping wounds. That very night the Lord appeared to him in the midst of a great light and so sweetly comforted him with his presence and his words that the saint thought nothing of his torments.

Dacian, now convinced that the infliction of pain was of no avail, summoned a certain magician and said to him: "It must be by their magical arts that the Christians make light of our tortures, and they hold sacrifice to our gods to be worthless." The magician replied: "If I cannot overcome his spells, let my head be forfeit." Thereupon, relying on his magic and invoking the names of his gods, he mix-

nequivero, capitis reus ero." Ipse igitur maleficiis suis injectis et deorum suorum nominibus invocatis venenum vino immiscuit et sancto Georgio sumendum porrexit, contra quod vir Dei signum crucis edidit haustoque eo nil laesionis sensit. Rursum magus priore fortius venenum immiscuit, quod vir Dei signo crucis edito sine laesione aliqua totum bibit. Quo viso magus statim ad pedes ejus cecidit, veniam lamentabiliter petiit et se christianum fieri postulavit, quem mox judex decollari fecit.

Sequenti die jussit Georgium poni in rota, gladiis bis acutis undique circumsepta, sed statim frangitur et Georgius illaesus penitus invenitur. Tunc iratus jussit eum in sartaginem plumbo liquefacto plenam projici, qui facto signo crucis in eam intravit, sed virtute Dei coepit in ea quasi in balneo refoveri.

Quod videns Dacianus cogitavit eum emollire blanditiis, quem minis superare non poterat vel tormentis, dixitque illi: "Vides, fili Georgi, quantae mansuetudinis sunt dii nostri, qui te blasphemum tam patienter sustinent, parati nihilominus, si converti volueris, indulgere. Age ergo, dilectissime fili, quod hortor, ut superstitione relicta diis nostris sacrifices, ut magnos ab ipsis et a nobis consequaris honores." Cui Georgius subridens ait: "Ut quid a principio non magis mihi persuasisti blandis sermonibus quam tormentis? Ecce paratus sum facere, quod hortaris."

Hac Dacianus permissione delusus laetus efficitur jussitque sub voce praeconis, ut omnes ad se convenirent et Georgium tamdiu reluctantem tandem cedere et sacrificare viderent. Ornata igitur tota civitate prae gaudio cum Georgius ydolorum templum sacrificaturus intraret et omnes ibidem gaudentes adstarent, flexis genibus Dominum exoravit, ut templum cum ydolis sic omnino destrueret, quatenus ad sui laudem et populi conversionem nihil de eo penitus remaneret, statimque ignis de coelo descendens templum cum diis et sacerdotibus concremavit terraque se aperiens omnes eorum reliquias deglutivit.

Hic exclamat Ambrosius in praefatione dicens: "Georgius fidelissimus miles Christi, dum christianitatis professio silentio tegeretur, solus inter chris-

ed poison into some wine and gave it to blessed George to drink; but the saint made the sign of the cross over the wine, drank it, and suffered no harm. The magician then put a stronger dose of poison into the wine, but the saint, again making the sign of the cross over the cup, drank with no ill effect. At this the magician prostrated himself at George's feet, begged his pardon with loud lamentation, and asked that he be made a Christian: for this he was beheaded in due time. The following day the prefect ordered George to be bound upon a wheel that was fitted with sharp knives, but the wheel fell apart at once and the saint remained unharmed. Dacian then had him plunged into a caldron of molten lead, but George made the sign of the cross and, by God's power, settled down as though he were in a refreshing bath.

Now, realizing that he was getting nowhere with threats and torments, Dacian thought he might bring the saint around with soft speech. "George, my son," he said, "you see how long-suffering our gods are; they put up with your blasphemies so patiently yet are ready to forgive you if you consent to be converted. Follow my advice, then, dearest son. Give up your superstition, sacrifice to our gods, and win great honors from them and from ourselves." George smiled and replied: "Why did you not say kind things to me before, instead of trying to overcome me by torture? So be it: I am ready to do as you say." Dacian, deluded, was glad to hear this and ordered the herald to call the whole populace together to see George, who had resisted so long, finally yield and worship the gods. The city was strung with garlands and filled with rejoicing, and all stood by as George came into the temple to offer sacrifice. He fell to his knees and prayed the Lord to destroy the temple with its idols so completely that, for the glory of God and the conversion of the people, nothing would be left of it. Immediately fire came down from heaven and consumed the temple, the idols and the priests, and the earth opened and swallowed up anything that was left. Saint Ambrose says in his Preface for Saint George: "While Christianity was professed only under cover of silence, George, most loyal soldier

ticolas intrepidus Dei filium est confessus. Cui et tantam constantiam gratia divina concessit, ut et tyrannicae potestatis praecepta contemneret et innumerabilium non formidaret tormenta poenarum. O felix et inclitus Domini proeliator! Quem non solum temporalis regni blanda non persuasit promissio, sed persecutore deluso simulacrorum ejus portenta in abyssum dejecit." Haec Ambrosius.

Hoc audiens Dacianus Georgium ad se adduci fecit eique dixit: "Quae malitia tua, pessime hominum, quod tantum facinus commisisti?" Cui Georgius: "Ne credas, rex, sic esse, sed mecum perge et iterum me immolare vide." Cui ille: "Intelligo fraudem tuam, quia vis me facere absorberi, sicut templum et deos meos absorberi fecisti." Cui Georgius: "Dic mihi, miser, dii tui, qui se juvare non potuerunt, quomodo te juvabunt?"

Iratus rex nimis dixit Alexandriae uxori suae: "Deficiens moriar, quia ab hoc homine me superatum cerno." Cui illa: "Tyranne crudelis et carnifex, numquid non dixi tibi, ne saepius christianis molestus esses, quia Deus eorum pro ipsis pugnaret, et nunc scias, me velle fieri christianam." Stupefactus rex ait: "Heu proh dolor! Numquid et tu es seducta?" Fecitque eam per capillos suspendi et flagellis durissime caedi. Quae dum caederetur, dixit Georgio: "Georgi, lumen veritatis, quo, putes, perveniam nondum aqua baptismi renata?" Cui Georgius: "Nihil haesites, filia, quia sanguinis tui effusio baptismus tibi reputabitur et corona." Tunc illa orans ad Dominum emisit spiritum.

Hinc attestatur Ambrosius in praefatione dicens: "Ob hoc et gentium regina Persarum crudeli a viro dictata sententia nondum baptismi gratiam consecuta gloriosae passionis meruit palmam, unde nec dubitare possumus, quod rosea perfusa sanguinis unda reseratas poli januas ingredi meruit regnumque possidere coelorum." Haec Ambrosius.

of Christ, alone and intrepid among Christians openly professed his faith in the Son of God; and the grace of God, in return, gave him such fortitude that he could scorn the commands of tyrants and face the pain of innumerable torments. O blessed and noble fighter for the Lord! Not only was he not won over by the flattering promise of earthly power, but he fooled his persecutor and cast the images of his false gods into the abyss." Thus Ambrose.

When Dacian heard what had happened, he had George brought before him and said: "How evil can you be, you wickedest of men, that you could commit so great a crime!" George retorted: "You do me wrong, O king! Come along with me and watch me offer sacrifice again!" "You trickster!" Dacian exclaimed. "What you want to do is to get me swallowed up as you made the earth swallow the temple and my gods." "Miserable man!" George answered, "how can your gods, who could not help themselves, help you?" Enraged, the king said to Alexandria, his wife: "I shall faint, I shall die, because I see that this man has got the best of me." Her response was: "Cruel, bloodthirsty tyrant! Did I not tell you not to go on mistreating the Christians, because their God would fight for them? And now let me tell you that I want to become a Christian." Stupefied, the king cried: "Oh, worse and worse! So you too have been led astray!" Thereupon he had her hung up by the hair of her head and beaten with scourges. While she was being beaten, she said to George: "O George, light of truth, what do you think will become of me since I have not been reborn in the waters of baptism?" "You have nothing to fear, lady!" he answered. "The shedding of your blood will be both your baptism and your crown." With that she prayed to the Lord and breathed her last. Ambrose testifies to this, saying in his Preface: "For this reason the queen of the pagan Persians, though she had not yet been baptized, was shown mercy and received the palm of martyrdom when her cruel spouse had condemned her to death. Hence we may not doubt that she, crimson with the dew of her blood, gained entrance through the celestial portal and merited the kingdom of heaven." Thus Ambrose.

Sequenti vero die Georgius accepit sententiam, ut per totam civitatem traheretur, postmodum capite puniretur. Oravit autem ad Dominum, ut quicumque ejus imploraret auxilium, petitionis suae consequeretur effectum; divina autem vox ad eum venit, quod sic fieret, ut oravit.

Completa oratione capitis abscisione martirium consummavit sub Dyocletiano et Maximiano, qui coeperunt circa annum Domini CCLXXXVII, Dacianus autem cum de loco, in quo decollatus est, ad palatium rediret, ignis de coelo cecidit et ipsum cum ministris suis comsumpsit.

Refert Gregorius Turonensis, quod, cum quidam quasdam reliquias sancti Georgii deferrent et in quodam oratorio hospitati fuissent, mane nullatenus capsam movere potuerunt, donec ibidem reliquiarum particulam dimiserunt.
Legitur in hystoria Antiochena, quod, cum christiani ad obsidendum Jerusalem pergerent, quidam juvenis speciosissimus cuidam sacerdoti apparuit, qui sanctum Georgium ducem christianorum se esse dicens monuit, ut ejus reliquias secum in Jerusalem deportarent et ipse cum iis esset. Cum autem Jerusalem obsedissent et Saracenis resistentibus per scalas adscendere non auderent, beatus Georgius albis armis indutus et cruce rubra insignitus apparuit innuens, ut post se securi adscenderent et civitatem obtinerent. Qui hoc animati civitatem ceperunt et Saracenos occiderunt.

The following day George was sentenced to be dragged through the whole city and then beheaded. He prayed the Lord that all who implored his help might have their requests granted, and a heavenly voice came to him saying that it would be so. His prayer finished, his head was cut off and his martyrdom accomplished in the reign of the emperors Diocletian and Maximian, which began about the year of our Lord 287. As for Dacian, while he was on his way back to his palace from the place of execution, fire fell from above and consumed him and his attendants.

Gregory of Tours relates that some men were carrying away relics of Saint George and were given hospitality at a certain chapel overnight; and in the morning they were absolutely unable to move the casket containing the relics until they had shared them with the oratory. And in the *History of Antioch* we read that during the Crusades, when the Christians were on their way to besiege Jerusalem, a very beautiful young man appeared to a certain priest. He told the priest that he was Saint George, the captain of the Christian host, and that if the Crusaders carried his relics to Jerusalem, he would be with them. Then, when they had laid siege to the city, they did not dare mount the scaling ladders in the face of the Saracens' resistance; but Saint George appeared to them wearing white armor marked with the red cross, and made them understand that they could follow him up the walls in safety and the city would be theirs. Thus reassured, the army took the city and slaughtered the Saracens.

The Mediaeval Swedish Versions of the Legend of Saint George

Four Swedish versions of the saint's legend – two in verse and two in prose – have come down to us from the Middle Ages. On the whole, of course, they follow the Golden Legend more or less faithfully. The ways in which they deviate from the original and from each other deserve closer examination, however, especially descriptions of the battle with the dragon, in order to establish which version is closest to Bernt Notke's rendering of events.

The earliest of them is a prose translation made around 1300, in which a large number of the narratives in the Golden Legend have been transposed into Swedish, in an adapted and often abbreviated form, which is also true of the Saint George legend.[1] In this version he is called "Georgius" and on the whole the translator renders the text of the Golden Legend faithfully. He can add explanations, such as the information that Lydia is sited "where Troy stood of yore" as has been mentioned (page 175). And when Jacobus tells us that among the guests that the king had wanted to invite to his daughter's wedding, now alas to be cancelled, were princes (principes) the translator explains this by calling them "kings and dukes", for he himself lived during a period when Sweden had both a king and two dukes, who competed with each other in arranging magnificent weddings.[2] The only noteworthy deviation concerns the dragon's sustenance. According to the early Swedish legend it was given seven sheep each day and when all the sheep had gone, a human being chosen by lot provided an adequate substitute for this daily ration. But George's intervention, his conversation with the princess and his battle with the dragon, which he threw to the ground and wounded with his lance, are presented to us in a more or less word-for-word translation from the Golden Legend.

The legend of Saint George is also included in a devotional work entitled "Själens tröst" (The Soul's Consolation) which is a Swedish version of a low-German original produced during the first half of the 15th century.[3] Here the translator has expanded the more laconic narrative with borrowings from the early-Swedish version such as a description of the position of Troy and by telling us that the king placed a gold crown on the princess's head before she set out to meet the dragon. Nevertheless the version about "Yrian" in "The Soul's Consolation" is shorter than the previous Swedish version and the Golden Legend, with which it otherwise agrees completely. This is true about the dragon's diet – to begin with two sheep and later one sheep and a human being chosen by lot – and about the way in which the saint arrived on the scene, his conversation with the princess and the battle with the dragon. After making the sign of the cross, he charged at the dragon and struck him through the throat with his spear.

A third version of the legend is in rhyming verse and differs to a greater extent. It forms part of a

---

[1] This has been preserved in several manuscripts, the defective *Codex Burenianus* from the 14th century and the more complete *Codex Bildstenianus* from the 15th century. They were published by G. Stephens with the title *Ett fornsvenskt Legendarium* in SFSS VII: 1-2, Stockholm 1847-58, pp. 491-496.

[2] But in manuscripts from the 15th century when there were no longer any dukes in Sweden, they are replaced by counts. Op. cit. Vol. 2, p. 1017.

[3] The version of "Själens tröst" found in *Codex Holmiensis* (*f.d. Ängsö, ca. 1430) has been published by G.Klemming, *Själens tröst. Tio Guds bud förklarade genom legender, berättelser och exempel* i SFSS XIX, Stockholm 1871-73, pp. 122-127. S.Henning, *Sjaelinna throst* in SFSS, Uppsala 1954, pp. 90-94 is a modern critical edition. A version of the legend in modern Swedish can be found for instance in *Legender från Sveriges medeltid*, published by E.Fogelklou, A.Lindblom and E.Wessén, Stockholm 1917, pp. 85-88.

manuscript dating from just before the middle of the 15th century.[4] Here the saint is presented as one who comes to our aid in battle and in difficult predicaments. This "Knight Sir Yrian", as he is referred to, bears obvious traces of the late-mediaeval Swedish cult of the warrior, chivalric saint which Karl Knutsson seems to have introduced into the country. "The Knight Sir Yrian " appears to be related both by its style and by its rhymes with the rhyming chronicle about King Karl Knutsson and his period ("The Chronicle of Karl") and may have been similarly inspired by the king himself and written by one of his clerks or his entourage. In this version the dragon is supplied with a bull ("a whole ox") to prevent it from spewing out its smoke. In his combat with the dragon, the knight is mounted on a white horse, clad in white armour, and carries a white banner emblazoned with a red cross. In other respects the narrative agrees with the Golden Legend – even about Saint George's battle with the dragon, which he charged and wounded in many parts of its body.

The fourth Swedish version is the "Lay of Saint George", which the chronicle tells us was sung by Sten Sture's army at the Battle of Brunkeberg in 1471.[5] Unlike the earlier versions, which describe in prose or verse the whole of the legend including the martyrdom, the 33 stanzas of the "Lay of Saint George" deal only with the encounter with the dragon but compensate for this with more detail and greater visual effect than previous versions and a somewhat different approach. Even if, in some of the other versions, it is assumed, in the light of the earlier narrative in the Golden Legend, that the princess is accompanied by a lamb, the Lay of Saint George is the only version that lays stress on this:

And so she takes her favourite lamb
And from the castle goes

Out by the lake, she climbs a small hill. At that moment, Saint George comes riding up in armour that glistens like the sun and with a white banner with a red cross. Whereas the other versions describe him wholeheartedly rescuing the princess from certain death, in the Lay of Saint George he lays down a condition for doing so:

This day will I save you from your fate
If faith in Christ you will profess

The princess says that she is more than willing to do so.

And when the dragon from the lake emerged
Saint George at once against him charged

Into his mouth he struck a blow
His lance in pieces flew

No bird can fly away so swift
As he his sword then drew

He then urges the princess to place her belt around the dragon's throat and in this way they lead it into the city and induce the king and his people to embrace Christianity, and so the Lay of Saint George ends in full agreement with the other versions.

The description of the battle with the dragon, however, is described differently as can be seen from verse 28 quoted above. Only the Lay of Saint George tells us that the lance broke into pieces, and that the knight then swiftly drew his sword, in other words in exactly the same way as the drama is presented in Stockholm City Church. In the Gol-

---

[4] This can be found in Cod. Holm. D.4 and has been published by G.Klemming, *Svenska medeltidsdikter och rim*. SFSS XXV, Stockholm 1881-82, pp. 185-189. This and other versions is dealt with in Valter Jansson's "Görans saga" in Kulturhist. Lexikon för Nordisk Medeltid, 1956-78, Vol. 6, col. 2 f.

[5] It has, however, only been recorded in written versions made after the Middle Ages published by E.G.Geijer and A.A.Atterbom in "*Svenska folkvisor från forntiden,* I-III, Stockholm 1814-16, no. 60, and several times more recently, for instance by G.Sahlgren, who reissued the above work with a new commentary (*Svenska folkvisor,* published by Kungl. Gustav Adolfs Akademien, Uppsala 1958), Vol. III, 60. The Lay of Saint George is a ballad, and as such, it can be found in *Sveriges Medeltida Ballader*, published by Svenskt visarkiv, chief editor Bengt R. Jonsson, Vol. 2, Stockholm 1986, as no. 40 (SMB 40) in different main versions with variants. The quotations here are taken from the oldest complete version C:a, first found in a broadside from 1686 (pp. 68-70).

den Legend and in all the other Swedish versions, the saint uses only his lance to vanquish the dragon. This is also how it is described in all the versions of the legend found in Germany and other countries. They all tell us that Saint George did not use his sword until he had entered the city, when he beheaded the dragon after converting the population. There are, however, two exceptions. One is the version by Petrus de Natalibus, who, in a version written around 1370 in Latin describes Saint George both wounding the dragon beside the lake, and then, in the same context, immediately beheading it with his sword.[6] He has excluded the intervening episode with the girdle as being too fantastic to credit belief. But the fact that Notke did not use Petrus de Natalibus as his source is obvious, for instance, from the relief on the castle that depicts the princess leading the dragon by her girdle.

The other exception is William Caxton's English translation printed at Westminster in 1483. This tells us that Saint George made use of both weapons on the lakeside, before the princess was then able to lead the dragon into the city with her belt: "S. George was upon his horse, and drew out his sword and garnished him with the sign of the cross, and rode hardily against the dragon which came towards him, and smote him with his spear and hurt him sore and threw him to the ground."[7]

This unrealistic way of doing combat – first drawing his sword and then charging and wounding the dragon with his spear – is obviously something that Caxton, with no experience of tournaments and the proper way of using weapons, had invented. This has been shown by Feldmann, who therefore concluded that this means that there is no literary source for Notke's representation of the combat with the dragon. However, this German scholar was not familiar with the Swedish "Lay of Saint George". Apart from the unlikelihood of Bernt Notke, a German, studying a newly published English version in Stockholm, the version he gives us of the battle is different and fits in better with the techniques used by knights in combat.

Notke's Saint George has charged with his lance, wounding the dragon and overturning it, but at the same time the lance has disintegrated, so that he has then swiftly drawn his sword. In other words, at the behest of the victor of the Battle of Brunkeberg, Notke has portrayed exactly the same sequence of events as in the unique description given in the "Lay of Saint George", which was the battle song of the Swedish army. The uniqueness of the description in the Lay and the extent to which it coincides with the representation of events in Notke's group has not been noticed previously. It can provide an important contribution to our understanding of the gestation of the group.

It should be remembered, however, the Lay was not written down until the 16th or 17th century and may then no longer have been identical with the Lay of Saint George sung at the Battle of Brunkeberg, as its publishers believed. It is possible that this later version had been embroidered with details deriving from the influence of the sculpture.

What is worth noting, however, is that certain earlier pictorial representations have shown Saint George fighting the dragon with both lance and sword outside the city. This was the case in the very first monumental image of this motif. In the Romanesque relief in the porch at Ferrara, signed by Master Nicolaus in 1135, the saint is riding with drawn sword over the dragon, after his lance has pierced the dragon's throat and shattered (illustration 13). And several German engravings by Notke's contemporaries can be cited, which depict Saint George similarly using both weapons on his first encounter with the monster.[8]

---

[6] This has been studied by D.Feldmann, "Zur Bedeutung von Notkes St. Georgsmonument in Stockholm" in *Konsthistorisk tidskrift* 1976: 1-2, pp 22 f. In notes 13 and 14 he describes various continental versions of the legend and in note 11 he provides a precise reference to his source in Petrus de Natalibus and quotes the relevant wording in Latin.
[7] The Golden Legend ... as Englished by William Caxton, ed. F.S.Ellis, London 1900, Vol. 3, p. 128.
[8] Engravings by Martin Schongauer and Meister E.S., see Roosval, *Nya Sankt Göranstudier*, Stockholm 1924, Pl. 18 & 22.

The Original Position of the Saint George Group

What was the original position of the Saint George group in the City Church, and how were the figures arranged? The conclusions we have come to on these issues have already been presented both in words and diagrams. What follows is an account of the opinions of earlier scholars, a discussion of their points of view and a presentation of new arguments. In other words, the grounds on which our conclusions are based will be presented here.

According to Johnny Roosval, the *original position* of the monument was probably in the large pentagonal eastern bay of the chancel, which was demolished at Gustav Wasa's command in 1555 to provide a free field of fire for the castle's newly erected cannon tower.[1] If this were the case, however, the monument, obscured by the enormous reredos erected in 1468, would only have been partly visible from distant parts of the nave and inaccessible to the laity. During the Middle Ages the chancel was a sanctuary to which access for all but the clergy was denied by a screen.

In a well documented study, Sten Anjou maintained that the screen between the chancel and the sections of the church open to the laity was sited beneath the chancel arch in the middle of what is now the nave and that this is where the altar for the laity stood, as it did in other churches.[2] According to a number of available sources, from the 14th century onwards a number of different cults were linked with the lay altar, among them those of the Holy Cross and of Saint George. This must, therefore, have been where the service described in the verse chronicle was read for Sten Sture and his men on the morning before the Battle of Brunkeberg. Along with "laity and clergy" he witnessed the following:

> *A priest read the Mass by the holy cross*
> *The strongest and quickest of those in the host*
> *Whereupon a miracle then did befall*
> *Which God made manifest clearly for all.*
> *And from the cross fell one drop of blood*
> *Into the chalice right where he stood.*[3]

---
[1] J.Roosval, *Nya Sankt Göransstudier*, Stockholm 1924, pp. 171 ff.
[2] S.Anjou, "Sten Stures riksmonument" in *Fornvännen* 1938, pp. 343 ff.
[3] Verses 4749-54 of the Sture Chronicle. The crucifix to which this miracle was attributed was in all probability the chancel crucifix that had then been in the City Church since the beginning of the 15th century and which is now exhibited in Stockholm's Museum of the Middle Ages, published in J.Svanberg "Medeltida bildkonstverk i Stockholms kyrkor", *Sankt Eriks årsbok* 1993, p. 197 ff., ill. P. 198; p. 209 f.

This was seen as a positive sign from Christ Himself before the battle. This therefore was the right place to appeal for Saint George's protection that morning.

Anjou then goes on to establish that his sources reveal that during the course of the 15th century the different cults associated with the lay altar were moved to new altars of their own in chapels throughout the church – the cult of the Holy Cross was moved in 1478. The only cult which is not mentioned as moving is the Cult of Saint George. Obviously this altar became his and his alone. The appeal that has already been referred to in the Vatican archives dating from 1492 states that Sten Sture and his wife "founded a chapel at the altar of Saint George". What this implies, therefore, is that the chapel, or in other words the plinth of the monument, had been erected at an altar of Saint George that already existed, and Anjou points out that there is no evidence of any such altar in the City Church apart from the lay altar.

In addition, the ceremony in 1495, at which St Erik's banner was placed on the altar of Saint George, where Sten Sture was accompanied by "a forest of yeomen", knights and soldiers, implies that the altar of Saint George was in a place in the City Church that was open to all, which would be true of the lay altar but not of a bay in the chancel. This was also the best position for the monument from an "architectonic point of view, evenly lit from all angles, immediately visible on entry to the church and permitting unobstructed view of every aspect". Finally, only a position in the nave adequately explains the justification given in 1528 by Olaus Petri for "the removal of the great Saint George statue in the City Church to Our Lady's Chapel". Because, the reformer explains, "he takes up too much room in the church". In the chancel bay it would not have interfered with the liturgy of the reformed church in the same way as it would in the centre of the nave before the lay altar, in other words next to the place where the Swedish Reformation's first pulpit (the "basket" as it was called) was erected.

Additional support for the convincing arguments presented by Anjou for the original siting of the monument in the triumphal arch of the City Church is provided by the numerous accounts of a similar placing of the Saint George groups in country churches in Sweden. Several examples are mentioned in the chapter on the imitations of the great monument (page 144 and note 4). In the churches at Adelsö, Hammarby, Funbo and Danmark in Uppland and in the churches of Hälsingland, we know that the Saint George groups were placed on the rood screen in the chancel arch. This is also where the group at Östra Silvberg in Dalarna was placed. This was a small group and it stood on a beam right across the chancel arch of the little miners' chapel. Most of these groups had been inspired by the great Saint George in Stockholm and were probably placed in the same way as their original.

With regard to the original arrangement of the figures, it was Roosval's belief that in the bay in the chancel the statue of the knight had been aligned parallel with the east-west axis of the church facing the rear of the high altar. On one side stood the castle, the princess on the other . Both these sculptured figures would have been standing some distance from the main statue on small pillars or consoles projecting from adjacent walls.

Anjou does not discuss the arrangement of the figures but restricts himself to a diagram in which the position of the main group is given on the east-west axis of the church under the chancel arch.

Erik Lundberg, who has presented the most recent carefully thought out proposal for the reconstruction of the monument, sites the main statue and the chapel that supported it athwart the church.[4] He imagined that low pedestals extended from each end of the plinth, the one on the right for the princess with the lamb, and on the left for the castle surmounted by the statue of Karl Knutsson. Whereas Roosval considered that the enclosing framework of the statue was provided by the vaulting of the church itself, Lundberg argued that it had been crowned by its own richly-carved wooden canopy, supported by tall masts, projecting from the plinth. The dramatic events the group portrays were enacted within this setting as if in an enlarged reredos.

So according to Anjou the chantry and the group of sculptures upon it were sited on the main axis of the church, but according to Lundberg athwart it. In the former case, from the nave the group would have been seen from behind, hardly the most interesting view, or face on, one of its two best aspects (illustration 64). The other is from the side, to where both the knight and the dragon are turning (illustration 37). Lundberg and Eimer claimed that this was the side facing the nave. But I now think that at least the chantry was sited on the main axis. The sculptures may have been aligned with it or perhaps placed on a separate beam across the chancel arch with the knight riding southwards (as in illustration 37).

Lundberg believed that the princess was placed on a lower extension from the right end of the chapel. But the fact that she too is executed larger than life, as is the knight and his horse, suggests that she was placed on the same level as they were. And only in such an elevated position is her unnaturally large crown going to seem to be in proportion. Old depictions of the statue indicate that initially the base projected much further beyond the dragon than it does now, and that the princess was placed there (page 159f.). Ancient account books belonging to the City Church also state that she was placed "before" the knight and the dragon. Was she

---

[4] E.Lundberg, *Albertus Pictor*, Sveriges Allmänna Konstförenings publication LXX, Stockholm 1961, pp. 16f. There he adopted Roosval's belief that the monument stood in the bay in the chancel but later considered it to have stood beneath the chancel arch.

turning her back on the combat or facing it? Both the Saint George groups at Finström and Hattula around 1500 that still have their original bases (illustration 147) and the earliest documented careful sketch of the statues in the City Church from the 1650s (illustration 162) show her with her back turned to the combatants.[5]

The comparatively small crucifix that we believe was made by Notke for the City Church – to replace the older crucifix which, along with the cult of the Holy Cross, was moved in 1478 to another position in the church – probably hung in the centre of the chancel arch. There it completed the symbolism of the Saint George group just as the chancel crucifixes did for the imitations in the country churches. This made it possible to view this crucifix in the City Church, where it probably hung from the vault above – or in front of – the princess and the knight, emblematic of the grace and spiritual power that brought him victory (illustrations 139-141). Provided, of course, that it was not hanging on the southern pillar of the chancel arch, so that Saint George's glance was really directed towards it, if the group was turned athwart the church.

No indications can be found in earlier pictures or documents of the position of the castle. It must have been visible from all angles as it is decorated on every side, which is why Lundberg's proposed reconstruction, which places it with one side abutting one of the plinth's gables, is difficult to accept. The smaller scale in which the relief figures and coats-of-arms on the castle are carved could, admittedly, indicate a low position. But as there is no damage to the noses on the reliefs, they must have been out of reach. And on Notke's Triumphal Crucifix in Lübeck Cathedral many small figures are placed high above the ground. We have chosen to place the castle behind the knight, imagining the base to have extended further behind him.[6] But there is less certainty about the original placement of this item than there is for the others.

Enough has already been said about the chapel on which the Saint George group stood and in which his altar was placed and where it was

---

[5] Unlike their Swedish counterparts, many of the Finnish Saint George groups have retained their original bases. Thanks to the willing help of Marja Terttu Knapas, fil.lic., at Finlands Kyrkor in Helsinki and Doctor Åsa Ringbom at Åbo Academy, I have been enabled to examine the five best preserved groups in Finland and also see the observations made by the restoration experts who have worked on them. In all of them the princess was placed in front of the dragon. In three she is now facing the dragon, on the bases of the groups in Hinnerjoki and Sagu only shallow markings indicate her position, while she is attached with a round peg at Rusko. (At Sagu, she is also kneeling on top of a small hillock as described in the Lay of Saint George, cf. p. 185). In these three groups we cannot be sure which way the princess was originally facing, but at Finström she was originally turned away from the dragon, according to information from Åsa Ringbom. Finally, at Hattula the princess has her back to the dragon and cannot be moved, as the peg by which she is attached (which here is the original one) is oval, according to the information given to me by Knapas on the basis of the inspection by the restorer in 1991.

[6] Roosval considered that the castle had been surmounted by a tower — there was room for one next to the statuette of the king and possibly the statuette of a queen — which gave it enough height to balance the princess standing on the other side of the main statue.

planned to bury the founders, so that little needs to be added now. We only agree with Lundberg's reconstruction of the outer form of the chantry, except that we have placed the princess and the castle on the same level as the rest of the group. In page 79 we also indicate the problems involved in any reconstruction of the chapel and the surrounding screens, as we do not know how many parts it consisted of originally. As Lundberg suggests, the plinth's walls – the screens – were probably taller to begin with than they are now. He also points out that above "the reliefs they reveal sections painted to look like brickwork which contain the lower sections of four gothic windows on each side of the monument. These must have terminated higher up." On the other hand we do not believe in Lundberg's idea that masts projected from the top of the chapel to support a canopy of complex sculpted arches above the main statue.[7]

---

[7] Göran Lindahl has had the kindness to inform me (in a letter in June 1991) that in 1966 he and a group of students at the School of Architecture looked into the question of the original arrangement of the Saint George group. Their endeavours resulted in a model being made by the architect Peter Gavel of the group and the chapel in the interior of the Cathedral. This interesting proposed reconstruction was never published and all that remains of the model are some photographs (deposited in the archives of the School of Architecture at Skeppsholmen). Like me, Lindahl conceived of the main statue with the princess in front of it standing right above the nave and with the figures facing the direction I have proposed, but according to Lindahl they stood on a high beam, supported by open arches, in roughly the same way as Notke's crucifix group in Lübeck cathedral. Like the screen there, according to Lindahl the chapel decorated with the reliefs formed an independent structure placed in the central nave of the Cathedral a little to the west of the Saint George group and at right angles to it (i.e. the chapel had the same alignment as the rest of the church). Lindahl shared Lundberg's opinion that the sides of the chapel terminated in tall windows and that it was therefore considerably higher than it is now.

My objection to this proposal is that the tall chapel would have obscured the group when seen from the west — its main aspect — if it was placed in front of the group rather than beneath it. In Lübeck Cathedral, Notke's screen with its sculpted figures is a little to the east of, or behind, the Triumphal Crucifix group. The chapel and the group of sculptures could of course have been arranged like this in Stockholm, but in that case the group must have been placed on a beam.

Saint George from the Reformation to the Present Day

The Reformation came to Sweden in the 1520s. The way in which its proponents attacked Catholic images in Stockholm's churches and systematically cut off the noses and gouged out the eyes of the figures on the reliefs on the plinth has already been described (page 77). Mention has also been made of Olaus Petri's decision that the enormous group "that takes up all the room in the church" had to be moved to the Chapel of Our Lady, the largest chapel in the building, which was sited east of the southern entrance (page 188).

In the middle of the 16th century, the City Church's sexton, Torbjörn Tidemansson, wrote a lively rhyming chronicle about how the statue was beginning to be treated with less and less respect. Visitors to the church "can stroll into Our Lady's chapel and right into the back of you" he wrote and seems to mean that they were allowed to walk into the plinth from the back. He also complains about the work of masons close to the statue and says that "you are allowed no peace in the church any more". The work of art, he tells us, has been debased even further by a move to St. Anne's chapel, or in other words to the south-west corner of the nave (where the Sun Dog picture now hangs). It was to remain there for centuries. The reliefs on the plinth display graffiti carved by visitors – their marks and dates (1559, 1633, 1636 and 1643).[1] The most stringent period of Swedish protestantism at the time of the Uppsala meeting in the 1590s was also a critical era. As in many other churches, alterations started at the City Church "involving the removal of a pile of Papist effigies and other items but in which the idol of Saint George with its horse and what belonged to it was allowed to remain".

During the first half of the 17th century, however, great appreciation of the Saint George group was expressed repeatedly. In his chronicle on Stockholm, Johannes Messenius wrote that "in the Roman Empire/its peer cannot be found". And no less a dignitary than Gustav II Adolf was, according to a much cited note, wont to say "In Sweden there are three outstanding masterpieces, and the first is the Knight Saint George in Stockholm". This was the unhesitating evaluation with which the keen-

---

[1] This paragraph, like the whole chapter, is based up to page 194 on J.Roosval, *Riddar Sankt Göran i Stockholms Stora eller Sankt Nicolai kyrka. En skildring af monumentets yttre öden och en beskrifning öfver dess olika delar med anledning av den ursprungliga polykromins framtagning*, Stockholm 1919. When writing this book, however, he did not yet know where the chapel of St. Anne was located, and its position was described for the first time in J.Roosval, *Nya Sankt Göranstudier*, Stockholm 1924, pp. 141 f.

est champion of protestantism gave pre-eminence to a century and a half old Catholic image of a saint .[2]

From this time onwards, it is also possible to trace the fate of the sculpture in the City Church's accounts. It remained in an elevated position, obviously on a platform between the pillar at the extreme south-west and the southern wall.

Benches were placed under it, and later this space was enclosed to form a room where in summertime the priest could "shrive people for this was impossible in the consistory because of the smell and odour of the corpses always standing there". It is also clear that during the 17th century the group stood close to or on a gallery used by servants. But the statue itself was in a state of "some decay" and therefore it was restored around the year 1700.

A sculptor called Johan Meijer was paid 200 riksdaler in copper coins in 1699 for unspecified sculptural work. This was for repair work (which Roosval demonstrated in his painstaking catalogue in 1919). Two years later an apprentice sculptor was paid for spurs and a small bell, and a turner for 50 pearls of walnut timber "which were for the virgin". Some of them were scattered over her costume, while others may have been used to make a pearl necklace. In the 18th century reliefs on the stoves from Småland she is wearing a necklace of this type and they are clearly depictions of the Saint George group in the City Church as it was then (illustration 166).[3] In them she can be seen kneeling on the platform of the castle, which is where she was probably moved in connection with this work. In 1700, the sum of 960 riksdaler in copper coin was paid to a master painter called Nicolaus Schultz because he had "gilt the Knight Saint George with fine gold and materials". In other words, the group was re-gilded and repainted. On the whole the original colour scheme was retained, but in a simplified form, as the new colours were duller and the gold matt.[4] In the same year the relics were removed and the glass lid that had protected them replaced with a newly made wooden lid. In 1704 the gallery was also removed, so that the sculpture was left resting solely on its raised wooden platform and this was decorated with panels and a picture.

This seems to be where the sculpture stood for the whole of the 18th century, and historians of the period referred to it with interest and great appreciation. Not until the 1820s did classically influenced connoisseurs begin to regard it as hopelessly archaic. At that time a journal called "Boy-

---

[2] An exact reference to the source is given in note 28 to chapter 5.
[3] Johnny Roosval failed to notice the pearl necklace on the princess in the oven reliefs, which is pointed out for the first time here. It can be seen particularly clearly in a wooden matrix for the oven reliefs which is now in the Museum of National Antiquities in Stockholm.
[4] "On the whole the restoration followed the colouring as it was originally, but it was simplified extensively altering the character and intensity. Lustrous gold was replaced by matt gold, light bluish grey by dark greenish grey, crimson by darker brick red etc." Roosval 1919, p. 24.

es magasin" published the following comment: "This parody of good style was commissioned by Sten Sture .... from a sculptor of effigies in Antwerp to prove the esteem in which he held the arts .... there is indeed good reason to congratulate our country on having had its Sergel, and still possessing Göthe, Byström and Fågelberg, but no more artists like the one who served Sture". A guide of Stockholm published in French from the same period (1830) narrates the legend first recounted by Messenius that the effigy-maker was murdered by Sten Sture's men to prevent him from creating another similar work. "Aujourd'hui la vie d'un artiste si médiocre ne courrait aucun risque" ("Today such a mediocre artist would have no need to fear for his life") is the author's scornful comment on the story.

The church, however, took good care of its heirloom and in 1824 the master-painter C.F.Forsselius was entrusted with the renovation of the group, involving cleaning, touching up the gilt and paint and varnishing it. In the following year he painted the reliefs on the plinth in "stone colour" so that they would appear to be sculpted of marble. Around 1860 the horse's braided tail was replaced by a loosely hanging tail made of genuine horsehair (which is still in the possession of the City Church).

In 1866 the Saint George group was moved to the Museum of National Antiquities, which was then housed in a newly erected building on Blasieholmen. There it was placed directly on the floor of what was called the Ecclesiastical Room. After 40 years, however, against the wishes of the Royal Antiquarian, it was returned to the City Church at the government's decision. This took place during a period when many churches were demanding the return of works of art which had previously been entrusted to museums. At the same time, modern scholarship had begun to take an interest in Sten Sture's group of statues, for both historical and artistic reasons. As a result, a thorough and painstaking examination and restoration soon started with the object of returning it as far as possible to its original condition. The work went on from 1914 until 1931, under the direction of Allan Norblad, a curator, and later Alfred Nilsson and the architects Ragnar Östberg and Erik Fant, with Professor Johnny Roosval as the historical consultant. More recent paint work was removed, the original colours were restored in so far as they could be determined, the statue was touched up in some places and the large group of statues arranged and positioned as they remain today. The horse, which had collapsed as a result of the way it had been moved around during the centuries, was straightened up with the help of the iron strut that can be seen supporting the left side of its stomach, the base beneath the dragon was extended and missing pieces of armour were replaced.

During the Second World War, the Saint George group was placed in a shelter. In 1940 a crane was used to lift it from its position in the northern aisle through a window and then it was transported by lorry to a tunnel under Södermalm that was later to form part of the underground system.

At the end of the war, the monument was returned to its previous place in the City Church. A small ceremony took place in 1954, when the package of relics was replaced in the locket hanging in the chain on Saint George's chest (see above page 45). Later a figure disappeared from one of the small reliefs on the castle (page 69). Those that remained were removed so that they could be stored securely behind lock and key in the church, and they were not replaced on the castle until 1988. Not long before that, the whole group had been enclosed by metal railings to prevent too inquisitive inspection. When the railings were erected, the princess was moved on the castle to be closer to the main group. The representative of the Central Board of National Antiquities, Åke Nisbeth, also considered rotating the whole group 45° so that it would stand athwart the church, as he thought that it originally did – even though it was then in a more central position. Nothing came of this idea, however.

In the 1960s further examinations were carried out – mainly of the colour pigments of the polychromy by Eva Brita Blomberg, a restoration expert, whose results were later published.[5] Today Lars Göthberg and Ingrid Hemgren are the curators responsible for the care of the monument. Ingrid Hemgren has cleaned the monument carefully, affixed paint that was flaking and examined, among other things, the reliefs on the plinth to study the possibilities of removing disfiguring traces of dark varnish from areas of skin. As she was involved during the 1970s in the thorough and technically advanced restoration work on Notke's Århus altar, she has a sharp eye for Notke's special techniques. She has shared her observations unstintingly with the present author. On October 5th 1989, the contents of the reliquaries were removed to be examined at the Museum of National Antiquities, to be photographed for the first time to illustrate this work, and to be exhibited in the City Church. They were replaced in the reliquary on Saint George's chest at a small ceremony on December 29th so that they would be in their rightful place when two days later the 500th anniversary of the entombment of the relics to consecrate the monument was celebrated.

---

[5] E.B.Blomberg, "Resultat av färgundersökningar på S:t Göransgruppen i Stockholms Storkyrka", in *Meddelelser om konservering*, 2:2, Copenhagen 1973, pp. 64-68.

Strindberg on Finding the Relics

Searching for traces of Sweden's Cultural History
Random notes by August Strindberg[1]

1.
In the loft above the City Church

Matins in the City Church. St Nicholas is presented as the oldest of Stockholm's patron saints. Old acquaintances in the loft. An unexpected encounter with Saint George and Sten Sture.

The gaslight is still flickering on a grey February morning, when he sets out from his remote dwelling on Norrmalm to meet the sexton at the City Church, who receives him in the chancel, where he (often) serves as the sole member of the congregation at matins.

It is a marvellous sight to see three puny human beings in a cathedral, illuminated by a gas flame and the light from a stained glass window that can endow the snow-laden ashen air with oriental brilliance. The priest invokes Divine blessing and peace on the work of the day that is dawning, its clamour making itself heard from the streets, insinuating itself through the cloth-lined doors and the puttied windows to echo in the vaults like the murmur of worldly souls, awaiting deliverance but with no time to seek it.

He and the sexton proceed to the twisted ironwork that takes them up to the tower and the lofts, and he finds occasion to confirm for the sexton a long-harboured suspicion that the City Church in Sweden's capital is named after the patron saint of Russia, St Nicholas, who was also the patron of seafarers, which he can prove by citing a hymn from the newly discovered gradual for the Swedish church, in which holy Nicholas is invoked for his power over winds and waves,[2] so that any idea of any other saint, a pope or the like, is rejected.

But the path is narrow, and the path is dark, and now, as in all church towers, they are treading treacherous planks laid across an abyss, until they come to a halt before an ancient door, which is unlocked with an enormous key. The eye tries to find a fixed mark on which to rest after being

---

[1] This article was first printed in *Nya Dagligt Allehanda* October 15th 1881. Strindberg included it in his collection *Tryckt och otryckt II*, Stockholm 1890 (which is where this text is taken from). It can also be found in *Samlade Skrifter av August Strindberg*, part 17 (=*Likt och olikt II*), Stockholm 1922, where it was printed for the first time in the new, revised spelling.

[2] "O beate Nicolae, nos ad maris portum trahes" etc. Cf. *Fornsvenskt Legendarium*, p. 575

cast repeatedly from light to darkness. What appears to be an unbounded perspective opens before them: the ground, the floor, or what should be the floor, billowing like a tidal sea, but its waves are ashen and pursue each other to the remote horizon, where a wan yellow moon or sun casts a faint glow on their knobbly backs. He asks where he is. In the loft above the City Church vaults, their extrados illuminated by a small round gable window in the distance. It is a magnificent sight. But the sexton begins to step out on to the crests of the petrified waves, and *he* follows after, not without some hesitation. Now he can see that the ancient walls rise like mountains at the sides of the vaults and that they are provided with small windows that would admit a little light if they were not blocked by snow. They proceed on planks laid across the stormy surface that never ceases to resemble an ocean, onwards leads the light. But when they are half way, the path declines below the pitched roof and absolute darkness falls. The sexton goes first – Mind your head! Watch your footing! There's a step! Hold on to the handrail! Darkness, darkness everywhere. But then like a ray of electric light, a white beam appears, he explores it with his hand to feel something soft and cold. It is snow, that has forced its way through a fissure in the roof and is illuminated by daylight, seeping through the same fissure, and in the same light he can see how the beams reach across his head to form crosses and scissors, as if they want to wound and horrify him. Darkness falls again! And then they halt before a door. Now we are there: Please come through – into the darkness! Heavy iron bolts creak, protesting hinges allow the tower shutters to lift, and in pours daylight, to rest on the purlins below.

He looks around; this is where he will find what he is looking for. Against the wall stands a cross painted black; he approaches and then draws back; on it a man is hanging, the agony of death in the twisted contours of his face and an open wound in his side. "Is this where you have been moved to, my old and bleeding friend? Are they ashamed of you, or don't you fit in any more among the great men whose marble monuments speak of great feats of the kind that form no part of your biography?"

What piece of furniture is that? The old pillory. And that? A bier! A very large one that served before hearses came into use. And here we have the stocks with holes for the feet and chains for the hands. And here: a tithe container, a rather deep one. On the ceiling a ship! A vow from a shipwreck – probably to St. Nicholas![3] And finally an old wooden picture with the heads of angels and an inscription, in which he can decipher A(nno) D(omini) 1561. Quite an old picture in other words!

This is all that the room contained, and it invited no enduring sojourn, as the snow and icy winds began to enter through the open shutters.

---

[3] This ship is now in the Nordic Museum.

So he wrote rapidly with freezing fingers: inventory! One Christ, one pillory, one stock, one bier, one votive offering from a shipwreck, one grain container for tithes, one wooden picture; and when he contemplated what he had written he saw a whole series of pictures and narratives and amplifications, which he stored away in his memory, as now they had to begin the retreat and close the shutters, and so any hope of finding paper or parchment had to be abandoned.

Immediately to the left of the main entrance, close to the sacristy door, a staircase leads up to the City Church archives.[4] He entertained no wild illusions when he walked into the minute room where so many illustrious predecessors had searched and made discoveries, but he still had his reasons, however, as conceptions of what is remarkable change through the years. He knew that Peringskiöld had once upon a time (when he was writing the history of the City Church) searched the room; nevertheless he knew that since then during the 1840s one of the most important documents concerning Stockholm's Mediaeval history had been discovered there, the Documents of the Guild of Corpus Christi, and handed over to the Royal Library to be housed there permanently. He knew that the gentlemen at the Museum of National Antiquities had gleaned what they could during the 1860s when they had removed Saint George and the Dragon. It was, therefore, with little excitement that he began to leaf through the old documents in the chill of the room. Should he open thirty seamen's knots and retie them again? Blacken his fingers with no hope of being able to wash them before he got home? Yes, he would! The cold is dreadful! He moves from one foot to the other; clasps his arms around his chest, blows on his fingers, and works his way through several bushels of burial certificates, notifications of birth; hopeless, endless. There is one ray of light when he finds the accounts for the Stockholm hospital from 1556-58, beautifully written and bound using parchment taken from ancient Catholic missals and psalters. He sits on one edge of the table, absorbed by them, until a throbbing pain in his foot reminds him that the room is unheated. He looks at Danviken's accounts for some of the following years and then turns his gaze elsewhere. He skims page after page of whole series of consistorial circulars in the hope of finding, hidden among them, what he is seeking. In vain! But then another small encouragement: a fossil, a psalter printed in the 15th or early 16th century that survived the Reformation. It is much used but still beautiful in all its simplicity with its large red initials; but now the deadly chill has reached his knees and time is running out. He sacrifices his clean handkerchief to a binding in pressed leather with wrought fittings torn from a Karl XII bible, a magnificent piece of work. With icy fingers and waning hopes he opens a small

---

[4] Not to be confused with Consistory Archives, which are to be found in the Consistory Building at Trångsund.

round wooden box which according to the inventory contains "labels". Indeed it does, labels made of brocade, crimson damask (as it should be called) with a pattern of woven gold and also some tufts of cotton. But it also contains some small finger-length receptacles of the same material with parchment labels sewn to them. Here are parchments, and plunderers have been at work. He opens one of the receptacles, and in a tuft of cotton he finds a fragment of bone wrapped in a piece of linen with a parchment around it, on which is written (in Latin): "Anno domini 1490 ... did Antonius Masth, apostolic protonotary and nuncio, consign these remains of the holy Saint George for the good of the souls of the noble lord Sten Sture, governor of the realm, and his wife Ingeborg! – and laid them in an image of Saint George, erected on the same day." That is roughly what it said. So there he sat, with a bone from no less than Saint George in his frozen hand, reading a hand-written missive to Sten Sture.[5] It was not so remarkable, but it did confirm the story that Sten Sture had caused the image of Saint George to be erected in 1490 or that he was at least connected intimately with the saint. The other receptacles contained bones and a green silk purse with wood-flour and labels saying that they belonged to Saints Cyriacus, Herman, Blasius and others. But this is not very remarkable! No, that's true, but the discovery he made in the attic of the old War Office was much more remarkable, and this will be described in the next chapter.

---

[5] Masth is mentioned in Diarium Vadstenense as having visited Sweden in the year in question. The situation of the relics is mentioned in Rüdling "I flor stående Stockholm" and Grundel's thesis on Stockholm without their being described. They have therefore fallen out of "Saint George and the Dragon" on some occasion and been mislaid.

Strindberg's Report

This is August Strindberg's handwritten report about how he "rescued from a closet (the archive) in Stockholm City Church and deposited in the Royal Library" what was left of Saint George's relics in 1880. A detailed description of the original placing of the relics in four fabric bags, each occupying a compartment in the pendant attached to the chain hanging on the saint's chest, what each bag contained, their removal and their subsequent fate can be found on page 45 and the accompanying notes 2 – 4 and illustrations 32 and 33, and also on page 139 with note 45 (about the glass covering the compartments) and page 194.

"The other relics had been opened and their contents removed when they were found by AS in 1880" Strindberg reports. He is referring to the three bags that have since disappeared. When they were removed from the reliquary in 1700, an inventory was made of their contents according to the labels sown to them. But then no attempt was made to open them, as Strindberg did with the only one that still retained its contents in 1880. He was, therefore, the first to see the document about the consecration since it had been placed there nearly 400 years previously. His rough translation of the Latin text is more or less correct (compare the article on page 198 with page 45). This was the most important and totally new element in Strindberg's discovery.

What happened to the relics after they had been deposited at the Royal Library is described on page 45. In 1954 they, together with Strindberg's report on his discovery, which has accompanied the relics ever since it was written, were replaced in the reliquary on Saint George's chest. How they were placed when the reliquary was reopened on October 5 1989 in order to photograph and examine its contents can be seen from illustration 32. Late in December they were all replaced in the reliquary once again which was then sealed with the lid made in 1700 (see illustration 30) so that they would be in their rightful place for the 500th anniversary of the consecration of the monument.

The third compartment was said to contain only a relic of St. Cyriakus, in other words the scrap of bone that Strindberg wrapped in a piece of paper on which he wrote in his neat, clear handwriting "St. Cyriakus". Not only are the contents of the two remaining compartments missing, but even the bags as well (for what they contained see illustration 33).

Strindberg's handwritten report on the discovery of the relics. It has accompanied them and is now in the reliquary on Saint George's chest. (See illustration 32.)

Notes

CHAPTER I
Saint George – Martyr and Dragon-slayer

1 Within the Roman Catholic church during the second Vatican Council from 1962 – 1965, a liturgical committee was set up which removed the saints for whom no historical evidence could be found. The result is that Saint George's day is no longer celebrated as a saint's day in the Roman ritual. He remains, however, in the venerable *martyrologium Romanum* and was so well-known and popular that he is still to some extent revered as a saint. His status as a saint in the Greek Orthodox ritual has not changed.

2 The icon measures 94 x 66.5 cm (NM 191) and forms part of a large collection of icons donated to the NM in 1933 by Olof Aschberg. At that time it was covered in a thick coat of more recent paint, most of it a solid dark green background colour (see H.Kjellin, *Ryska ikoner i svensk och norsk ägo*, Stockholm 1956, colour plate XLVI) which was removed during restoration in the 1960s. The school to which the artist belonged is not clear. *Den ryska ikonen 1000 år. Nationalmusei katalog nr 513*, ed. U.Abel, L.E.Blomqvist & L.Holger, Stockholm 1989 (2nd impression), no. 12.

3 The combats of Horus are described in M.A.Murray, *Ancient Egyptian Legends*, London 1920, p.59 ff. For details about Marduk see *Lexikon der griechischen Mythologie*, published by W.H.Roscher, Leipzig 1894-97, Vol. II, col. 2358 ff. Apollo is dealt with in more detail in K.Kerényi, *Grekiska gudar och myter*, Stockholm 1955, p.122 f. and M.P:sson Nilsson, *Olympen,* (2nd impression) Stockholm 1964, p.90.

4 For Perseus see op.cit. p.191f. His liberation of Andromeda from an enormous dragon is portrayed with archaic expressiveness in a blackfigure vase painting on a Corinthian amphora from around ca. 550 BC, see K.Schefold, *"Frühgriechische Sagenbilder*, Munich 1964, Abb. 44b. There are several wall-paintings from Pompeii and Herculaneum with motifs depicted in the same way as in figure 4 here, all of them probably deriving from a Greek original from the 5th century BC.

5 M.Blindheim, "Sigurdsdiktningen i middelalderens billedkunst" in ICO (*Den Ikonographiske Post*) 1973:3.

6 The battles of heroes against dragons is a widespread motif in legends from many countries. Among other dragon-slayers apart from those mentioned in the text can be named: *Kadmos* in Thebes according to a Classical Greek myth, and *Didrik of Berne* and *King Arthur* in Germanic and Celtic myths from the early Middle Ages. In addition, *Dobrinjas* and *Aljosja* killed named dragons in Russian myths that derive from historic events in Novgorod and Kiev in the 10th and 11th centuries. The hero *Faridun* vanquished the Dragon king Zahak with a club of nails according to the Iranian saga from the 12th century. But in the Old English epic *Beowulf* the dragon and the eponymous hero kill each other in their final combat and in the Japanese saga on Prince *Yamato Date* the hero is killed by the great serpent — in both cases the texts were written down in the 8th century. See *Legends of the World*, ed. R.Cavendish, London 1982.

7 Medieval representations of Michael are dealt with in J.Svanberg "Kampen mellan gott och ont på dopfunten i Hög", in ICO 1980:1 and L.Karlsson, *Medieval Ironwork in Sweden*, Stockholm 1988, pp.254 ff. – In addition to Michael and George, other saints slew dragons: *Margareta* of Antiokia, who became a martyr at the same time as Saint George, defeated a dragon in her prison by making the sign of the cross when it threatened to swallow her. She is represented in art with the dragon at her feet and wearing a crown (she was sometimes identified as Saint George's princess). *Martha*, who the gospels tell us was the sister of Mary and Lazarus, travelled with them to southern France according to legend and in Tarascon she vanquished a fire-breathing dragon by making the sign of the cross and sprinkling it with holy water and then leading it away with her belt (cf. Saint George's princess) to Arles. Pope *Sylvester*, who died in 335, is said to have killed a dragon that inhabited a hole in the Capitol in Rome and revived two men who had been killed by the dragon's breath. Other saints who may have dragons as attributes are Beatus, Cyriakus, Eleuterius, Eucharius, Narcissus and Servatius.

8 The oldest Greek legend in what is known as the Athenian Folkbook contained a dozen or so different torture scenes and seven miracles, and it describes how Saint George died four times and Our Lord raised him after three of them. At the Council in Rome in 494, the Pope, Gelasius, in the presence of 70 bishops, attempted to remove the apocryphal scriptures, and in the legend of Saint George the torture scenes were reduced to five, the miracles to three and the resurrections eliminated completely. But both the apocryphal and the canonical versions of the legend were in circulation during the whole of the Middle Ages, the former mainly in Syrian, Arabic and Coptic texts, the latter mainly in Western Europe. There were also intermediate versions which mainly followed the edited text but incorporated some material from the apocryphal versions. J.E.Matzke, "Contributions to the history of the legend of Saint George ...", in *Publications of the Modern Language Association of America*, Baltimore, 17, 1902, pp.464 ff.

9 Unless otherwise mentioned, the rest of this chapter is based on S.Braunfels-Esche, *Sankt Georg. Legende Verehrung Symbol*, Munich 1976.

10 Saint George was Jaroslav's patron saint. He was married to Ingegerd, the daughter of Olof Skottkonung and his coins were popular in Sweden, where in addition to the example of the coin illustrated items have also been found on Gotland and at two Sami votive sites. For more details see B.Malmer, *Mynt och människor*, Uddevalla 1968, pp.80-82, from which this illustration has been taken.

11 (with figures 9a-b). The two statues of the equestrian saints at the outermost end of each side of the "porch of the martyrs" in the southern transept of Chartres Cathedral have been confused with each other hitherto as they have been identified on the basis of the consoles on which they stand. Scholars have not noticed that when they were placed there they ended up on each other's console. Now the perpetually clean-shaven Saint George is standing on the left on the console depicting the martyrdom of his bearded brother (he is being forced to pray to the idol) and to the right stands the bearded statue on the console depicting the martyrdom of the beardless George (he is being tortured with a wheel of knives that is not mentioned in the martyrdom of the legend of Theodore). It is the consoles that have been confused as the way in which the statues' faces are turned towards the porch shows that they are in the right position.

12 K.Weitzman, *The Monastery of Saint Catherine at Mount Sinai. The Icons.* Vol. 1, Princeton 1976, p.71ff., illustrations 43, 44 and fig. 28.

13 The battle of Puig is portrayed in a painting in the centre of a large reredos from Valencia which is now in the Victoria and Albert Museum in London, which was created in the 1410s and is attributed to Marzal de Sas. It shows Saint George himself taking part in the battle with the Moors. In addition it illustrates 17 scenes from his legend (with the battle with the dragon as large and as central as the above mentioned battle scene and also, on a smaller scale, on the wings five scenes from the encounter with the dragon and eleven from his martyrdom). See the illustration here and for more detail M.Kauffmann "The Altarpiece of St. George from Valencia" in *Victoria and Albert Museum Yearbook*, 2, 1970, p.65 ff, with copious illustrations.

14 Among the icons there are some that depict a young man behind Saint George on his horse while he is fighting the dragon. This refers to one of George's miracles which is popular in the east and concerns a youth serving in a church dedicated to Saint George in Paphlagonia who was abducted by the Saracens to be a slave and cupbearer for one of their generals. One evening he was rescued by Saint George and lifted on to his horse to be taken back to his church. He is depicted with a beaker of wine still in his hand behind the dragon-slayer on a Greek Byzantine icon in the Museum of National Antiquities (NM 190).

15 (figure 13) During the conservation of the portal at Ferrara, traces of paint were found on the sculpted reliefs, which Professor Marcello Rotili of the University of Naples has been kind enough to notify me about and document in the new photographs that are reproduced here.

16 The oldest French sculpture in stone of Saint George can be found on a mid-12th century arch in Mervilliers. It depicts Saint George as an enthroned officer receiving gifts of money from a knight called Rembaut, the founder of the arch. See Y.Labande-Mailfert, "L'iconographie des laics dans la société religieuse aux XIe et XIIe siècles" in *Pubblicazioni dell'universitata cattolica del sacro cuore*, series 3, varia 5, Milan 1968, p.507f,. fig. 19.

17 The famous George statue in Prague is dealt with in more detail in J. Homolka's article in *Die Parler und der schöne Stil* 1350 – 1400, publ. A. Legner, Cologne 1978, Vol. 2, p.63 f. (with a bibliography). There it is assumed that the statue was created by Peter Parler and only cast by the Klausenberg brothers.

18 Saint George on the bronze created by Barisanus for the Cathedral in Monreale (like the one he made for Ravello) from the late 12th century and in an Icelandic pattern-book from around 1450, see J. Roosval, *Nya Sankt Görans Studier*, Stockholm 1924, pl. 3:4 and fig. 2. Vittore Carpaccio produced (1502-07) ten paintings with different motifs from the legend of Saint George – including several from his encounter with the dragon – in Scuola di San Giorgio degli Schiavoni in Venice, see B. Blass-Simmen, *Sankt Georg. Drachenkampf in der Renaissance. Carpaccio – Raffael – Leonardo.* (Diss. in Zürich 1988). Berlin 1991. Saint George motifs from all periods are discussed and reproduced in D. Scott Fox, *Saint George. The Saint with three Faces,* Windsor 1983, and G. Didi-Huberman & R. Garbetta & M. Morgaine, *Saint Georges et le dragon. Versions d'une légende,* Paris 1994.

19 The flag of Moldavia dating from the period, which still exists, shows Saint George enthroned, his feet resting on the dragon. For more details of these remarkable exterior frescoes see S. Ulea "Originea si semnificatia ideologica a picturii exterioare romanesti" in SCIA, 1963, no. 1, p.57–93 (the ideological relationship between the church paintings and Saint George in the struggle of the Romanians against the Turks) and by the same author in *Die Wandmalerei in der Moldau im 15. und 16. Jahrhundert,* Bucharest 1983 (in less detail).

20 (with illustration 16) A relief of Saint George and the dragon with the same appearance can be found in the tympanum of Saint George's church in Brinsop. In art from the Norman period in England, there are few representations of the saint on horseback but several in which he is depicted on foot fighting the dragon with his sword (for instance the relief in Ault Hucknall), see C.E.Keyser, *A List of Norman Tympana and Lintels*, London 1904, p.LXXV ff. and fig. 145, 149-153.

21 (Illustration 18) Uccello has also depicted Saint George in combat with the dragon in the same setting in another painting (in the Musée Jacquemart-André, Paris). But there the dragon is erect, advancing on its hind legs against the knight attacking with his lance and the princess has not yet removed her belt.

22 For details of Saint George as a "vegetation divinity" see Roosval, op.cit. (1924), p.48 ff. C.G.Jung's interpretations can be found mainly in the chapter "The Origin of the Hero" and "The Battle for Deliverance from the Mother" in *Symbols of Transformation* first published in German 1911-12 and which forms part of the collected edition of his works in English, *The Works of C.G.Jung*, Vol.5, part II. See also C.G.Jung *Aspects of the Feminine* (Bollingen Series XX), Princeton 1982, p.109 f. and *Människan och hennes symboler* (the 1978 edition of this richly illustrated overview of Jung's psychology), p 118 ff.

According to Jung Saint George was one of the archetypal hero figures, who in extreme peril restores the normal conscious order while at the same time renewing the principle of life. The image of such a hero evokes strong feelings and nourishes identification. In this way the observer and supplicant can be freed of their own feeling of impotence. The hero represents a higher and greater identity, which can endow individuals with strength and develop their ego-awareness and this equips them to face major challenges. For the basis of this summary I would like to express my gratitude to the Jung scholar Gunnar Olofgörs. See also Å. Ström, "Sankt Göran – från myt till legend" in ICO 1990:4 (p.43 ff.).

23 (Illustration 20) J.Svanberg, "Roger och Angelica – ett Ariosto-motiv i konsten", in *Studier i konstvetenskap tillägnade Brita Linde*, Stockholm 1985, p.181 ff.

24 (Illustration 22) Previous scholars have considered that "Peter" created many of the paintings at Ösmo but that others were painted later by Albert, who had been Peter's pupil. But "Peter" has been invented as a result of a misreading of some of the letters in an inscription at Ösmo. Recently several scholars have demonstrated that the works previously ascribed to Peter are actually by the young Albert: S.Warmenius, "Den unge Albert – Erik Axelssons (Tott) målare", in ICO 1991:3; E.Helenius-Öberg "Den unge Albertus Pictor och hans lärare", in ICO 1992:2, p.29 ff. and J.Svanberg in Bergström, Hallerdt, Svanberg, *Albert målares kyrkor*, Stockholm 1992, p. 30.

The fact that Saint George is riding a white horse in Albert's paintings (later ones as well) as in Johannes Ivan's (see illustration 25 below) may be due to the reliance of both painters on a contemporary rhyming version of the legend in Swedish dating from the second quarter of the 15th century, in which great stress is laid on the white horse he rode while fighting the dragon (for more information about the Swedish versions of the legend see the documentation section at the end of this volume).

25 For more information about Lund and Vallentuna see B.I.Kilström, the article "Georg" in KLNM, Vol. 5, col. 268 ff.

26 The Källunge paintings are dealt with in *Sveriges Kyrkor, Gotland*, Vol. II, Stockholm 1935, p.208 & 212 and fig. 308. For this chapter see J.Svanberg "Sankt Göran i medeltida konst i Sverige och Finland" in ICO 1990:4, p.29 ff.

27 (With illustration 23) The knight in combat with the dragon on the font at Vättlösa is identified here for the first time as Saint George. Compare it with the contemporary English reliefs of Saint George on horseback carved in stone depicted in illustration 16 and referred to in note 20. According to the book by Keyser referred to in note 20, representations of Saint George fighting the dragon on foot are considerably more frequent in English Norman art. This is a good reason why the standing warrior fighting with his sword and sometimes shield against a dragon depicted on a number of Romanesque fonts in Västergötland should probably be identified as Saint George and not Saint Michael, as he has been up to now, even though the warrior lacks wings and angels are portrayed with wings on the same fonts. He can be found on fonts ascribed to Master Othelric and his successors in Hornborga, Härjevad, N. Härene, Skeby, Skälvum, Högstena, Flakeberg, etc. See S.A.Hallbäck "Medeltida dopfuntar i Skaraborg" in *Västergötlands Fornminnesföreningens Tidskrift* 1971–72, figs. 55, 61, 63, 69, 75, 87, 112. The font at Vättlösa is also correctly ascribed to one of Othelric's successors; the knight is not identified, p.142 and figs. 104–109. It is also possible that a standing dragon-slayer in Rydaholm church in Småland represents Saint George. See below table 7, note 1.

28 The chasuble belongs to Uppsala Cathedral and comes from France, bought from Lyon for the consecration of Folke Ängel as Archbishop in 1274. (I.Estham, "Textil skrud och prydnad" in *Uppsala domkyrka*, Uppsala 1982, p.137; J.Svanberg, "Sankt Göran och draken i Sveriges och Finlands medeltida konst", in *Med hammare och fackla* XXXIV, Stockholm 1996, ill. 1). Saint George is depicted galloping with his lance at the ready, his horse caparisoned as was customary at the period, and his banner on the lowered lance. His name has been embroidered on the picture. A chalice belonging to the church at Östra Ryd which is also in Uppland, portrays the saint on foot with his sword and a shield with the cross of Saint George on it. This depiction in multicoloured enamel is on the foot of the chalice, and is accompanied by an inscription with George's name and the name of the knight who made the donation and the date 1345. The donor is kneeling before the saint with the inscription "the knight Georg Tzendlin", a Slavic name. For more details about the chalice, which was brought back from eastern Europe during the Thirty-Years War see C.R. af Uggla's "Nattvardskalkarna i Östra Ryd. Herrarnas av Sesswegen kalk" in *Bidrag till den medeltida guldsmedskonstens historia II*, Stockholm 1948, p.251 ff.

The two high-Gothic wall paintings at Ängsö in Västmanland, and Vendel in Uppland from the first half or middle of the 14th century are on the southern walls of both churches. Å.Nisbeth, *Ängsö kyrka och dess målningar*, published by KVHAA. Antikvariska serien 33, Stockholm 1982, p.112 and illustration 68. At Vendel the dragon with the lance thrust into its jaw is all that remains of the painting. At Ängsö most of the motif has survived, but the colours have faded a great deal. The small dragon supporting itself on its tail resembles the one at Vendel – in the self-confident high-Gothic period, monsters were small, if they were not omitted completely as in the two imported works referred to above.

29 Portrayals of the martyrdom of Saint George are very rare in Sweden. Our most extensive series (apart from the monument in the City Church) was to be found in the church at Lofta in Småland, in the form of wall paintings dating from the second half of the 15th century. Before the church was demolished, water-colour reproductions of the paintings on the vaults were made by Mandelgren. The following scenes are depicted: 1. Saint George is tortured on the wheel of knives. 2. He is immersed in a cauldron of molten lead which is being ladled over him. 3 – 4. He accepts and drains a beaker of poison and when this has no effect the sorcerer is executed. 5. He is dragged naked by horses. 6. He is suspended from a scaffold and martyred with a lance. 7. He is placed on the rack and salt is strewn on his wounds. 8. He is beheaded.

30 For more details about the George group in Artushalle in Gdansk (from around 1481) see Roosval, op.cit. (1924) plate 4:2. This excellent wooden sculpture with its knight, dragon, princess and city of Silene underwent conservation in the 1980s.

31 The way in which the cult of the international Saint George became in Sweden a cult with nationalistic character has been described thoroughly by A. Etzler, "Sancte Örjenskulten i Sverige" in *Med Hammare och Fackla III*, Stockholm 1931. This is the source of the information and the quotations in this paragraph. See also K.Kumlien, *Karl Knutssons politiska verksamhet*, Stockholm 1933 and *Karl Knutsson i Preussen* 1457-1464 KVHAA. Handl. 46:2, Stockholm 1940.

32 For more details about the Guild of Saint George see Etzler, op.cit.

33 On the use of Göran as a name see KLNM, Vol. 5, col. 269. For pictorial representations see table 11 in which I have listed them. Whereas all the previous periods and the first three decades of the 15th century had produced only a handful

of pictures, at least 25 representations of Saint George date from the era of Karl Knutsson. The number may be higher as it is difficult to say precisely whether certain pictures date from before or after 1470, so that some may have been assigned to a later era although they had been produced earlier.

CHAPTER 2
The Battle of Brunkeberg and its Aftermath

1 This chapter is based on the descriptions of the battle and the events preceding it found in S.Kraft, *Senare medeltiden 2*. Tidsskedet 1448-1520, *Sveriges historia till våra dagar*, del *3:2*, Stockholm 1944, p 151 ff., and S.U.Palme, *Sten Sture den äldre*, Stockholm 1968 (2nd. ed.) p.50 ff. and the sources and works referred to in these books (p.294).

2. The two quotations from the chronicle are taken from *Svenska medeltidens rimkrönikor* del 3: *Nya krönikans fortsättningar eller Sturekrönikorna*, ed. G.E. Klemming in SFSS 17:3, Stockholm 1867-68, verses 4809-20 and 2308-11 and have been translated for this edition. K.Hagnell, *Sturekrönikan 1452–1496. Studier över en rimkrönikas tillkomst och sanningsvärde*, Lund 1941.

3. For more details about the Archbishop see G.Kellerman, *Jakob Ulvsson och den svenska kyrkan* I. Undre äldre sturetiden 1470-97, Uppsala 1935. The position he adopted before the battle is described on p.111 ff.

4 For details about the decision to elevate the feast of Saint George (and also the other three patron saints of the realm) to a major (double) celebration op.cit. p.391.

5 More details are given about the origin of the Uppsala reredos on pages 123-125 of this work. A thorough analysis of the process in which Peringskiöld's copies were made and their reliability has been made in A.Lidén's *S:t Eriks tavla i Peringskiöld's Monumenta Ullerakerensia* 1719 (presented at a seminar in the specialised course in Art History at the Stockholm University, autumn semester 1984).

CHAPTER 3
Saint George and the Dragon in Stockholm City Church

1 For the Lay of Brunkeberg see *Svenska folkvisor*, published by the Royal Gustaf Adolf Academy, edited by G.Sahlgren, Uppsala 1958, no. 61 (in Vol.III). The description of the mass (verses 4745-58) is quoted *in extenso* in the documentation section at the end of this volume, p.187.

- The Greyfriars' diary, *Diarium Fratrum Minorum Stockholmiensium*, pub. in SRS (*Scriptores Rerum Suecicarum Medii Aevi*), 1818, p.67 f. The first reference describes that the Papal Nuncio, Lord Anthonius Mast, arrived in Stockholm in 1489, preached a crusade against the Turks and raised a cross in Stockholm City Church on October 28th of the same year. Then: "*Eodem anno ymago erecta per illustriorem Dominum Gubernatorem regni Swecie militem in Gripsholm Sancti Georgii venit ad Ecclesiam magnam Stockholm.*" These entries for 1489 were made by the Warden of the Priory, Kanutus Johannis, who also added a short poem in hexameters about the same events (see J.Rosén's article "Diarier" in KLNM Vol.3, col.67).

The information in the Sture Chronicle about the same events (the erection of Saint George and the dragon in the City Church is mentioned in verses 3398-99) was probably taken from the Greyfriars' Diary in Hagnell's opinion, op.cit. p.317 f. The information in *Olai Petri Svenska Krönika*, ed. G.E.Klemming, Stockholm 1860, p.251 probably derives from the same source.

Johannes Messenius claims in his rhymed chronicle about Stockholm, published by C.Silfverstolpe in *Historiskt Bibliotek I*, Stockholm 1875, p.118 f. that the Saint George statue was a votive offering: Lord Sten had "once / been in very great peril" and therefore offered God and Saint George that if he were delivered from his predicament "through the prayers of the holy knight, / he would in praise and reward / have his image so wrought / when he was fighting his battle / with the dragon; and his prayer was granted" (verses 1551-61). Nothing is said here about the vow having been made before the battle of Brunkeberg, but this has been assumed unreservedly by Roosval, *Riddar Sankt Göran i Stockholms Stora eller Sankt Nicolai kyrka*, Stockholm 1919, p.13 f. and other scholars.

2 The scholarly publication of I.Collijn, "Riddar Sankt Görans reliker", in *Fornvännen* 1919 (reprinted in *Historia kring Stockholm*, Stockholm 1982, p.156 ff.).

3 When Eva Lundvall, a conservation expert, opened the relic pouch of satin brocade in October 1989, one of the two small packages of relics described by Collijn was missing, the one made of green silk (his no. 3) which, according to the paper label inside it, contained a relic of bone from Saint George. Only the label remained.

4 This is a new translation of Mast's certificate. The original Latin can be found in illustration 33.

5 Transcripts of these supplications (regests) made by K.H.Karlsson are now in the National Archives. Their contents were summarised and the most important of them printed in *Historisk Tidskrift 1901* p.74 ff. and this formed the basis of the brief presentation in Roosval 1919 p.16 f.

6 The contents of this petition were printed in their entirety in *Historisk Tidskrift 1901*, p.76. The Swedish names have been distorted by the Papal scribe. The Latin wording of the extract translated on page 46 of this volume reads: "*quod idem vicerex cum sibi subditis hominibus pro fabrica imaginis s. Georgii plus quam ad valorem quatuor milia mar. ar. de facto exbursarunt et omni anno die s. Gereonis solempnes processiones cum omni clero, sacramento et reliquiis totius opidi ad montem Bukaregm (Brunkeberg) quam cum principissa facere solitum est*". This is a source that was not used to its full extent by Roosval (1919, p.16) or any subsequent scholar.

Gerhard Eimer dismisses the Vatican document in his essay on Notke 1983 (p.79 f.) and in his book on the artist in 1985 he omitted it from the list of documents relating to the origin of the sculpture (p.108). Instead, Eimer includes as two different sources (3 and 4) the entry in the Greyfriars' Diary and Kanutus Johannis's hexameters – unaware that it was he who wrote both the related entries and the poem in the same diary. Eimer had failed to familiarise himself with the Swedish textual sources.

This has also contributed to the following misapprehension in his book. He maintains that the link claimed by Roosval and other scholars between the Saint George monument and the Battle of Brunkeberg is a myth invented under the influence of early 20th century Swedish nationalism, aggravated by the dissolution of the union with Norway. This is said to have led Roosval to interpret the monument on the basis of *"in einem unfassbaren Chauvinismus"*(p.29). Eimer claimed that the concept of national awareness stems from the 19th century and was totally alien for the late 15th century, and most alien on its battlefields (p.103 f.). Eimer ignores the fact that the phenomenon existed long before the concept did. In actual fact, Swedish nationalism is expressed frequently and firmly in many written sources from the period, not least in the Sture Chronicle (see for example the quotation above on p.37). It was fomented consciously by political leaders such as Karl Knutsson and Sten Sture in their struggle to prevent the re-establishment of the Scandinavian Union. This is a fact that one can deplore but not deny. It is also clear that Sten Sture and his supporters regarded the victory at Brunkeberg as a national triumph and that the Saint George statue was to be linked to it. This connection is shown most clearly in his petition to the Pope of November 3 1492.

7 Roosval 1924, p.151 ff. He assumes that a special chapel dedicated to Saint George had been built at Brunkeberg ridge. It was, however, most probably the chapel of Saint George's hospital, which was situated on lower Norrmalm, see below note 5:5.

8 Anthonius Mast came originally from Antwerp where he belonged to the chapter of the Cathedral Church of Saint Mary to which he returned after years in the service of the Pope. He himself said that he brought 20,000 letters of indulgence with him on his mission to Sweden and in Stockholm he also had 200 "articuli abbreviati" printed in Swedish, presumably to be nailed to church doors, according to Hagnell, op.cit. p.317 and note 71. Problems arose in accounting for the income from Mast's sale of indulgences – the Pope requested the funds and a Swedish Commission of the Realm was appointed to enquire into the matter.

Eimer, op.cit. p.108 ff. and in his "hoc magnum opus. Zur Entstehung von Bernt Notkes Monumentalwerken" in *Imagines Medievales* (Festschrift for Carl-Otto Nordström). Acta Universitatis Upsaliensis, Ars Suetica 7, Uppsala 1983, p.81 ff., adduces Mast's visit and the sale of indulgences as playing an important role in the origin of the Saint George monument (instead of nationalism which Eimer rejects). But Eimer has interpreted the role played by Mast and his actions very differently from Tore Nyberg in his thorough analysis about "Papst Innocenz VIII. und Skandinavien", in *Archivum Historiae Pontificiae 22*, Rome 1984, p.89 ff., which is the basis of the description given here. Eimer believes that the role played by the sale of indulgences corresponded to the role it played for the Triumphal Crucifix in Lübeck (see the text p.115). But a special indulgence was linked to the Crucifix whereas the indulgences sold by Mast for the Jubilee were not linked to any image.

Eimer has also failed to observe that Mast's two-month indulgence campaign in Stockholm finished on the same day as the inauguration of the Saint George statue. It is not unlikely that the indulgence was nevertheless linked to the statue, as was customary during this period. In 1474 Archbishop Jacob and four other Swedish bishops had issued letters of indulgence for all those who knelt and recited certain prayers in front of images in Stockholm City Church (Lilljenwalldh, *Specimen I de templo urbis Stockholmiensis...* Thesis Uppsala 1788, p.20).

We also know of an image of Saint George in the church at Marstrand which has now disappeared that Archbishop Henrik Kalteisen issued an indulgence for all those who knelt before the image to revere the saint (KLNM, article on George, Vol.5, col.272). According to the record of the examination of parishioners from the church at Oviken in Jämtland, Archbishop Jöns Bengtsson Oxenstierna consecrated an image of Saint George, now lost, with a grant of indulgences. This information, for which I would like to thank Maj Nodermann, can be found in N.Ahnlund's *Jämtlands och Härjedalens historia*, I, Stockholm 1945, p.396.

9 The Sture Chronicle, verse 3668 ff.

10 J.Rosén i *Den svenska historien*, part 3, (2nd ed.) Stockholm 1978, p.185 ff. – Palme, op.cit. p.204 ff. – G.Carlsson, *Hemming Gadh. En statsman och prelat från sturetiden*, Uppsala 1915, p.100 f. (about how the death of Sten Sture was concealed).

11 The rhyming chronicle's earliest comment in the first person, verse 5507 f. The next two verses read "I stood there a few days / until the lords had taken a new Protector", in other words until Svante Nilsson had been elected Governor of the Realm.

12 Lady Ingeborg did not die until 1507, several years later than her husband. The suggestion that the reason for the original apertures in the plinth and their being closed up was linked to its intended use as a burial chapel and the later change of mind was originally made by Roosval 1924, p.79 ff. Here he also provides different examples of foreign parallels, mainly taken from Italy.

13 The assumption about impulses from China via Venice and the observation about Bellini's great dragon was made by Roosval, 1924, p.45 f. (and plates 9 and 33). – See M.Siggstedt, *Drakens år. Den kinesiska drakens symbolik*. Museum of Far Eastern Antiquities, Stockholm 1988.

14 All the figures, sections and features of the Saint George group are described in detail in terms of shape, colours, damage and restorations in Roosval 1919 which is in the form of the catalogue for the exhibition arranged at that time by the Museum of National Antiquities of the sections of the work undergoing restoration.

15 (with illustration 38) The plinth under the bust of the dead man was created recently during restoration. Where the bust was placed originally is not known. On the collar of the jacket, fashioned in parchment, there is an S between two curlicues – perhaps the way in which his wife had labelled the garment. His hair has been glued around his neck and over his temples as if he had been tonsured. As he is not wearing the clothes of a clergyman, this may be intended to represent a miscreant with a shaven head. I am grateful to the conservations expert Ingrid Hemgren for these observations.

16 As a result of the movement of the monument, the front half of the horse's body had collapsed on to the dragon. This has been corrected during restoration, but to keep it in its original position a visible iron truss had to be added under its left side. – I am referring here to Leonardo's unfinished work on the two equestrian monuments to Francesco Sforza, Duke of Milan, 1483–96 and to Marshal Giacomo Trivulzio probably 1508–12, see L.Goldscheider, *Leonardo. Paintings and Drawings*, London (1943) 1975, Plates 106, 111, and p.177.

17 Roosval (1924) devotes a great deal of attention to the

way in which the knight is wielding his sword, According to him the vertical blow was an Italian speciality, whereas in Northern Europe it was more customary to portray lateral blows in pictures and sculptures during this period. But closer examination of the extensive pictorial material (which Roosval has arranged on the basis of the way in which the blow is being struck) shows that it is not easy to discern any such difference in martial technique or artistic conventions between north and south – there are variations in both directions. In an encounter with a dragon lying on the floor of the City Church, a vertical blow is the only choice open to a mounted knight.

18 The princess is 68 inches (174 cm.) tall. This is tall for a kneeling figure but includes her exaggeratedly high crown. Her head and upper body are basically life-size. The knight who measures almost 90 inches (228 cm) from the crown of his head to his toes is, on the other hand, considerably larger than life in every respect. The difference is due to the fact that he is a saint and also that he was placed higher and would otherwise have appeared to be smaller than the princess.

19 The brand on Lord Sten's horses is described in Palme, op.cit. p.271.

20 Sture Chronicle, verse 2198 f.

21 The unicorn, the least tame and most elusive animal of all, was a suitable symbol for a war-horse, and spiral horns were often included to adorn the brows for real war-horses, as for instance in the caparison for Gustav II Adolf's horse, to cite one of the many examples in the Royal Armoury in Stockholm.

22 A detailed description of Saint George's armour can be found in H.Hildebrand, "Herr Stens Sankt Göran", *Antiqvarisk Tidskrift för Sverige* 7:4, 1884-85.

23 Even though the helmet has been hollowed out so that it could to some extent encompass the knight's head, the visor on the helmet which has been carved from a piece of oak is fixed and depicted in a lowered position. This alone indicates that the knight with his finely formed facial features cannot have been wearing the helmet. Moreover a tall plume of feathers surmounts his head, which is intended to be bare. Nevertheless after the renovation in 1700 the helmet was placed on SG's head behind the high plumes on his brow as is shown in old copies and the bronze casting of the group at Köpmannabrinken (see illustrations 163 and 169 below). Roosval drew attention to this mistake in 1919, p.40. He later suggested that the helmet was perhaps held by an angel hanging from the vaults to appear to hover above Saint George (according to the legends he had, after all, been given his armour by angels), see Roosval 1924, p.61 f. However, the fact that the interior of the helmet is unpainted argues against this, as this would hardly have been the case if the helmet had been intended to hang so that its interior was visible. It cannot, therefore, be said with assurance where the helmet was originally placed. Today it rests on a recently constructed section of the base plate at the front of the statue.

Originally the knight also had a shield, probably borne by the left arm which is holding the reins and certainly decorated with the red cross of Saint George on a white ground. We can be certain that he had a shield because of a poem written about the sculpture in the middle of the 16th century by the Sexton of the City Church, Torbjörn Tidemansson, who saw the statue undergo its first move:

Holy Saint George, the knight so great
In Stockholm stands in great estate
The shadow of his tall horse grey
From those who approach takes light away
Our Lady is your strength and stay
And with shield and helm you survive today.

For more details about the poem see J.Roosval, "Torbjörn Tidemanssons rim om den store Örjanen och andra bidrag till detta monuments historia under 15- och 1600-talen" in *Samfundet S:t Eriks årsbok 1906*, p.56.

24 "I have with God's help ..." see Palme, op.cit. p.261.

25 Palme, op.cit. p.262 ff.

26 Gold (yellow) and blue have been Sweden's national colours since the Folkunga period, when they formed part of this dynasty's coat-of-arms and the Three Crowns coat-of-arms.

27 The assumption that the knight and the princess represent Sten Sture and Ingeborg Tott can be found in S.Anjou, "Sten Stures riksmonument" in *Fornvännen* 1938, p.345. For "Dear comrade" on and in Sten Sture's letter to his wife, see Palme, op.cit. p.272.

28 For the assumption about the Danish coat-of-arms on the escutcheon on the dragon's back see Roosval 1924, p.94 f. and later Palme, op.cit. p.263. If the three leopards had been painted on the dragon's escutcheon, one of the reigning Danish kings heraldic emblems would have adorned the other, as their coat-of-arms also included a dragon. The unlikelihood of the Danish standard's cross being painted on the satanic dragon has been pointed out by W.Paatz, *Bernt Notke und sein Kreis*, Berlin 1939, p.88, and by Eimer 1983, p.80 f. The latter considers it more likely that the intention was to paint the same Muscovite two-headed eagle on the shield that he claims is represented in one of the plinth reliefs (see illustration 106 below and its caption). But this is hardly likely in either case.

Irrespective of the design intended for the emblem on the dragon's escutcheon, with regard to the political symbolism, a striking parallel to both the monster itself and the entire group can be found in Feldmann's essay (referred to below in note 34). He cites in his Abb. 20 and note 53 a print dating from 1577 depicting William of Orange as Saint George – and the symbolism is explained carefully in the accompanying texts (the princess is *Belgica*, the dragon Spanish tyranny, George is William, his sword is hope, his helmet justice …).

29 In front of the painted castle gate to the left in the floor of the niche there is a hole for a plug. It may once have been used to attach the carved figure of a gatekeeper.

30 Chalk sketches were made by the artists on the timber panel behind the relief before it was fixed in place. Roosval 1919, p.69, contains more detailed comments on these sketches and they are also reproduced in S.Karling, "Några Notke-kommentarer", in *Den ljusa medeltiden. Studier tillägnade Aron Andersson* (SHM Studies 4), Stockholm 1984, p.88 f. and fig. 12. The chalk sketches consist of a naïve representation of a pair of birds, and a finely drawn escutcheon surmounted by a helmet with two objects forming a cross on its diagonal field. "To the left of the helmet a word had been written in miniscule script which starts with an elegant S and which can be deciphered as Sten. An inscription to the right of the helmet contains a similar S followed by a t. At the bottom right a B can be

made out" (Karling). According to Roosval this could be a sketch by the master himself of a disposition of the coats-of-arms in the style of the large escutcheons.

31 The picture in the Guild's charter and its connection with the depiction of the masons in the Saint George group and the rebuilding of the City Church is dealt with in J.Svanberg, "Murare i senmedeltidens Stockholm" in *S:t Eriks årsbok* 1984, p.9 ff.

32 The screens and the plinth reliefs are dealt with in Roosval 1919, p.72 ff., and Roosval 1924, p.99 ff.

33 J.Roosval, "Reliefer och statyetter till Sankt Görans sockel" in *Konsthistorisk Tidskrift* årg. 1, 1932, p.102 ff. and on the sides immediately preceding them the same author's "Sankt Göran färdig" deals with the restoration work that had been going on since 1914 and what it had achieved when completed in 1932 with regard to the arrangement and the restructuring of the plinth. Roosval believed that the statuettes had stood on the frames fashioned in the form of small gothic buttresses around the screens' reliefs – in other words where the smooth wooden pilasters can now be found at each corner and in the centre of each side. He believed that the martyrdom scenes which have since disappeared were placed in the end walls. This is where the coats-of-arms of the founders were placed in the course of the restoration, but he emphasised that this was certainly not their original position.

34 The most important modern scholarly work on the plinth reliefs is by D.Feldmann, "Zur Bedeutung von Notkes St. Georgs-Monument in Stockholm", in *Konsthistorisk Tidskrift* 1976, p.19 ff. – Cf. K.J.Dorsch, *Georgzyklen des Mittelalters. Ikonographische Studie zu mehrzenigen Darstellungen der Vita des hl. Georg in der abendländischen Kunst unter Einbeziehung von Einzelszenen des Martyriums* (Thesis) Frankfurt/Main - Berne - New York 1983, above all no. 76 (the monument in the City Church), p.350 f.

35 Messenius's Chronicle about Stockholm, see above note 1 for this chapter. The corresponding section of Peder Swarts' chronicle is quoted with a commentary by K.B.Westman, *Reformationens genombrottsår i Sverige*, Uppsala 1918, p.319 ff.

36 An illustrative model demonstrates the height to which an iconoclast's weapons of destruction could reach in Roosval 1924, plate 41.

37 Roosval 1919, p.28 and 82 (about the copy of the inscription).

38 A detailed account of the original construction of the screens and how they were closed up can be found in Roosval 1919, p.72 ff. At the top both details in their construction and the paintwork decorating the lower parts of windows reveal that the screens were once surmounted by a structure which has since disappeared. The base beneath the dragon and the horse was therefore originally higher than it is now.

39 For the order in which they should be read see Feldmann, op.cit. p.30 f. and Abb. 19.

40 (Illustration 84b) The hypothetical reconstruction of the plinth – chantry differs from the one proposed by Erik Lundberg in his book *Albertus Pictor*. Sveriges Allmänna Konstföreningens publikation LXX, Stockholm 1961, p.16 f. which I followed in the 1st Swedish edition of this book (Ill. 84b).

41 For the German version of the legend see Feldmann, op.cit. p.30. The appearance of the angel bringing Saint George the banner with its cross immediately before his execution is also described in a rhyming 15th-century version in Swedish about "ridder sancte Yrian", ed. by G.E.Klemming in SFSS XXV, Stockholm 1881-82, verses 429-438 (for more about this version see the documentation section at the end of the volume, p.184 f.)

42 Roosval (1919, p.85 f.) suggested that to produce the impressions of the coins (cf. illustrations 95 and 96 below and their captions) "probably gilt coins or lead impressions of coins had been affixed". It is, however, unlikely that lead impressions were used. Nor was it necessary to have affixed real coins, instead it was enough to paint the impressions silver to create the illusion of a heap of coins. This is the first time that the impressions have been identified, see illustrations 95–96 with their captions, and note 45 below.

43 For this relief see Roosval 1932 "Reliefer ...", p.102 ff.

44 For this relief see Roosval 1932 "Reliefer ...", p.108 ff. However, Feldmann, op.cit. p.29, was the first scholar who could identify the motif of the relief correctly.

45 (Illustrations 95 and 96 and captions). For assistance in publishing the first identification of the coins I would like to express my gratitude to Lars Lagerqvist, Head of the Royal Cabinet of Coins and Medals, and the numismatist Christian Hamrin. See Lars Lagerqvist, *Svenska mynt under vikingatid och medeltid samt Gotländska mynt*, Stockholm 1970, p.126 ff. (for coins minted during the era of Sten Sture the elder). I.A.a (an örtug, both faces) and II.A.a. (a half örtug). After Hamrin had identified these, Lars Lagerqvist was kind enough to inspect the relief in December 1989 and was able to establish that among the impressions that could be identified at least eight coins had been minted in Stockholm under Sten Sture, one came from Denmark (1430s) and one from the Hanseatic Port of Anklam (1395) close to Lassan in Pomerania.

In this context it should be pointed out that in the year after the inauguration of the monument, Bernt Notke was appointed Master of the National Mint in Sweden.

46 (Illustration 106 with caption). Feldmann, op.cit. note 52, assumes that the double-headed eagle on Dacianus's throne may not only be a reference to his position as a Roman governor but also to Ivan III who had adopted the double-headed eagle, (see below note 5:40). He would then be linked to the individual who condemned Saint George to death, a slur on one of Sten Sture's current political protagonists. But in my opinion there is a great deal that contradicts this assumption.

47 (Illustration 107 with caption). It is Karling, op.cit. p.90 f. who has assumed that the A implies that Albert the painter was involved in the work on the reliefs (mainly with the polychromy). Karling has also observed a couple of less distinct letters on other tiles in the same relief – a Z and possibly a D and another A.

CHAPTER 4
Bernt Notke – The Saint George Master

1 (Illustration 108) The workplace is of course totally unrealistic: artists and craftsmen like these worked indoors in workshops (cf. the painter in illustration 109), but their implements and methods of working are reproduced faithfully. With regard to beliefs about the special relationship of artists to a planet see R.& M.Wittkower, *Born under Saturn. The Character and Con-*

duct of Artists: A Documented History from Antiquity to the French Revolution, London 1963.

2 (Illustration 109) P. Tångeberg, *Mittelalterliche Holzskulpturen und Altarschreine in Schweden. Studien zu Form, Material und Technik,* published by KVHAA, Stockholm 1986, p.242, drew attention to the clay dish, where oil paint is being kept immersed in water. He has been kind enough to allow us to use his photograph of the painting.

3 Johannes Messenius's rhyming chronicle about Stockholm, verses 1562-70. Cf. note 3:1 above, which cites the verses immediately before them (1551-61) about Sten Sture's votive offering to Saint George and the reference to the publication of the chronicle. In the concluding verses about the monument (verses 1571-76) it is said to have cost Lord Sten an enormous sum "that was larger than anyone thinks" and that it now stood in Saint Anne's chapel in the City Church where it was seen by many people.

4 Johannes Messenius tells us that the artist was executed in another work, one in which he wrote in Latin about the five most ancient Swedish cities, *Sveopentaprotopolis,* Holmiae 1611, p.102. After a few lines devoted to the Saint George statue, executed by a "sculptor from Antwerp" he writes: *Qui opere eleganter completo, ne statuam majoris elegantiae usquam sculperet Iocorum, in cellario pretorij, a principis famulo pugione inter pocula transfossus perhibetur.*

5 V. von Heidenstam, *Sankt Göran och draken,* Berättelser, Stockholm 1900, is based on Messenius' information cited in the previous note both concerning the origin of the artist (Andorf is another form of Antwerp) and his death. In the short story he is stabbed to death with a dagger in the cellar of the Town Hall by one of Sten Sture's retainers, although the reason for the deed is a different one according to Heidenstam.

6 J. Roosval, "Studier rörande Storkyrkans Sankt Jöransgrupp" in *Meddelanden från Nordiska Museet* 1901, p.209. The same author's "Hvem har skulpterat S. Göran och draken?" in *Festskrift för Henrik Schück,* Stockholm 1905.

7 For Roosval's books and articles see the notes and the list of references. Paatz's major work from 1939 contains in Vol. I text and notes, 42 copies of documents and a catalogue of 106 works that Paatz attributes to Notke and his circle of artists, and in Vol. II plates. A shorter, summarising work is W. Paatz, *Bernt Notke,* Vienna 1944. E. Moltke, *Bernt Notkes altertavle i Århus domkirke og Tallinntavlen,* Copenhagen 1970, Vol.I (text and illustrations) – Vol.II (plates). Eimer, op.cit. 1985, contains text without notes, two documents that eluded Paatz, and a catalogue listing 25 works that Eimer believes to be by Notke himself. The extensive literature on Notke is catalogued in a bibliography in Paatz 1939, and subsequent works in Eimer 1985. A German scholar who has devoted a large number of post-war works to Notke is Max Hasse – among them the pamphlet *Bernt Notke, St Jürgen zu Stockholm.* (Werkmonographien zur bildenden Kunst; Reclams Universal-Bibliothek Nr 81), Stuttgart 1962 and the article "Bernt Notke" in *Zeitschrift des deutschen Vereins für Kunstwissenschaft XXIV* 1970, p.19 ff. Other essays by Hasse are cited in the notes below.

8 *Internationales Kolloquium zum Werk des Bernt Notke anlässlich der Restaurierung der Triumpkreuzgruppe im Dom Lübeck 22.-24. September 1976 (Vorträge)* gives an account of new observations made during restoration of this work and of other works for which there are documented links with Notke (the Århus altar and the Tallinn altar). Most of these articles are cited below with reference to the specific works. M.J. Liebmann, *Die deutsche Plastik 1350-1550,* Leipzig 1982, p.246 ff., provides an up-to-date and lively overall picture of Notke's oeuvre with the Saint George statue as its culmination and ascribes to the sculptor a significant role in the development of German sculpture during its period of greatness.

9 (Illustration 110) Bernt Notke's trade mark in his seal on a document dated from Lübeck May 3 1484, now once again in the keeping of the City Archive in Tallinn. Reproduced from S. Karling, *Medeltida träskulptur i Estland,* Gothenburg 1946, p.185.

10 The account of Notke's life and work is based mainly on the books by Paatz and Eimer unless otherwise stated in the notes.

11 Attention has been drawn to the significance of Pasquier and the Tournai tapestries for Notke by M. Hasse, "War Notke ein Maler und Bildschnitzer oder war er nur Unternehmer?" in *Zeitschrift des Vereins für Lübeckische Geschichte und Altertumskunde 52,* 1972, p.137 ff. He refers to the similarities between the equipment of Caesar's horse and Saint George's on p.140 f. See also Eimer 1985, p.16 and 117.

12 M. Lumiste & G. Globatschowa, "Der Revaler Totentanz von Bernt Notke" in *Zeitschrift des deutschen Vereins für Kunstwissenschaft XXIII* 1969, p.122 ff. According to Hasse 1970, p.20 ff., the fragment in Tallinn is a piece of the original Lübeck dance of death that had been removed early in its history. It is stated that they were two parallel works in the latest and most thorough study of the issue; *Der Totentanz der Marienkirche in Lübeck und der Nicolaikirche in Reval (Tallinn)* ed. von H. Freytag (Niederdeutsche Studien, Vol. 39) Cologne 1993.

13 *Internationales Kolloquium zum Werk des Bernt Notke...* 1976 (the complete title can be found in note 8 above), p.1-100, contains the articles referred to below on various aspects of the Triumphal Crucifix group in Lübeck Cathedral in the light of the new findings resulting from the restoration work. Two of the contributions can also be found in the lavishly and beautifully illustrated book *Triumphkreuz im Dom zu Lübeck. Ein Meisterwerk Bernt Notkes,* Wiesbaden 1979 (E. Vetter about the iconography and E. Oellermann on the history and restoration). Cf. Paatz 1939, p.52 ff. and 329 ff. (catalogue no. 36) and Eimer 1985, p.55 ff.

14 E. Vetter, "Zur Ikonographie des Triumphkreuzes" in *Internationales Kolloquium ... 1976,* p.62 ff. The triumphal crucifix group comprised 72 figures, but the small ones at the top (including God the Father) were destroyed by bombing in 1942.

15 D. Eckstein & A. von Ulmann, "Holzbiologische Untersuchungen und werktechnische Beobachtungen am Triumphkreuz im Lübecker Dom" in *Internationales Kolloquium ... 1976,* p.81 ff.

16 E. Oellermann, "Restaurierungsbericht" and "Die originale Bemalung des Triumphkreuzes von Bernt Notke" in *Internationales Kolloquium ... 1976,* p.21 ff.

17 A. Grassmann, "Bernt Notkes Triumphkreuz: Die Inschriften und ihre Lesung" in *Internationales Kolloquium ... 1976,* p.58 ff. Previously E. Oellermann had published the newly discovered inscriptions in two "Fundberichte" in *Kunstchronik 26,* 1973, p.93 ff. and *Kunstchronik 27,* 1974, p.425 ff. See also the comment by M. Hasse "Das Pergament zu Bernt Notkes Triumphkreuz im Lübecker Dom" in *Kunstch-*

ronik 26, 1973, p.389 ff.

18 For more about the Århus altar see in addition to Paatz 1939 and Eimer 1985, principally Moltke 1970. Moltke's book was published before the altar was restored, when the original colouring became apparent and new findings were made, and these are described in E.Skov and V.Thomsen, "Bernt Notkes altertavle i Århus domkirke. Nye undersøgelser" in *Nationalmuseets Arbejdsmark 1981* (Copenhagen 1981), p. 107 ff.

19 The inscribed signatures, which during the latest restoration were revealed under overpainting, are beneath the feet of the three large figures in the corpus and were therefore once visible to those standing before the altar. Below the figures at each end, Clement and John, are the words "Bernardus" and "fecit me", but the base below the central figure, Anne, has obviously been replaced as it no longer has the original blue colour. The central part of the inscription, which probably contained the artist's surname, his profession and where he came from, is therefore missing.

20 For the reredos at Tallinn see in addition to Paatz 1939, Karling 1946 and Eimer 1985, mainly Moltke 1970 and for information about the conservation work N.Bregmann & O.Lelekowa, "Die Restaurierung des Altars von Bernt Notke in Tallinn" in *Internationales Kolloquium ...* 1976, p. 126 ff. It was painted in tempera in 1625 and in oil in 1815. Both layers have been removed.

21 Like the Århus altar the Tallinn altar is also surmounted by a carved representation of Mary being crowned and the statues on the reredos are surrounded by smaller statuettes representing different prophets and saints. The large statuettes on the wings depict Saint Olof, Saint Anne, Saint Elisabeth and Saint Victor.

22 According to Notke's letter the reredos had been commissioned by Hagenbeke, and Karling (1946, p. 168, illustration 162), assumes that he is depicted as the kneeling figure. However, his bald head is interpreted by Eimer (1985, p. 100) as the tonsure of a clergyman, and he prefers to assume that this is Diderik Notke, at that time a priest in Tallinn, although it is not known which church he was attached to.

23 For details of the Uppsala reredos see G.Boëthius & A.Romdahl, *Uppsala domkyrka 1258-1435,* Uppsala 1935, p. 173 ff. and Paatz 1939, p. 180 ff. and 378 ff. (cat. no. 100) and in Vol. II Abb. 10–13 and Eimer 1985, p. 49 ff. and 174 f. Paatz dates it to 1475–77 mainly on the grounds that the killing of Saint Erik in the composition presupposed knowledge of the painting by Dirc Bouts with a similar subject. Sten Sture's son-in-law Erik Eriksson Gyllenstierna, whose coat-of-arms is included in the battle scene, died in 1477. Like the other coats-of-arms depicted, it is assumed to refer to one of the founders. Both the sculptures and the painting in the destroyed reredos have been attributed to Notke.

24 The works in Sweden that Eimer 1985, p. 100 ff. attributes to Notke (apart from the major works dealt with in this volume) are two reredoses that still exist (in the churches at Skellefteå in Västerbotten and Rytterne in Västmanland) and two almost life-size sculptures (Saint Erik in Strängnäs Cathedral and Saint Thomas à Becket from Skepptuna in Uppland, now in the Museum of National Antiquities). Paatz (1939, p. 99 ff.), however, attributes neither of these works to Notke himself but instead other sculptures in Sweden (a saint and a reredos from Skummeslöv, now in Lund Museum of Antiquities and two saints from the church at Köping on Öland, now in the Museum of National Antiquities). In addition Paatz attributes to Notke a large number of wooden sculptures in other countries around the Baltic and works in other materials. He may have made models for silverware (a Saint George reliquary from Elbing), textiles (embroidered with St George and the dragon in the church at Vassunda in Uppland), grave panels (the Hutterock brass in Saint Mary's church in Lübeck) and the woodcut illustrations for the Lübeck Bible. Other scholars have tried to attribute additional works to Notke, some of them in Sweden. Disagreements reveal how uncertain these attributions are, and Moltke 1970, passim, has expressed serious criticism and rejected them. Cf. J.Svanberg, "Bernt Notke" in *Svenskt Biografiskt lexikon,* pamphlet 134 Vol. 27 Stockholm 1991.

25 The attribution of the Karl Knutsson statuette to the Saint George master was first proposed by Roosval 1901. A closer description of the statuette is given in Roosval 1919, p. 90 f. (cat. no. 57). Paatz 1939, p. 81, 97 f. and 319 (cat. no. 19) and Andersson 1980, p. 129 f. (apart from the Saint George group in Stockholm, the only sculpture in Sweden "which could be unanimously ascribed to Bernt Notke") and in Eimer 1985, p. 28, 52 f., 171, 175 (cat. no. 5). On the base a label has been glued in the 19th century with the information that it portrays "Carl VIII Knutsson Bonde" and donated to Gripsholm by Baron Carl Bonde. It has been exhibited in Stockholm at the National Art Museum in 1919 and 1935 and at the Museum of National Antiquities in 1953, and most recently in Washington at the National Portrait Gallery in 1988. More details can be found in the catalogue from this exhibition *Masterpieces from Gripsholm Castle,* Uddevalla 1988, ed. P.Bjurström & Ulf G.Johnsson, p. 14 f.

26 S.Wallin, "The Karl Knutsson statuette at Gripsholm. A comment on its fate" in *Kyrkoinredning för herremän,* Stockholm 1958, p. 187 ff.

27 A.Lindblom tries in *Kult och konst i Vadstena kloster,* Uppsala 1965, p. 178 ff., to argue that the statuette came from Vadstena Abbey Church. A.Andersson, in *Medieval Wooden Sculpture in Sweden,* Vol. III, Stockholm 1980, p. 129 f. that it formed part of the king's grave monument in Riddarholmens church. Eimer (1985, p. 54) claims that the statuette probably formed part of the reredos in Uppsala.

28 Roosval (1901 and 1932, p. 111), who was the first to attribute the statuette to Notke, linked it with the sculptures in the City Church and concluded that it originally stood in a niche in one of the six small decorative towers which he assumed to have existed along the sides of the great plinth. Sten Anjou, "Sten Stures riksmonument" in *Fornvännen* 1938, p. 347 ff. was the first to show that the Karl Knutsson statuette had probably stood on the roof of the castle to complete the political symbolism of the group as a whole. E.Lundberg adopted this idea in his proposed reconstruction of the Saint George group (Lundberg 1961, p. 15 ff.).

29 The size of the base under the statuette of the king is 35 x 15 cm. and the platform on the castle 115 x 75 cm. Roosval (1924, p. 160 f.) argues that the castle was also surmounted by a tower like that shown in the stove relief in illustration 166 and drew comparisons with the old Three Crowns Tower of the Palace in Stockholm.

30 Analysis of the king's cranium and a reconstruction of his

profile based on the one made by C.M.Fürst and V.Berglund and published in C.M.Fürst, *När de döda vittna*, Stockholm 1920, p. 135 ff. and in C.M.Fürst & M.Olsson, *Magnus Ladulås och Karl Knutssons gravar i Riddarholmskyrkan*, Stockholm 1921, p. 206 f.

31 For details about the rebuilding of the City Church see *Sveriges Kyrkor, Stockholms Kyrkor,* Vol. 1:1, *S:t Nicolai eller Storkyrkan,* (ed. J. Roosval), Stockholm 1924, p. 336 ff. and Svanberg 1984, p. 18.

32 Eimer (1985, p. 23 ff.) is the most recent scholar to have emphasised the role of the patrons and their mutual contacts.

33 Ibid., p. 25., Paatz 1939, p. 294 (document nr. 23), in which Bernt Notke is named as a witness for the Swedish Councillor of the Realm Bengt Karlsson March 19 1486.

34 For more details about Notke's stays in Sweden, see the documents in Paatz 1939, p. 292 ff. and Moltke 1970, p. 58 f. and 206, with a critical summarisation of what is known about Notke's whereabouts year by year (and for the years about which nothing is known).

35 Paatz 1939, p. 302 f. (document np. 39): Henrik Wilsing's letter to the Stockholm burgher Tile Hampe (in the National Archive in Stockholm). It is commented on and reproduced photographically in Moltke 1970, p. 82 ff.

36 The identification of the imprints of the coins presented here for the first time greatly strengthens this hypothesis (see note 3:45). As has often been pointed out, the use of elk antlers also suggests that the work was created in Sweden. Elks with the same type of antlers were not to be found in Germany.

37 For more details about the allocation of the work to different craftsmen see Paatz 1939 p. 91 ff. ("Die persönliche Leistung Notkes") and p. 129 ff. & 142 ff. (the proportionate responsibility of the two assistants). According to Paatz, the younger of the two, known as "the imperialissima master" (i.e. Henrik Wilsing?), created not only the small reliefs on the castle but also the Man of Sorrows and the Madonna on the horse's equipment and the relief from Ed (illustration 89 above), whereas the other reliefs on the plinth were the work of the older journeyman (i.e. Thönnies Hermensson?), apart from the relief now in Danderyd, which was Notke's work. Notke also created all the figures in the main group and of course made the sketches on which all the other sections were based. The fact that the Danderyd relief is the only one in which the timber is exposed so that the fine detail of the carving can be admired is almost certainly the reason why Paatz believed that it was an exception and superior to the others (illustration 103 below).

38 J.Roosval, "Hinrich Wylsynck" in *Nordisk Tidskrift för Bok- och Biblioteksväsen* XXIII, 1936, p. 181 ff. attributed the main group to Notke, the reliefs on the castle and those found at Ed and Danderyd to Henning von der Heide (senior), and the other reliefs to Henrik Wilsing. Moltke 1970, passim, totally rejects all these attributions based on stylistic features. Karling 1984, p. 90 f. (cf. note 3:47 above). He seems to be of the opinion that Albert was not only the painter but was also involved in carving the reliefs on the plinth (on the strength of an entry in the rolls that Albert supplied a reredos to Nådendal).

39 For more details about the methods customarily used in workshops in Lübeck for producing and painting wooden sculptures see H.Huth, *Künstler und Werkstatt det Spätgotk* (1st ed. 1925) Darmstadt 1967 (Neudruck bei Wissenschafliche Buchgesellschaft) and for works that can be found in Sweden Tångeberg, op.cit. p. 129 ff.

40 A detailed description of the extraneous materials used on each item can be found in Roosval 1919 passim and a more general discussion of the use in the period of "nicht geschnitzte plastische Formen" on sculptures in Tångeberg op.cit. p. 246 ff.

41 The significance of the overwhelming scale of Notke's works has been asserted by Paatz 1939, p. 84 ff. ("Italienische Monumentalität") and by Eimer, in particular in his essay "Das Monumentale in der Kunst Bernt Notkes", in *Internationales Kolloquium ...* 1976, p. 133 ff.

42 The Maria reredos in Cracow is dealt with in E.Lutze, *Veit Stoss,* Munich-Berlin 1952, p. 10 ff. and Illustration 1–15, and in Z.Kepinski, *Veit Stoss,* Warsaw 1981, p. 20 ff. A sum of 2,808 guilder was paid for the enormous work, made up of contributions from the German congregation in Cracow. The apostles standing around Mary as she falls asleep in the corpus reach a height of just over 9 feet (2.8 meters) and the reredos is over 52 feet (16 metres) tall, in other words half the height of the chancel.

43 For a more thorough discussion of the original placement of the Saint George monument and the arguments involved see the special chapter in the documentation section at the end of this volume, p. 186 ff.

44 This crucifix in the City Church, carved from oak, was attributed by Paatz (1939 p. 151) to Henning von der Heide (senior) and dated between 1490-95 (p. 156). The first person to attribute it to Notke instead was R.Norberg "Johannesfatet från Norrby" in *Fornvännen* 1953, p. 102 f., because of the intensity of its expression, the powerful plasticity, the correct proportions, the draping of the textile around the loins and the masterful freedom of the flowing locks – all reminiscent of the crucifix at Lübeck according to Norberg, who was of the opinion that the crucifix in the City Church had been created by Notke in connection with the work on the Saint George monument (he also gives an account of the restoration work of 1934 mentioned in the caption to illustration 140). Norberg's attribution has been accepted by subsequent scholars such as Andersson 1980, p. 139 (with some reservations, however – he explains the stylistic differences from the Lübeck crucifix by the fact that 15 years separate them). Eimer (1985, p. 129 f. and 185; cat. no. 20) subscribes to Norberg's argument that it was created by Notke without reservation. My hypothesis about its relationship to the Saint George monument is new.

45 For more about the pane of glass see illustration 32 above and the caption, and Roosval 1919, p. 38. It is referred to in C.Chr.Liljenwalldh's dissertation (supervised by E.Fant), *De templo urbis Stockholmiensis primario, S. Nicolai dicto,* spec. 1, Uppsala 1788, p. 10 f.

CHAPTER 5
A Perennial Motif

1 (illustration 142) The Lillkyrka reredos was made in Sweden, probably in Stockholm. According to local tradition, it was brought to Lillkyrka in 1547 by a monk who had been expelled from his monastery by Gustav Vasa. Mary stands in the corpus holding the Infant, and the wings depict her birth, purifi-

cation and betrothal. The dating and iconography is dealt with in Å.Nisbeth, *Kyrkan i Lillkyrka*, Linköping 1963 (the churches of the diocese of Linköping). In this context it is surprising that the fourth relief depicts Saint George on the rack. Unlike the other reliefs, this one is also too large for its niche, which suggests that it comes from another reredos.

2 O.Broman, *Glysisvallur*, ed. by Gästrike-Hälsinge nation in Uppsala, Uppsala 1911-1954, part II p. 354 f. He also describes, church by church, what the Saint George groups that have since disappeared looked like: Ljusdal (p. 384) and Bollnäs (p. 496) possessed knight and dragon, maiden and lamb; at Ljusdal Saint George had a lance in his hand but at Bollnäs one hand held his drawn sword, the other a lance, etc. – An inventory from the church at Almundsryd in Småland in 1829 lists a wooden sculpture of "Saint George and his horse, which is also sculpted in an antique fashion". Entries like this one, for which I should like to express my gratitude to Birgitta Sandström, can be found in many churches.

3 Broman II, p. 354 f. (on the group preserved at Bjuråker). Other Saint George groups which according to Broman were sited on the northern side of the chancel could be found in the churches at Ljusdal, Hälsingtuna, Alfta, Segersta and Söderala. The frequency of this position and the observation that on the top of the chancel screen they stood close to (north of) the triumphal crucifix was pointed out by P.G.Hamberg *Norrländska kyrkoinredningar. Från reformation till ortodoxi*, Stockholm 1974, p. 76 ff., which also shows how the link between the Saint George group (which has been preserved) and the crucifix was maintained in the account book of the church at Skellefteå after the reformation, as was a "Saint George's altar" as well (1544).

4 The position of the group that has since disappeared in the church at Hammarby is dealt with in I.Henschen & A.Tuulse, *Sveriges kyrkor – Uppland* Vol. V:1, Stockholm 1953, p. 201 & 204. Roosval 1924, p. 75 f. adduces Adelsö and other examples from the churches at Funbo and Danmark in Uppland, where a Saint George group that no longer exists was placed on the chancel screen. At Danmark it is stated explicitly that it stood on the right (i.e. north) side of the crucifix in a 17th century description. In the chapel at Ö.Silvberg in Dalarna in 1833 a Saint George and the Dragon was still "attached" high up on a beam between chancel and the nave, see G.Boëthius, *Sveriges Kyrkor – Dalarna I:2*, Stockholm 1920, p. 450 and fig. 435. The group that has survived at Vika is presumed to have had a similar position in the same work p. 202. At the church of Haraker in Västmanland, a Saint George group had survived placed on a transverse beam in the western half of the church (together with a mounted Saint Martin, executed on a smaller scale), see B.Flodin, *Harakars kyrka*, Västerås 1980, p. 10 f.

5 Roosval 1924 contains illustrations of a number of the Swedish groups (plates 12–14 and 20–21). The Finnish groups are described, commented on, and in many cases illustrated in C.A.Nordman, *Medeltida skulptur in Finland* (Finska Fornminnesföreningens Tidskrift 62), Helsinki 1964, p. 586-595 with illustrations 692–693 and 697–703 and p. 617 f. with illustrations 743–744. One group that has disappeared completely and one of which only a little remains may be mentioned here, as they constitute the only groups for which there is a documentary link to a specific master.

According to an entry in rolls of Stockholm on June 20 1517 two named individuals were to pay "Lasse the carpenter for the Saint George he made for the church", in other words the chapel of Saint George's hospital on Norrmalm (which has now disappeared without trace as all the evidence suggest that it was built of wood. Documentary sources tell us that it was founded around 1420 and was situated somewhere between the modern churches of Saint James and Saint John in central Stockholm). See J.Svanberg, "Varför just Sankt Görans sjukhus?" in *S:t Görans sjukhus. Ett stycke svensk sjukhushistoria*, Stockholm 1992, p. 246 ff. Other documents tell us that Lars the carpenter was one of Hemming Gad's and the younger Stures' men. The group of sculptures referred to in the entry has now disappeared, but in the church at Värmdö, where there is still a reredos signed by master Lars dedicated to Saint Olof, a knight from a Saint George group has been preserved, which has been convincingly attributed to the same master's hand. "Perhaps the Värmdö figure of Saint George is a smaller copy" of his figure in the Chapel of Saint George in Stockholm according to A.Lidén, "Lars Snickare och S. Olofskåpet i Värmdö kyrka", in *Antikvariskt arkiv* 71 (pub. KVHAA), Stockholm 1984, p. 15 (entry) and p 29 f. with illustration 16 (quotation p. 30).

In the church at Falsterbo there is still a princess from a Saint George group which according to a document was commissioned by a named burgher of Falsterbo in 1509 from "Heninck Roleves, a painter" of Rostock for a sum of 30 gulden. Both "the George and the maiden" were to be gilded with the finest gold. They were unfinished, however, when Henink Roleve died. His widow, who continued to run his workshop requested an additional 50 gulden as the Saint George was now larger than had originally been intended ("worde grotter alse se menet hadde"). When Linné saw the group on his journey through Scania in 1749 it was standing on the floor before the altar in the church at Falsterbo. C.G.Brunius has left a description of an oblong baldaquin which has since disappeared which was borne aloft by two stout oak timbers across the chancel, on which the name of the burgher who commissioned the work (confirmed by the document) had been carved together with the date 1522. This is obviously the structure on which the group was placed originally. See M.Rydbeck, "Henning Roleves S.Göransgrupp i Falsterbo kyrka" in *Meddelanden från Lunds universitets historiska museum* 1942, p. 331 ff.

6 A.Tuulse, *Sveriges kyrkor – Uppland* Vol. VI:1, Stockholm 1954, p. 131, fig. 120, 121, dates the Färentuna group at around 1460. It "almost certainly came into existence at the behest of Karl Knutsson Bonde. For he owned the whole of the parish of Färentuna and his daughter was married in the church," according to Tuulse, *Färentuna kyrka, Upplands kyrkor,* part V, no. 62, Uppsala 1955, p. 105.

7 The dating of the knight at Sund is Nordman's, op.cit. p. 593.

8 The dragon is holding (or once held) the broken shaft of the lance in the other claw in most of these groups, as in Stockholm. In addition to the five illustrated in Nordman op.cit. (illustrations 692–693, 697–698, 700) see Paatz 1939, Vol. I, Plate VI (Hinnerjoki) and I.Rácz & R.Pylkkänen, *Skatter ur Finlands konst och kultur. Del III – Medeltiden,* Helsinki (1960) 1967, plates 239–40 (Hollola).

Paatz, ibid. p. 352, labours under the misapprehension that the Finnish groups are imitations of Henning von der Heide's Saint George group in Lübeck (see illustration 143 below). But their princesses, knights and dragons show a greater resemblance to the group in Stockholm than to the one in Lübeck (where the dragon is missing). The Stockholm group was also more familiar in Finland for several reasons than the later and more remote work in Lübeck.

9 (illustration and caption 150). The Tortuna group and its details are dealt with in M.Rydbeck, "Late Medieval Sculpture" in *Medieval Wooden Sculpture in Sweden,* Vol. IV (The Museum Collection), Stockholm 1975, p. 255 f.

10 Evidence of the relationship can be found in special details in the knight's armour as Nordman, op.cit. p. 618, has for instance pointed out with regard to the City Church monument in Österbotten. At Visnum-Kil in Värmland, the tip of the lance has pierced the dragon's throat in exactly the same way as in the City Church. And the dragon in the group at Haraker is similarly holding the broken shaft of the lance in its right front claw. This can be interpreted with the same political symbolism as in Stockholm since a Swedish army defeated the Danes led by Christian I outside the church of Haraker in the battle of 1464.

11 *Riddarlek och tornerspel.* A catalogue compiled by L.Rangström. The Royal Armoury. Stockholm 1992, p. 61, no. 24. (The same kind of woven garlands in text and illustration.)

12 Plaited hair and a gown with pleats sewn into the bodice and sleeves with openings for the blouse can also be seen in Henning von der Heide's princess in his group from 1505 (illustration 143 above). These seem to be a requirement for princesses in both the group at Bjuråker and at Kråksmåla. The princess's reticule corresponds to the one worn by the princess at Vika.

13 See I.Swartling, "Haaken Gulleson och hans verkstad" in *Gammal Hälsingekultur – Meddelanden from Hälsinglands Fornminnessällskap 1956,* Hudiksvall 1956, p. 51–53 and fig. 40–43. The knights at Bjuråker, Hälsingtuna and Lögdö have similarly shaped chains around their necks and pendants with the Lamb of God (although this is unclear in the group at Lögdö which is so dilapidated that it is also impossible to ascertain what weapon the knight had been holding in the right arm that has now disappeared). The first two in particular are accounted by Swartling to be the work of the master but she regards the knight at Stöde on the other hand (with the cross of Saint George as his pendant) as the work of a pupil. This is also the case in G.&H.Westelius, *"Iaak Haaken Gulleson Maler".* A study for the chronological ordering of the mediaeval master's works (a paper presented to a seminar in the specialised course in Art History at Stockholm University during the autumn semester of 1982). The date they ascribe to the group at Bjuråker is 1513-15, Hälsingtuna 1515-1517 and for the two others 1520-22. What is certain is that the Saint George at Stöde was purchased in 1521 for the sum of 26 marks.

14 Nordman op.cit. p. 617 attributes the Laihela group (his illustration 743) to Haaken Gulleson on the grounds of similarity to the group at Hälsingtuna and claims that the dragon "is in complete accord with" the dragon under the master's Margareta figure in the church at Bollnäs. This last sculpture is dealt with in S.Hallgren (illustration) and I.Swartling (text) *Haaken Gulleson skulptör.* Exhibition catalogue from the Museum of National Antiquities, Stockholm 1968, illustration 12. According to Nordman op.cit. p. 617 f., a Saint George group in the church at Lillkyro "was perhaps executed by the same master or a sculptor closely linked with him". The difference in style is, however, in my opinion, too great for this to be the case.

15 J.Roosval, *Medeltida skulptur i Gotlands Fornsal* Stockholm 1925, p. 145 f. (inv. No. 3233). The height of the horse just over 6 feet (185 cm.) and the rider slightly less (180 cm.). As in most mediaeval Saint George figures the rider can be detached from the horse. M.Korsman, "Undersökning rörande polykromin på träskulpturen Sankt Göran till häst i Gotlands Fornsal i Visby" in *Gotländskt Arkiv* 1973, p. 59 ff.

16 G.Svahnström, "Riddare med rödgul vimpel" in *Gotländskt Arkiv* 1978, p. 43 ff. and the same author together with Karin Svahnström, *Visby Domkyrka. Inredning. Sveriges Kyrkor, Gotland.* Vol. 202, Stockholm 1986, p. 27 ff. The five paintings are said to have been painted on lead supported by timber and depicted according to their inscriptions the Saints Mary, Maria Magdalena, Gertrude and Peter together with Ivar Axelsson's coat-of-arms. They are described in 1683, 1738 and 1759 as hanging together behind the altar of Saint Mary's church. All five have since disappeared.

17 The op.cit. above includes the entry in the inventory and the different hypotheses about the placement of the Visby knight (a third is that it comes from the chapel – now a ruin – of Saint George's hospital north of the city walls). Svahnström endorses the theory that it came from the Church of Saint Hans and was a funeral monument to Ivar Axelsson that was first presented by B.G.Söderberg, "Är Sankt Göran den övermodige Thott?" in *Gotlands Allehanda* August 19 1958. They question whether this is a representation of Saint George rather than an equestrian statue of Lord Ivar related to Italian funeral monuments. This point of view was also adopted by Andersson 1980, p. 169, but he maintained that the sculpture had been inspired by Notke's Saint George. Erik Nylén, "Gotlands Sankt Göran" in *Gotländskt Arkiv* 1990 asserts that no other mediaeval equestrian statue of Saint George has been identified on Gotland, which suggests that the Visby knight is identical to the Saint George statue mentioned in the inventory from the chapel of Visborg castle. Its presence there and the original colour of the horse is regarded by Nylén as a possible explanation of why the tower of the demolished castle was referred to as "Blacken grå". He points out that the knight was likely to have been bearing a shield with the cross of Saint George painted on it. Cf. above note 3:23 about the Stockholm knight's lost shield.

18 Presumably the relief that has since disappeared from the City Church in Stockholm depicted how the saint's head had just been cut off (as in Notke's picture of the martyrdom of Saint Erik in Uppsala). But the Ängsö master has, as in the preceding scene, chosen the moment before the consummation of the drama, which is easier to depict.

19 All of this is dealt with in J.Svanberg "Ett altarskåps historia. Från altare i Ängsö till predikstol i Tillinge" in *Kyrka och socken i medeltidens Sverige,* ed. O.Ferm, Stockholm 1991. I.Rosell, Tillinge kyrka in *Sveriges kyrkor – Uppland* Vol. XI:2, Stockholm 1968, p. 243 f. and fig. 178 & 217–24 describes and illustrates every section of this reredos, which "displays northern German influences. Probably executed by a workshop in Stockholm." But Rosell does not, as I do in the work cited above, try to reconstruct the reredos and link it with the

Saint George representation in the City Church. The figures are carved of oak and in a good state of preservation but much of the paintwork is recent, as the pulpit was painted in 1755 and whitewashed in 1783. It has been renovated both in the 1910s and the 1980s and in 1943 a replacement for Saint George's missing sword arm was added.

20 Svanberg, last op.cit. deals with the purchase of the reredos from Ängsö (for 150 daler) and its historical background. By August 1470, Fader Ulfsson had already joined Sten Sture's party and was represented among the victors at Brunkeberg according to K-G.Lundholm, Sten Sture och stormännen, (Bibliotheca Historica Lundensis III), Lund 1956, p. 50 & 58. A more detailed presentation of Fader Ulfsson, his wife and his son Bengt can be found in C.A.Klingspor & B.Schlegel, Engsö (Svenska slott), Stockholm 1877.

21 That Fader Ulfsson and his wife turned to Stockholm when commissioning objects for their church is shown by a chasuble at Ängsö decorated with their coat-of-arms that has been attributed to Albert the pearl-embroiderer. The reredos may have been a donation to the church in their wills, which was executed by their son.

22 See Paatz 1939, p. 154 ff. and 350 ff. (catalogue no. 60). In addition a goldsmith received a small sum for decorative additions to the Saint George statue in 1505 and in 1517 eight silver buttons were bequeathed to the statue. A silver helmet and a gold chain belonging to the group of sculptures were sold in 1775. A castle that has since disappeared also formed part of the group according to early testimony. Here the reference is to Henning von der Heide senior.

23 G.von der Osten, "Über Brüggemanns St Jürgensgruppe aus Husum in Kopenhagen" in Wallraf-Richartz-Jahrbuch Vol 37, Cologne 1975, p. 67 ff. points out the knight's striking likeness to a portrait of Karl V. He considers the group to be Brüggeman's final work, somewhere between 1523 (the first year in which the Emperor began to wear a beard like that of the sculpture) and 1527 (when the Reformation reached Husum). He also points out that Duke (later King) Fredrik was never portrayed with a beard. The princess belonging to this group has not been preserved.

24 Hamberg, op.cit., p. 77, and M.Lindgren, Att lära och att pryda. Om efterreformatoriska kyrkmålningar i Sverige cirka 1530–1630, pub. by KVHAA, Stockholm 1983, p. 240 f.

25 Here Lindgren's thorough investigation is referred to (latest op.cit.) In the 18th century Saint George and the Dragon were still being painted in the fisherman's chapel at Trysunda in Ångermanland (on the interior of the western end), see Hamberg, op.cit. p. 80 f. and the illustration there. In Denmark and Norway several new representations of Saint George and the Dragon date from after the Reformation, see M.Lindgren, "De ståndaktiga helgonen. Om danska helgonbilder efter reformationen" in ICO 1984:2, p. 60 ff. See also T.Riska "Sankt Göran i finländska kyrkor" in Pastor et Episcopus, Aninaurun Missiologian ja ekumeniikan seuran julk. 47, 1985.

26 The Pyhämaa painting: L.Pettersson, "Målaren Christian Wilbrandts kyrkointeriörer", in Fra Sankt Olav til Martin Luther. 3:e nord. symposion for ikonografiske studier 1972, Oslo 1975, p. 223 ff. with illustration 6; Hamberg op.cit. p. 79.

27 J.Roosval deals with the Veta painting in "Notkes Sankt Göran i fri kopia" in Fornvännen 1947, p. 142 ff. The Vårdsberg painting is dealt with in Lindgren 1983, fig. 192 with comments on this and other Saint George motifs on p. 241.

28 According to a transcript in Leijonmarck's Memorabilia in the Royal Library (collection of transcripts 67, pag. 70) Gustav II Adolf used to say "Above all others in Sweden there are 3 eminent masterpieces, 1o the Knight Saint George in Stockholm, 2o the reredos in Linköping, 3o Salvator at Vadstena." (The last two refer to the mannerist Heemskerck altar and Triumphal Crucifix from 1430).

29 For details of the origin of the Saint George painting at Saltvik – with which the painter was to atone for his wife's extra-marital relationships – see V.Nyman, "Landsprosten Boëthius Murenius i Saltvik 1636-1669" in Sanct Olof. Julbok för de åländska församlingarna 1978, p. 106 ff.

30 For details about Rehn and illustration 156 below see H.H. von Schwerin, "Mönstertecknaren och arkivritaren Olof Rehn" in Tidskrift för Konstvetenskap 1936, p. 66.

31 I owe the information about the funeral monument at Hovby to Barbro Westrin fil.lic., Stola, who drew it to my attention and provided photographs and information.

32 Saint George and the Dragon forms the subject of seven Dalecarlian paintings dating from between 1807 – 1847 according to Svante Svärdstrom's archive at the County Museum in Falun. – S.Svensson, "Sankt Göran på ugnshäll och stolsrygg" in Kulturens årsbok 1959, p. 60 ff. I would like to thank Torvald Nilsson of Kulturen in Lund and Christina Enhammer at the County Museum in Kristianstad for their help with the photographs.

33 Carl Larsson, Jag (pub. posthumously 1931), Stockholm 1987, p. 37 f. and 192 f.

34 In 1910, Anders Zorn erected a gable relief in wood on his farm at Mora depicting Saint George and the Dragon surmounted by his heraldic symbol (a gold star on a red field). "Zorn's version of Saint George was more than a decoration – it was a personal symbol" according to H.H.Brummer, ZORN MCMLXXXIX, Stockholm 1989, p. 281. In fact, Saint George is also carved on Zorn's gravestone (based on Christian Eriksson's original) – perhaps as a symbol for the artist's struggles as it is for Kandinsky. The statuette was taken from the chapel at Sollerön, where however, Zorn left the princess belonging to the group.

35 The bronze in the Old Town was donated by Hjalmar Wikander, cast by Otto Meyer, and erected 1912–13. The tall plinth of granite is decorated with reliefs in stone of the coats-of-arms of the founders, Stockholm, Sörmland, Uppland, Västmanland and Dalecarlia and the inscription: "The Lay of Saint George spurred Swedish men on at the Battle of Brunkeberg" and "Saint George's image commemorates the memory of the Swedish victory." In comparison to the original, the bust of the dead man is lying on the other side of the dragon and other remains of its meals have partially changed places. On the castle under the princess the side casts have been made of the reliefs that still exist and they have been supplemented with two newly made ones. One depicts the saint kneeling in prayer before the conflict, while several pages are holding his horse and weapons, and the other how Saint George kills the dragon with the king looking on. A painted plaster cast of Notke's Saint George group can be found in Katharinenkirche in Lübeck. It was a donation in 1926 by Hamburg and Bremen to celebrate Lübeck's seventh centenary as a free city.

36 Based on Christian Eriksson's plaster model, the enormous group at the City Hall was made by Ragnar Myrsmeden in beaten gilt bronze. The dragon has two heads so that it can see in both directions. The princess has a slightly lower position in a niche in the abutting lower tower which is called the "maiden's tower" for her sake. The main group has been placed at the top of this tower. A full-scale copy of her head can be seen in the artist's studio at Arvika, with an early sketch in plaster of the main group. In 1928, Christian Eriksson donated a replica of the main group measuring only 5 feet (1.5 metres) in height (made of oak, of which some had come from a tobacco press) to the church at Kiruna.

37 Gustaf Nilsson's figures are made of beaten copper.

38 M.Rickards, *Posters of the First World War*, New York 1968, p. 26 and illustrations 64 & 65, show Saint George fighting on the one hand "for British recruitment and on the other for the sixth Austrian War Loan". In the years following the Russian Revolution Trotsky was depicted in the form of Saint George on several Russian posters. Viktor Denis's version in a Soviet Calendar for 1920 shows Trotsky with a flowing cloak and the hammer and sickle on his shield mounted on Saint George's white charger. He is thrusting his lance into the jaws of a dragon with a top hat and the label "counter-revolution". See S.White, *The Bolshevik Poster.* (Yale University Press) New Haven/London 1988, p. 6 f. (with illustration).

39 Kandinsky's use of Saint George as a recurrent motif and its significance both for him and his era is dealt with in M.Werenskiold, "Kandinsky's Moscow" in *Art in America,* March 1989, p. 97 ff., with many pictures and extensive documentation. His "Saint George" from 1911 can be seen in the colour plate, cat.no. 10 in V.Endicott Barnett, *Kandinsky och Sverige*. Malmö Art Museum and the Museum of Modern Art in Stockholm 1989–90 (exhibition catalogue).

40 Since 1472 Ivan III, Grand Duke of Russia, had been married to the niece of the last Byzantine Emperor, and saw himself as the heir of political and religious claims of the Eastern Empire and demonstrated this by including the double-headed eagle of Byzantium in his seal. For the reverse side of the seal he adopted the Byzantine image of the ruler in the guise of Saint George as a mounted dragon-slayer. These two emblems were combined in 1560 to form the well-known coat-of-arms of the Tsar: a double-headed eagle with a shield on its chest emblazoned with the image of Saint George the dragon-slayer. However, he had become the patron saint of Moscow soon after Dimitri Donskoi's victory over the Tartars at Kulikovo in 1380 (here, as in other cases, Saint George stands for national liberation from an alien intruder).

Philotheus's letter, Moscow as the third Rome, Saint George as Moscow's patron saint and the significance of these concepts for Kandinsky are dealt with in Werenskiold, op.cit. p. 98 ff. and the works referred to there.

41 Werenskiold, op.cit. p. 107.

42 Torsten Renqvist's article "Ett möte i rätta ögonblicket" in the series "bildsyner" in *Dagens Nyheter,* August 23 1984.

43 In addition to conversations with the artist at his home and studio, this presentation and analysis of the work is based on O.Granath, "Torsten Renqvist. Vanlig och utvald" in *Konsten 1973*, pub. by Konstfrämjandet and FIB:s Konstklubb, Stockholm 1973, p. 36 – *Torsten Renqvist. Moderna Museets utställningskatalog* no. 115, Stockholm 1974, text by U.Linde, p. 23, 56 f. & 77 f. (cat. no. 156, 160–161), B.Sydhoff, *Torsten Renqvist. Konstnären, jorden och tiden*. Sveriges Allmänna Konstförening. Publikation 93. Stockholm 1984, principally p. 130 ff. – *Torsten Renqvist. Rovaniemi konstmuseums utställningskatalog*. Rovaniemi 1987, text by Maaretta Jaukkuri (five pictures of George and the Dragon).

44 The fact that the dragon is depicted copulating with itself was pointed out both by the artist during our conversation and by O.Granath, op.cit., p. 36.

45 His daughter, Anne-Li's, drawing of the dragon is reproduced in Sydhoff, op.cit. p. 150. The reference in the dragon's head to a painting of a dead bird is noted by Linde in the catalogue from the Museum of Modern Art referred to above, p. 23. The photograph of the Nazi executioner is reproduced in Sydhoff op.cit. p. 110 with a comment p. 111 f. In his diary, the artist has noted how he derived George's figure from the image, see "Brottstycken" from *Torsten Renqvists dagböcker,* ed. L.Nygren, Stockholm 1988, p. 299 f. (April 8 1972).

46 Renqvist's text for the sculpture is taken from "Brottstycken", p. 308. It has been quoted at exhibitions previously and reproduced in Sydhoff op.cit. p. 131 f.

Illustrations provided by

Alinari, Rome: 10
Asbjörn fotografi, Århus: 123
ATA, Stockholm: 68, 138, 144, 150
Bergström, Per, Stockholm University: 6
Bibliothèque Nationale, Paris: 21
British Library, London: 19
Cornelius, Erik, Nationalmuseum, Stockholm: 128, 131
Dalarnas Museum: 165
GE-foto, Mariehamn: 162
Göbel, Helmut, Lübeck: 117–118
Hamrin, Christian, Stockholm: 96
Hejdström, Raymond, Visby: 153, 155
Hilpo, Seppo, Helsinki: 176
Historisches Museum, Bern: 112
Jorabek, Jaroslav, Nationalgalleriet, Prag: 15
Karlsson, Lennart, Stockholm: 149, 151, 152
Kennerstedt, Lars, Stockholm: 8
Kristianstads Museum: 166
Kulturen, Lund: 167
Kungliga Biblioteket, Stockholm: 29, 163
Larsen, Lennart, Nationalmuseet, Köpenhamn: 122, 124, 125
Musée National d'Art Moderne, Paris: 174
Museum für Kunst und Kulturgeschichte der Hansestadt Lübeck: 143, 159
National Gallery, London: 18
National Monuments Record, London: 16
Nationalmuseet, Köpenhamn: 154, 160
Nationalmuseum, Stockholm: 2, 26
Rotili, Marcello, Benevento: 13
Scala, Florence: 4
Svanberg, Jan, Stockholm: 9, 17, 20, 116, 120, 121, 136, 148, 173
Säre, Peeter, Tallinn: 114, 126, 127
Tångeberg, Peter, Tystberga: 109
Verlag Photo-Castelli, Lübeck: 115
Victoria & Albert Museum, London: 1
Welin Foto, Åbo: 147
Åhlin, Christer, Eskilstuna: 133–134
Österreichische Nationalbibliothek, Wien: 108

The numbers after each supplier indicate the illustrations supplied.

Bibliography

Abbreviations used
ATA Antikvariskt Topografiska Arkivet *(The Archive of Antiquarian Topography)*
KLNM Kulturhistoriskt Lexikon för Nordisk Medeltid *(A Cultural and Historical Dictionary of the Middle Ages in Scandinavia)*
KVHAA Kungl. Vitterhets Historie och Antikvitets Akademien *(The Royal Swedish Academy of Letters, History and Antiquities)*
RA Riksarkivet, Stockholm, *(National Archives)*
SFSS Svenska Fornskriftssällskapets Samlingar *(The Collections of the Swedish Society for Ancient Documents)*
SHM Statens Historiska Museum *(Museum of National Antiquities)*
ICO Den Iconografiska Posten

Abel, U., Blomqvist, L.E. & Holger, L., *Nationalmusei katalog 513, Den ryska ikonen 1000 år.* Stockholm 1989 (second impression)
Ahnlund, N., *Jämtlands och Härjedalens historia.* Vol. I. Stockholm 1945.
– *Stockholms historia före Gustav Vasa.* Stockholm 1953.
Andersson, A., *Medieval Wooden sculpture in Sweden.* Vol. III. Stockholm 1980.
Andersson, L., *Pilgrimsmärken och vallfart. Medeltida pilgrimskultur i Skandinavien.* (Lund Studies in medieval Archaeology 7). Stockholm 1989.
Anjou, S., "Sten Stures riksmonument" in *Fornvännen.* 1938.

Bergman, M., *Venjans, Solleröns och Våmhus kyrkor. Dalarna, Sveriges Kyrkor.* Stockholm 1989.
Bjurström, P. & Johnsson, Ulf G., *Masterpieces from Gripsholm Castle,* exhibition catalogue. Uddevalla 1988.
Blass-Simmen, B., *Sankt Georg. Drachenkampf in der Renaissance.* Carpaccio – Raffael – Leonardo. (Diss. in Zürich 1988). Berlin 1991.
Blindheim, M., "Sigurdsdiktningen i middelalderens billedkunst" in *ICO (Den Ikonographiske Post)* 1973:3.
Blomberg, E.B., "Resultat av färgundersökningar på S:t Göransgruppen i Stockholms Storkyrka" in *Meddelelser om konservering,* 2:2 1973.
Boëthius, G. & Romdahl, A., *Uppsala domkyrka 1258–1435.* Uppsala 1935.
Branting, A. & Lindblom, A., *Medeltida vävnader och broderier i Sverige,* I (Swedish work) – II (from other countries). Uppsala 1928–29.
Braunfels–Esche, S., *Sankt Georg. Legende Verehrung Symbol.* Munich 1976.
Bregmann, N. & Lelekowa, O., "Die Restaurierung des Altars von Bernt Notke in Tallinn", in *Internationales Kolloquium...* 1976.
Broman, O., *Glysisvallur,* publ. by Gästrike-Hälsinge nation in Uppsala. Uppsala 1911–54.

Brummer, H.H., *ZORN MCMLXXXIX:* Stockholm 1989.
Carlsson, G., *Hemming Gadh. En statsman och prelat från sturetiden.* Uppsala 1915
A Catalogue of Wall-paintings in the Churches of Medieval Denmark 1100-1600. Scania Halland Blekinge, Vol. I–III. Copenhagen 1976.
Cavendish, R. (ed.), *Legends of the World.* London 1982.
Collijn, I., "Riddar Sankt Görans reliker" in *Fornvännen* 1919, reprinted in *Historia kring Stockholm.* Stockholm 1982.
Der Totentanz der Marienkirche in Lübeck und der Nicolaikirche in Reval (Tallinn). Publ. by H. Freytag in Niederdeutsche Studien, Vol. 39. Cologne – Weimar – Vienna 1993.
Diarium Fratrum Minorum Stockholmensium publ. in Scriptores Rerum Suecicarum Medii Aevii (SRS). 1818.
Didi-Huberman, G. & Garbetta, R. & Morgaine M., *Saint Georges et le dragon. Versions d'une légende.* Paris 1994.
Die Parler und der schöne Stil 1350–1400, (publ. by A. Legner). Bd II. Köln 1978.
Dorsch, K.J., *Georgszyklen des Mittelalters. Ikonographische Studie zu mehrszenigen Darstellungen der Vita des hl. Georg in der abendländischen Kunst unter Einbeziehung von Einzelszenen des Martyriums* (Diss.). Frankfurt/Main–Berne–New York 1983.
Dragut, V., *Dragos Coman maesrul frescelor de la Arbore.* Bucharest 1969.
– *Die Wandmalerei in der Moldau im 15. und 16. Jahrhundert.* Bucharest 1983.

Eckstein, D. & Ulmann, A. von, "Holzbiologische Untersuchungen und werktechnische Beobachtungen am Triumphkreuz im Lübecker Dom" in *Internationales Kolloquium...* 1976.
Eimer, G., "Das Monumentale in der Kunst Bernt Notkes" in *Internationales Kolloquium...* 1976.
– "hoc magnum opus. Zur Entstehung von Bernt Notkes Monumentalwerken" in *Imagines Medievales* (Festskrift till Carl-Otto Nordström). Acta Universitatis Upsaliensis – Ars Suetica 7. Uppsala 1983
– *Bernt Notke. Das Wirken eines niederdeutschen Künstlers im Ostseeraum.* Bonn 1985.
Ellis, F.S., (ed.) *The Golden Legend... as Englished by William Caxton.* Vol. 3. London 1900.
Endicott B., *V. Kandinsky och Sverige.* Malmö Konsthall and Moderna Museet in Stockholm 1989–90 (exhibition catalogue).
Estham, I., "Textil skrud och prydnad" in *Uppsala domkyrka.* Uppsala 1982.
Etzler, A., "Sancte Örjenskulten i Sverige" in *Med Hammare och Fackla III.* Stockholm 1931.

215

Feldmann, D., "Zur Bedeutung von Notkes St. Georgs-Monument in Stockholm" in *Konsthistorisk Tidskrift* 1976.
Flodin, B., *Harakers kyrka*. Västerås 1980.
Fogelklou, E., Lindblom, A. & Wessén, E. (publ.), *Legender från Sveriges medeltid*. Stockholm 1917.
Forssman, E., "Medeltida träskulptur i Dalarna" in *Dalarnas Hembygdsbok 1961*. Falun 1961.
Fürst, C.M., *När de döda vittna*. Stockholm 1920.
Fürst, C.M. & Olsson, M., *Magnus Ladulås och Karl Knutssons gravar i Riddarholmskyrkan*. Stockholm 1921.

Geijer, E.G. & Atterbom, A.A. (ed.), *Svenska folkvisor från forntiden*, I–III. Stockholm 1814–16.
Goldscheider, L., *Leonardo. Paintings and Drawings*. London (1943) 1975
Granath, O., "Torsten Renqvist. Vanlig och utvald" in *Konsten* 1973, publ. by Konstfrämjandet & FiB:s Konstklubb. Stockholm 1973.
Grassmann, A., "Bernt Notkes Triumphkreuz: Die Inschriften und ihre Lesung" in *Internationales Kolloquium...* 1976.

Hagnell, K., *Sturekrönikan 1452–1496. Studier över en rimkrönikas tillkomst och sanningsvärde*. Lund 1941.
Hallbäck, S.A., "Medeltida dopfuntar i Skaraborg" in *Västergötlands Fornminnesförenings Tidskrift* 1971–72.
Hallgren, S. & Swartling, I., *Haaken Gulleson skulptör*. Exhibition catalogue from SHM. Stockholm 1968.
Hamberg, P G., *Norrländska kyrkoinredningar. Från reformation till ortodoxi*. Stockholm 1974.
Hasse, M., *Bernt Notke. St Jürgen zu Stockholm. Einführung von M. Hasse* in Werkmonographien zur bildenden Kunst; Reclams Universal-Bibliothek Nr 81. Stuttgart 1962.
– "Bernt Notke" in *Zeitschrift des deutschen Vereins für Kunstwissenschaft* XXIV 1970.
– "War Notke ein Maler und Bildschnitzer oder war er nur Unternehmer?" in *Zeitschrift des Vereins für Lübeckische Geschichte und Altertumskunde* 52. 1972.
– "Das Pergament zu Bernt Notkes Triumphkreuz im Lübecker Dom" in *Kunstchronik* 26. 1973.
Hedquist, J., "Lövångers kyrka och dess inventarier", *Lövånger* Vol. II, 1949
Heidenstam, V. von, *Sankt Göran och draken. Berättelser*. Stockholm 1900.
Heland, M. von, "Manliga myter" in *Paletten* 1984:1.
Helenius-Öberg, E., "Den unge Albertus Pictor och hans lärare" in *ICO* 1991:4.
Henning, S. (ed.), *Sjælinna thrøst*, in SFSS. Uppsala 1954.
Hildebrand, H., "Herr Stens Sankt Göran" in *Antiqvarisk Tidskrift för Sverige* Vol. 7:4, 1884–85.
Huth, H., *Künstler und Werkstatt der Spätgotik*, Darmstadt 1967 (Neudruck bei Wissenschaftliche Buchgesellschaft).

Internationales Kolloquium... 1976: *Internationales Kolloquium zum Werk des Bernt Notke anlässlich der Restaurierung der Triumphkreuzgruppe im Dom Lübeck 22.–24. September 1976.*

Jansson, V, "Görans saga". Article in *KLNM* Vol. 6.
Jaukkuri, M., *Torsten Renqvist*. Exhibition catalogue, Rovaniemi konstmuseum. Rovaniemi 1987.
Jung, C. G., *Aspects of the Feminine* (Bollingen Series XX). Princeton 1982.
– *Människan och hennes symboler*. Stockholm 1978.
Karling, S., *Medeltida träskulptur i Estland*. Göteborg 1946.
– "Några Notke-kommentarer" in *Den ljusa medeltiden. Studier tillägnade Aron Andersson* (SHM studies 4). Stockholm 1984.
Karlsson, L., *Medieval Ironwork in Sweden*. Vol. I–II. Stockholm 1988.
Kauffmann, M., "The altarpiece of St George from Valencia" in *Victoria and Albert Museum Yearbook 2*, 1970.
Kellerman, G., *Jakob Ulvsson och den svenska kyrkan* I. Under äldre sturetiden 1470–1497. Uppsala 1935.
Kepinski, Z., *Veit Stoss*. Warsaw 1981.
Kerényi, K., *Grekiska gudar och myter*. Stockholm 1955.
Keyser, C.E., *A List of Norman Tympana and Lintels*. London 1904.
Kilström, B. I., "Georg". Article in *KLNM* Vol. 5.
Kjaer, U., "Det ondes overmand. S. Jorgen og S. Jørgensen-fremstillinger i Danmark" in *ICO* 1990:4.
Kjellin, H., *Ryska ikoner i svensk och norsk ägo*. Stockholm 1956.
Klemming, G.E. (ed.), *Själens tröst. Tio Guds bud förklarade genom legender, berättelser och exempel*, in SFSS XIX. Stockholm 1871–73
– *Svenska medeltids dikter och rim*, in SFSS XXV. Stockholm 1881–82.
Klingspor, C.A. & Schlegel, B., *Engsö*. Stockholm 1877.
Korsman, M., "Undersökning rörande polykromin på träskulpturen S:t Göran till häst i Gotlands Fornsal i Visby" in *Gotländskt arkiv* 1973.
Kraft, S., *Senare medeltiden 2. Tidsskedet 1448–1520, Sveriges historia till våra dagar*, Vol. 3:2, Stockholm 1944.
Kumlien, K., *Karl Knutssons politiska verksamhet*. Stockholm 1933.
– *Karl Knutsson i Preussen 1457–1464*. KVHAA: Handlingar 46:2. Stockholm 1940.

Labande-Mailfert, Y, "L'iconographie des laics dans la société religieuse aux XIe et XIIe siècles" in *Pubblicazioni dell'universita cattolica del sacro cuore* ser. 3, varia 5. Milan 1968.
Lagerqvist, L. O., *Svenska mynt under vikingatid och medeltid samt gotländska mynt*. Stockholm 1970.
Larsson, C., *JAG*. Stockholm (1931) 1987.
Leijonmarcks Memorabilia in Kungl. Biblioteket, Stockholm. Avskriftssamlingen 67.
Lexikon der griechischen Mythologie, publ. by Roscher, W. H. Leipzig 1894–97.
Lidén, A., *S:t Eriks tavla i Peringskiölds Monumenta Ullerakerensia 1719*. Department of Art History, Stockholm University 1984.
– "Lars Snickare och S. Olofskåpet i Värmdö kyrka" in *Antikvariskt arkiv* 71, publ. by KVHAA. Stockholm 1984.
Liebmann, M.J., *Die deutsche Plastik 1350–1550*. Leipzig 1982.

Lilljenwalldh, C.Chr., *Specimen I de templo urbis Stockholmiensis primario, S. Nicolai dicto.* Diss. Uppsala 1788.
Lindblom, A., *Kult och konst i Vadstena kloster.* Uppsala 1965.
Linde, O., *Rydaholms medeltidskyrka. En konstvetenskaplig undersökning.* Publ. by Jönköpings läns hembygdsförbund and Jönköpings läns museum. Värnamo 1978.
Linde, U., *Torsten Renqvist.* Exhibition catalogue, Moderna museet nr 115. Stockholm 1974.
Lindgren, M., *Att lära och att pryda. Om efterreformatoriska kyrkomålningar i Sverige cirka 1530–1630*, publ. by KVHAA. Stockholm 1983.
– "De ståndaktiga helgonen. Om danska helgonbilder efter reformationen" in *ICO* 1984:2.
Lumiste, M. & Globatschowa, G., "Der Revaler Totentanz von Bernt Notke" in *Zeitschrift des deutschen Vereins für Kunstwissenschaft XXIII* 1969.
Lundberg, E., *Albertus Pictor.* Sveriges Allmänna Konstförenings publikation LXX. Stockholm 1961.
Lundholm, K.-G., *Sten Sture och stormännen.* Bibliotheca Historica Lundensis III. Lund 1956.
Lutze, E., *Veit Stoss.* Munich/Berlin 1952.

Malmer, B. *Mynt och människor. Vikingatidens silverskatter berättar.* Uddevalla 1968.
Matzke, J.E., "Contributions to the history of the legend of St. George" in *Publications of the Modern Language Association of America, 17.* Baltimore 1902.
Messenius, J., *Sveopentaprotopolis.* Holmiae 1611.
– *Rimkrönika*, ed. C. Silfverstolpe in *Historiskt Bibliotek* I. Stockholm 1875.
Moltke, E., *Bernt Notkes altertavle i Århus domkirke og Tallinntavlen.* Copenhagen 1970.
Murray, M.A., *Ancient Egyptian Legends.* London 1920.

Nilsén, A., *Program och funktion i senmedeltida kalkmåleri. Kyrkomålningar i mälarlandskapen och Finland 1400–1534.* Stockholm 1986.
Nilsson, M.P:son, *Olympen.* Stockholm 1964, 2 ed.
Nisbeth, Å., *Kyrkan i Lillkyrka.* Linköpings stifts kyrkor. Linköping 1963.
– *Ängsö kyrka och dess målningar*, publ. by KVHAA in Antikvariska serien 33. Stockholm 1982.
– *Bildernas predikan. Medeltida kalkålningar i Sverige.* Värnamo 1986.
Norberg, R., "Johannesfatet från Norrby" in *Fornvännen* 1953.
Nordman, C.A., *Medeltida skulptur i Finland* (Finska Fornminnesföreningens Tidskrift 62). Helsinki 1964.
Nyberg, T., "Papst Innocenz VIII. und Skandinavien", in *Archivum Historiae Pontficiae 22.* Rome 1984.
Nygren, L., *Brottstycken ur Torsten Renqvists dagböcker.* Stockholm 1988.
Nylén, E., "Gotlands Sankt Göran" in *Gotländskt Arkiv 1990.*
Nyman, V., "Landsprosten Boëthius Murenius i Saltvik 1636–1669" in *Sanct Olof Julbok för de åländska församlingarna 1978.*

Oellerman, E., "Fundberichte" in *Kunstchronik* 1973 and 1974.
– "Restaurierungsbericht", in *Internationales Kolloquium...* 1976.
– "Die originale Bemalung des Triumphkreuzes von Bernt Notke" in *Internationales Kolloquium....* 1976.
Olai Petri Svenska krönika. ed. G.E. Klemming. Stockholm 1860.
– "Restaurierungsbericht", in *Internationales Kolloquium...* 1976.
– "Die originale Bemalung des Triumphkreuzes von Bernt Notke" in *Internationales Kolloquium...* 1976.
Osten, G. von der, "Über Brüggemanns St Jürgensgruppe aus Husum in Kopenhagen" in *Wallraf–Rirhartz–Jahrbuch* Vol. 37. Cologne 1975.

Paatz, W., *Bernt Notke und sein Kreis.* Berlin 1939.
– *Bernt Notke.* Vienna 1944.
Palme, S.U., *Sten Sture den äldre.* Stockholm 1968.
Pettersson, L., "Målaren Christian Wilbrandts kyrkointeriörer" in *Fra Sankt Olav till Martin Luther*, 3rd Nordic symposium for iconographical studies 1972. Oslo 1975.
Plezia, M. & Pleziowa, J., see *Zlota legenda.*

Rácz, I. & Pylkkänen, R., *Skatter ur Finlands konst och kultur, Vol. III – Medeltiden.* Helsinki 1960.
Rangström, L. (ed.) *Riddarlek och tornerspel.* Exhibition catalogue Livrustkammaren. Stockholm 1992.
Renqvist, T., "Ett möte i rätta ögonblicket" in *Dagens Nyheter* 1984-08-23.
Rickards, M., *Posters of the First World War.* NewYork 1968.
Riska, T., "Sankt Göran i finländska kyrkor" in *Pastor et Episcopus.* Aniaurun Missiologian ja ekumeniikan seuran julk. 47, 1985
Roosval, J., "Studier rörande Storkyrkans Sankt Jöransgrupp" in *Meddelanden från Nordiska museet* 1901.
– "Hvem har skulpterat S. Göran och draken?" in *Festskrift för Henrik Schück.* Stockholm 1905.
– "Torbjörn Tidemanssons rim om den store Örjanen och andra bidrag till detta monuments historia under 1500- och 1600-talen", in *S:t Eriks årsbok* 1906.
– *Riddar Sankt Göran i Stockholms stora eller Sankt Nicolai kyrka.* Stockholm 1919.
– *Nya Sankt Görans Studier.* Stockholm 1924.
– *Medeltida skulptur i Gotlands Fornsal.* Stockholm 1925.
– "Reliefer och statyetter till Sankt Görans sockel" in *Konsthistorisk Tidskrift* 1932.
– "Hinrich Wylsynck" in *Nordisk Tidskrift för Bok- och Biblioteksväsen XXIII.* 1936.
– "Notkes Sankt Göran i fri kopia" in *Fornvännen* 1947.
Rosell, I., *Tillinge kyrka. Sveriges kyrkor, Uppland XI:2.* Stockholm 1968.
Rosén, J., Maktkampen 1457–1471, den politiska utvecklingen från Kristian I:s trontillträde till slaget vid Brunkeberg, och Stureregimen, unionspolitiken 1471–1503, in *Den svenska historien.* Vol. 3. Stockholm 1978 (2 ed.).
– "Diarier". Artikel in *KLNM* Vol. 3.

Rydbeck, M., "Henning Roleves S. Göransgrupp i Falsterbo kyrka" in *Meddelanden från Lunds universitets historiska museum* 1942.
– Late Medieval Sculpture, *Medieval wooden Sculpture in Sweden,* Vol. IV Stockholm 1975.

Sahlgren, G. (ed.), *Svenska folkvisor,* publ. by Kungl. Gustav Adolfs Akademien. Vol. III. Uppsala 1958.
Schefold, K., *Frühgriechische Sagenbilder.* Munich 1964.
Schwerin, H.H. von, "Mönstertecknaren och arkivritaren Olof Rehn" in *Tidskrift för Konstvetenskap* 1936.
Scott Fox, D., *Saint George. The Saint with three Faces.* Windsor 1983.
Siggstedt, M., *Drakens år. Den kinesiska drakens symbolik.* Östasiatiska museet. Stockholm 1988.
Skov, E. & Thomsen, V., "Bernt Notkes altertavle i Århus Domkirke. Nye undersøgelser" in *Nationalmuseets Arbejdsmark.* Copenhagen 1981.
Stephens, G. (ed.), *Ett fornsvenskt Legendarium,* in SFSS VII:1–2. Stockholm 1847–58.
Stolpe, H., *Sankt Göran – med gloria eller utan* (Pamphlet). Malmö 1971.
Ström, Å., "Sankt Göran – från myt till legend" in *ICO* 1990:4.
Supplikregester, ed. in *Historisk Tidskrift* 1901.
Svahnström, G., "Riddare med rödgul vimpel", in *Gotländskt arkiv* 1978.
– & Swahnström, K., "Visby Domkyrka. Inredning." *Sveriges Kyrkor, Gotland.* Vol 202, Stockholm 1986.
Svanberg, J., "Ridder S. Jören. Kring Sten Stures monument i Stockholms Storkyrka till minne av slaget på Brunkebergsåsen år 1471" in *Med Hammare och Fackla 26,* 1971.
– "Asmundr gjorde dörren" in *ICO* 1974:4.
– "Kampen mellan gott och ont på dopfunten i Hög". *ICO* 1980:1.
– "Murare i senmedeltidens Stockholm" in *St Eriks årsbok 1984.*
– "Roger och Angelica – ett Ariosto-motiv i konsten" in *Studier i konstvetenskap tillägnade Brita Linde.* Stockholm 1985.
– "Sankt Göran i medeltida konst i Sverige och Finland" in *ICO* 1990:4.
– "Ett altarskåps historia. Från altare i Ängsö till predikstol i Tillinge" in *Kyrka och socken i medeltidens Sverige.* Ed. O. Ferm, Stockholm 1991.
– "Bernt Notke" in *Svenskt Biografiskt Lexikon.* Stockholm 1991.
– *Albert målares kyrkor.* Stockholm 1992.
– "Varför just Sankt Görans sjukhus?", in *S:t Görans sjukhus. Ett stycke svensk sjukhushistoria.* Stockholm 1992.
– "Medeltida bildkonstverk i Stockholms kyrkor", in *Sankt Eriks årsbok 1993.*
– "Sankt Göran och draken i Sveriges och Finlands medeltida konst", in *Med Hammare och Fackla 34,* 1996.
Swartling, I., "Haaken Gulleson och hans verkstad" in *Gammal Hälsingekultur – Meddelanden från Hälsinglands Fornminnessällskap 1956.* Hudiksvall 1956. (See also Hallgren, S.–Svartling, I…)
Svenska folkvisor, see Sahlgren, G. (ed.).

Svenska medeltidens rimkrönikor Vol. 3: *Nya krönikans fortsättningar eller Sture-krönikorna.* Publ. by G.E. Klemming in *SFSS 17:3.* Stockholm 1867–68.
Svensson, S., "S:t Göran på ugnshäll och stolsryggr" in *Kulturens Årsbok* 1959.
Sveriges kyrkor – Dalarna Vol. I:2 – Gotland Vol. II – Gästrikland – Medelpad – Stockholm Vol. I:1 – Uppland Vol. II:2, V:1, V:3, VI: 1, XI:2.
Sveriges Medeltida Ballader, publ. Svenskt visarkiv, ed. Jonsson, Vol. 2, Stockholm 1986.
Sydhoff, B., *Torsten Renqvist. Konstnären, jorden och tiden.* Sveriges Allmänna Konstförening. Publication 93. Stockholm 1984.
Söderberg, B.G., "Är S:t Göran den övermodige Thott?" in *Gotlands Allehanda* 1958-08-19.
– *Gotländska kalkmålningar 1200–1400.* Uppsala 1971.

Turek, E., *S:t Georg i ryska ikoner.* Deparment of Art History Stockholm University, 1986.
Tuulse, A., *Färentuna kyrka, Upplands kyrkor* part V, no 62. Uppsala 1955.
Tångeberg, P., *Mittelalterliche Holzskulpturen und Altarschreine in Schweden. Studien zu Form, Material und Technik,* publ. by KVHAA. Stockholm 1986.

Ugglas, C.R. af, "Nattvardskalkarna i Östra Ryd. Herrarnas av Sesswegen kalk" in *Bidrag till den medeltida guldsmedskonstens historia II.* Stockholm 1948.
Ulea, S., "Originea si semnificatia ideologica a picturii exterioare romanesti", in *SCIA* 1963, no 1.

Wallin, S., "Karl Knutsson-statyetten på Gripsholm. En notis om dess öden" in *Kyrkoinredning för herremän.* Stockholm 1958.
Warmenius, S., "Den unge Albert – Erik Axelssons (Tott) målare« in *ICO* 1991:3.
Weitzman, K., *The Monastery of Saint Catherine at Mount Sinai* in *The Icons,* Vol. 1, Princeton 1976.
Werenskiold, M., "Kandinsky's Moscow", in *Art in America* March 1989.
Westelius, G. & H., "Iaak Haaken Gulleson Maler". Studium för kronologisk gruppering av medeltidsmästarens verk. Department of Art History, Stockholm University, 1982.
Westman, K.B., *Reformationens genombrottsår i Sverige.* Uppsala 1918.
Vetter, E., "Zur Ikonographie des Triumphkreuzes" in *Internationales Kolloquium…* 1976.
Vetter, E. & Oellermann, E., *Triumphkreuz im Dom zu Lübeck. Ein Meisterwerk Bernt Notkes.* Wiesbaden 1979.
White, S., *The Bolshevik Poster.* Yale University Press. New Haven/London 1988.
Wittkower, R. & M., *Born under Saturn. The Character and Conduct of Artists: A Documented History from Antiquity to the French Revolution.* London 1963.

Zlota legenda, translation from Latin by J. Pleziowa and selection, introduction and notes by M. Plezia. Warsaw 1983.

Index of Individuals, Places and Objects

This index does not cover the documentation section

A
Abildgaard, Søren, Norwegian-Danish antiquarian draughtsman and painter (1718–1791) 151
Academy of Art 163
Adelsö church, Uppland 144
aid in adversity 16
Albertus Pictor, Swedish painter and embroiderer, (d. 1509) 28, 38, 39, 101, 135
Alexandria (Dacianus' wife) 94
altar foundation, Sten Sture's in Stockholm City Church 45–50
"Andreas from Andorf" 105
Andromeda (figure in Greek mythology) 12, 13, 26
Angelica (figure in Orlando furioso) 26
Angoulême, Cathedral at Anjou 21
Anneke, Bernt Notke's daughter 109
Antioch 15, 18, 21
    Count of 17
    Prince of 20
Antwerp 105
Apollo, Greek god 11, 24, 152
Arbore, church in Rumania 23
Ariosto, Italian Renaissance author 26
Artists Association 163
Artushof in Danzig 30
Arvid Birgersson (Trolle; d. 1505) 72
Asia Minor 15, 18
Atheneum, Helsinki 168

B
Bamber rider 61
banner (see National standard as well)
    Saint Erik's 48, 49
    Saint George's 21, 28, 30, 57, 67
Basle, Cathedral 21
Beckett, see Saint Thomas
"Bedford master", French illuminator (15th century) 26
Bellini, Jacopo, Italian Renaissance painter (1400–1470) 51
Bengt Fadersson (Sparre av Hjulsta och Ångsö; d. 1494) 72, 154
Berne museum 108
Bibliothèque Nationale 26
Birger Jarl 164
Birgitta (Birgersdotter), Holy, Swedish national saint 38
Bjuråkers church, Hälsingland 148, 149
Björn Starke, yeoman 37
Blasieholmen 35f
Bonde (lineage)
    coat-of-arms 127
    Sepulchral chapel 127, 128
    See also Karl Knutsson, Magdalena Karlsdotter, Carl Göran, baron
Botvid, saint 39
Bouts, Dirk, Netherlandish painter (1420–1475) 106
Boy, Willem, Flemish artist and master mason in Sweden (d. 1592) 32
Broman, Olof, priest at Hudiksvall 143f, 157
Brunkeberg, Battle of (1471) 31, 32, 35–42, 46, 56, 125, 145
Brussels 105
Brüggeman, Hans, German sculptor (early 16th century) 155, 156f
burial chapels 49
Byzantine art 17, 20
Byzantium 15, 76
Bälinge church, Sörmland 162

C
Caesar, Julius 107, 108
Campin, Robert, Flemish painter (1375–1444) 106
Cappadocia 15
Carl Göran Bonde 127
Carpaccio, Vittore, Italian artist (1455–1525) 21
Cassiopeia, Ethiopian queen 13
casts for pilgrim's badges 18, 20
Catherine of Alexandria, saint 153
Cefalù, Sicily 26
chantries, English burial chapels 49
Chapel of Saint George in Lübeck 142
Charles V, German Emperor 157
Charles VIII, king of France 25
Chartres Cathedral 17, 18, 88
Chivalric ideal 58, 61
Christian I of Denmark, 1448–1481 (Sweden 1457–1464) 25, 35, 36, 37, 48
Christian, "master", painter on Åland (17th century) 159
Christopher, saint 157
Clement, Pope, see Saint Clement
coats-of-arms on the Saint George group 50, 56, 67, 72
Coptic textiles 18
Cracow 137
Cross of Saint George 28, 56, 60, 73
Crusade, First, 1099 against the Turks 18f, 47
Cult of Saint George 15–21, 29ff, 45
Cyriakus, saint 47

D
Dacianus, Roman governor 11, 76, 82, 86, 90, 92, 94, 97, 141, 153
Dalecarlian paintings 161, 162
Danaë, figure in Greek mythology 13
Dance Macabre wall hanging 110ff, 137, 140
Danderyd church, Uppland 90, 101

Danderyd relief 90, 101, 135
Dannebrogen, Danish national standard 37, 63
Danzig 30
De Geer, Louis, Minister of Justice (1858) 162
de Guemez, Count 127
de Sas, Marzal, Spanish painter (ca 1400) 9
Delacroix, Eugène, French painter (1798–1863) 21
Delphi, Greek oracle 11
Demetrius, Byzantine soldier saint 17, 18, 19, 20, 80
Dendrochronological analysis 115
"Der blaue Reiter" (journal from 1912) 167
Diocletianus, Roman Caesar 18, 76
Dioscorus, the house of, Pompeii 12
Donatello, Donato di Niccolò di Betto Bardi, Italian Renaissance sculptor (1386–1466) 17, 19, 21, 63
Double-headed eagle 94, 101, 167f
Dürer, Albrecht, German Renaissance painter (1471–1528) 21

E
Ed church, Uppland 88, 99
Ed relief 88, 99
Egypt 15
Eimer, Gerhard, German art critic 106
Elin av Skövde, saint 39
Elin Nilsdotter (Natt och Dag) 154
Elisabeth, saint 120
Elya (princess) 54
Engelbrekt Engelbrektsson, Swedish rebel (d. 1436) 164
England 21, 139
Erik the Holy, Swedish patron saint (d. 1160) 38, 39, 42, 49, 96, 123f, 125
Eriksson, Christian, Swedish sculptor (1858–1935) 163, 164
Eskil, saint 39
Ethiopia 24
extraneous materials 116, 121, 122, 134, 137
Eyck, Hubert van, 1370–1426, Flemish Renaissance painter 106
Eyck, Jan van, 1390–1441, Flemish Renaissance painter 106

F
Fader Ulfsson (Sparre av Hjulsta och Ängsö) 72, 154
Fafner, dragon 13f
Falsterbo, Skåne 144
Ferdinand II, King of Aragon 25
Ferrara Cathedral 20, 21
Finström church, Åland 147
Fituna gård, Sörmland 127
Florence 17, 19
Fläcka village, Enånger, Hälsingland 148
"Fourteen aids in adversity" 16
Fredrik I of Danmark, earlier Duke of Sleswig 157
Fredrik III, German Emperor 25
Frescoes 22f
Färentuna church, Uppland 146

G
Gad, Hemming, Sten Sture's emissary in Rome, elected bishop of Linköping (1450–1520) 46, 48
Gavnö castle, Denmark 130, 131
Georgien 18
Gertraut, see Saffenbergh
gesso 116
Geverdes, Andreas, mayor of Lübeck 114
Geverdes, Georg, brother of the above 114
Golden Legend, see Legenda aurea
Gotland 29, 48, 151
Gotlands Museum of Antiquities, Visby 149f
Grenier, Pasquier, Flemish artist (15th century) 107, 108, 111
"Greyfriars' diary" in Stockholm 45
Grip (lineage, bearings) 72
Gripsholm, castle in Södermanland 32, 72, 127, 129
Gustav II Adolf, Swedish king (1611–1632) 158
Gustav Vasa, Swedish king (1523–1560) 32

H
Haaken Gulleson, Swedish sculptor and painter (early 16th century) 148f
Hagenbecke, Dierik, alderman in Tallinn 123
Hammarby church, Uppland 144
Hans (Danish king 1481–1513, Swedish king 1497–1501) 48, 63
Hattula church, Finland 143, 146, 147
Hedesunda church, Gästrikland 147
Heide, Henning von der (senior), German sculptor 142, 155f, 170
Heidenstam, Verner von, Swedish author 105
Henry VII King of England 25
Hippogriff (mythological animal) 26
hobs 162
Hollola, Tavastland 147
Holy Spirit, Church of in Tallinn 120
Horus, Egyptian god 11, 24
Hovby church, Västergötland 160
Huesca, in Spain 19
Huseby bruk, Småland 161
Husum, Schleswig-Holstein 155, 156
Hylestad, Norway 14
Hälsingland 143f, 148
Hälsingtuna church, Hälsingland 148

I
Iceland 21
iconoclasts 77
icons 17, 18, 20, 165
Ilges, finisher 116
"Imperial Eagle" 108
Ingeborg Åkesdotter (Tott), d. 1507, wife of Sten Sture 36, 46, 50, 63, 71
Innocent VIII, Pope (1484–1492) 47
Isaiah 11
Ivan III (the Great), Grand Duke of Moscow, Tsar (1440–1505) 101
Ivar Axelsson (Tott; d. 1407) 130, 131, 150f, 152

J

Jakob Ulfsson, Archbishop of Uppsala (1470–1514) 38, 39, 125
Jens Iversen Lange, bishop of Århus (d. 1482) 119f, 128
Jens mason 72
Jerusalem 19
Johan III's ecclesiastical ordinance 157
Johannes Ivan, Swedish painter (d. 1465) 31
John the Baptist 119
John, apostle and evangelist 113, 115, 120, 122, 124, 137
Johnson, Eyvind, Swedish author 168
Joyce, James, Irish author 168
Jubilee Indulgences 47
Jung, C.G., psychologist 24f
Justinianus, Emperor of the Eastern Empire, (527–565) 17
Jämshögs socken, Blekinge 162
Järva, Uppland 35
Jönköping 49

K

Kalmar 30, 48
Kandinsky, W., Russian painter (1886–1944) 166f
Karl Knutsson (Bonde), king of Sweden and Norway 30, 31, 42, 67
  statuette depicting Karl Knutsson 72, 127–131
Karling, Sten, Swedish art critic 135
Kefeus, Ethiopian king 13
Klara convent in Stockholm 35, 37
Klas Rönnow, Danish marshall 38
Kleodolinda (princess) 54
Knights of Malta 19
Knights of Saint George 19
Knivsta church, Uppland 49
Knut Posse, castle warden (d. 1500) 36, 38
Kristianstad museum 161
Krummedik, Agneta 133
Krummedik, Albert, bishop of Lübeck 112f, 115, 116, 117, 133
Kråksmåla church, Småland 145, 146f, 149
Kulturen, Lund 162
Kumla church, Västmanland 39
Källunge church, Gotland 29
Käpplingeholmen (Blasieholmen) 35, 38
Köpmanbrinken 163f

L

Laihela church, Österbotten 148f
Larsson, Carl, artist (1853–1919) 163
Lassan, city in Pomerania 106
Laurens Axelsson (Tott; d. 1483) 72
Lay of Brunkeberg 36, 45
Legend of Saint George 15–21, 75, 88, 90
Legenda aurea 15, 19, 20, 51, 54, 75f, 82, 84, 86, 90, 92, 94
Leonardo da Vinci, Italian Renaissance artist (1452–1519) 54
Lillchurch, Östergötland 141, 152
lion masks 108
Luke, evangelist 104, 105
Lund Cathedral 29
Lübeck 30, 106, 133, 134, 155
Lübeck Cathedral 112, 114, 133, 139
Lydda-Diospolis 15
Lydia 51
Lögdö church, Medelpad 148

M

Magdalena Karlsdotter (Bonde), daughter of king Karl Knutsson 130, 131, 151
Magnus Henrikssen, pretender to the throne 49
magus (sorcerer) 86, 98
Mammon 90, 101
Marduk, Babylonian god 11, 13, 24
Marées Hans von, German painter (1837–1887) 21
Mariefred abbey church 49
Mary Magdalene 113, 116, 117
Mary, Blessed Virgin, mother of Jesus 58, 113, 115, 121, 122, 141, 152
Marzal, see de Sas
Mast, Antonius, Papal Nuncio 45, 47
Master of the National Mint 134
Matarengi, Norrbotten 144
Maximilian, king of Rome 25
Medusa, figure in Greek mythology 12, 13
Meer, Lucas, finisher 116
Megalo-martyr 15
Mercury, Roman god 102
Merkurius, Byzantine soldier saint 19
Messenius, Johannes, Swedish historian (1579–1636) 77, 105
Michael, archangel 14ff
miles Christi 19
Moldavia 22, 23
Moldovita, church in Romania 22
Moltke, Erik, Danish philologist and art critic 106
Monumenta Ullerakerensia 41, 42
moors 19
Mora, Dalecarlia 163
Moreau, Gustave, French painter (1826–1898) 21
Moscow 101, 164, 165, 167
Munich 167
Musée National d'Art Moderne, Paris 166
Museo Nazionale, Naples 12
Museum of National Antiquities, Stockholm 148, 164
Muslims 19
Myrsmeden, Ragnar, artist 163
Mystery plays 80
Mårten i Nääs, artist on Åland (17th century) 159
Mälaren 35

N

National Gallery, London 24
Nationalmuseet i Köpenhamn 155, 156
Nationalmuseum, Stockholm 10f
National standard
  Danish (three leopards) 42, 63
  German (double headed eagle) 94
  Norwegian (lion) 127
  Russian (double headed eagle) 101, 167f

Swedish (three crowns) 49, 96
Natt och Dag (lineage, bearings) 35, 49, 72, 154
Netherlands 25, 105
New York 165
Nibelungenlied 14
Nicolaus, Italian mason (12th century) 20, 21
Nils (Bosson) Sture (Natt och Dag, d. 1494) 35, 36, 37, 74, 154
Nils Bosson (Grip) 74
Nilsson, Gustaf, artist 164
Nordic Museum, Stockholm 88
Norra Härene church, Västergötland 162
Norrmalm 36, 38
Notke, Bernt, artist (ca 1440–1509) 105–125, 154f, 163, 166, 170, 171
   in Sweden 109, 133ff
   signature 107
   trade mark 106
Notke, Diderik, priest 111, 120, 123
Notke, Michel, merchant 106

O
Olaf, master 49
Olaus Petri (mäster Olof), reformer, Swedish historian (1493–1552) 79, 191
Old Testament 11
Olov the Holy (d. 1030) 39
Or San Michele, Florence 17, 19
Orlando furioso 26
Oslo universitets oldsaksamling 14
oven reliefs 161f
Oxenstierna, lineage 35

P
Paatz, Walter, German art critic 106, 135
Palestine 15
Peder Swart, Gustav Vasa's chronicler 77
Peringskiöld, Johan, Royal Antiquarian (1654–1720) 39, 41, 78, 92, 123
Perseus, Greek hero 12, 13
Petrella Tifernina, Abruzzo 16
Petrikirche in Lübeck 109
Petru Rares, Moldavian Prince 22
Philip the Fair, Archduke of Burgundy 25
Philotheus, monk from Pskov 167
Pilate 94
plinth reliefs on the Saint George group 73–101, 141, 152f
Pompeii 12
Popular art based on the Saint George motif 162
Post-Reformation images of George 157ff
Prague 20, 22
Processional horse 47
Pskov, Russia 167
Puig, Spain (battle of) 19
Pyhämaa votive church, Finland 157
Python, dragon 11

R
Ramsundsberget, Sörmland 13
Raneke, Jan, heraldry expert 72
Raphael (Raffaelo Santi), Italian Renaissance painter (1483–1520) 21
Regensburg 19
Rehn, Olof 159, 160
relics, Saint George's 45ff, 139
   in the Lübeck crucifix 115, 139
Renqvist, Torsten, artist 168ff
Reredos in
   Cracow, St. Mary's Church (by Veit Stoss) 137
   Lillchurch, Östergötland (provincial work) 141, 152
   Schleswig Cathedral (by Hans Brüggeman) 157
   Stockholm City Church (Lübeck work) 30
   Tallinn, Church of the Holy Ghost (by Bernt Notke) 120f, 123, 124
   Tillinge, Uppland (from Ängsö, Västmanland; Stockholm work) 152ff
   Uppsala Cathedral (by Bernt Notke; destroyed by fire) 39, 41, 42, 123ff, 128
Århus Cathedral (by Bernt Notke) 119f, 121, 122, 133
Reval, see Tallinn
Revelations According to Saint John 14
Rhyming chronicles (see also Sture chronicle) 38, 45, 56, 61
Riddarholm church, Stockholm 128, 131
Roger, hero of Orlando furioso 26
Rogslösa church, Östergötland 14
Romania 22, 23
Rome 15
Roosval, Johnny, Swedish art historian 105f
Royal Library, Stockholm 45, 159, 160
Ruardean, England 23
Rubens, Peter Paul, Flemish baroque painter (1577–1640) 21
Rubicon 107, 108
Rusko, Finland 147
Russia 29, 167

S
Saffenbergh, Gertraut 106
Sagu church, Finland 147
Saint Anne 119
Saint Anne museum, Lübeck 142, 155
Saint Blasius 47
Saint Catherine's Monastery in Sinai 18
Saint Clement, Pope (88–97) 119, 121
Saint Emmeram's monastery, Regensburg 19
Saint Erik, see Erik the Holy
Saint George('s) (Georg, Georgius)
   armour 58
   as a Christian name 11
   as an officer 17
   brothers 17, 80, 96
   cost 46
   diadem 58, 60
   helmet 58, 61, 64, 80, 96
   origins of the group 45–50, 133–140
   placement of the princess and sheep 54, 56
   plume 57f, 61, 63
   relics 45, 46f, 139
   reliefs 57, 68, 71f; see also plinth reliefs on the Saint

George group
  reliquary 45, 47, 58, 139
  restoration 64, 88
Saint George group in Stockholm passim and ffa 43–101 and 133-140
Saint George's banner 21, 25, 30
Saint George's guild 30
  saint's day 15, 24, 29, 38, 47
  shield 58
  symbolism 58, 61, 63f, 164–171
  weapons 21, 56, 73, 80
Saint George's Chapel, Lübeck 155
Saint George's Church (ruins), Visby 16
Saint George's Cross 28, 56, 60, 73
Saint George's monastery in Prague 20, 22
Saint Gereon, equestrian saint 46f
Saint Germanus 47
Saint Hans church, Visby 152
Saint John Baptist, Ruardean 23
Saint Mary's Church Cracow 137
Saint Mary's Church Husum, Schleswig-Holstein 155, 156f
Saint Mary's Church Lübeck 111, 112
Saint Mary's Church Visby, now its Cathedral 151f
Saint Matthew's Gospel 94
Saint Nicholas' Church in Tallinn 110, 111
Saint Peter's Church, Lübeck 109
Sala parish church 105
Saltviks church, Åland 159
San Giorgio Martire in Petrella Tifernina 16
Saracens (muslims) 19
Scanian wars (1452) 30
Scharpeselle, Bernt, finisher 116
scouts 164
Set, mythological figure in prehistoric Egypt 11
Sicily 21, 26
Sigfrid, Swedish patron saint 38, 39
Sigurd Fafnesbane (Siegfried) 13f
Silene, city of 26, 28, 51, 67–72, 128, 137, 158, 160, 162
Sinai 18
Skellefteå parish church 147
Skänninge, Östergötland 30
Slatte, Peder, mayor of Stockholm (1506–1516) 72
Smyrna 18, 20
Sollerön, Dalecarlia 163
Sparre (av Hjulsta och Ängsö), coat-of-arms 72, 154
Spånga church, Uppland 127, 128
St. Anne Museum, Lübeck 142, 155
stave churches 14
Stefan the Great, Moldavian Prince (1457–1504) 22
Sten Sture d. ä. (Sten Gustavsson Sture; Tre Sjöblad) 25, 31, 35ff, 42, 45, 46, 50, 56, 61, 63, 105, 115, 124, 131, 133, 147f, 151, 154, 171
Stender, Hartich, painter 116
Stiklastad, Norway 39
Stockholm 30, 67
Stockholm City Church 48, 128, 153, 154, 156
  addition of new vaults 133
  crucifix 139
  rebuilding 71f
Stockholm Town Hall 163, 164
Stora Kopparberget 30
Stoss, Veit (Wit Stwosz), German-Polish sculptor (1447–1533) 137
Strindberg, August, author, amanuens at the Royal Library (1849–1912) 45, 47, 105
Strändernas svall, novel by Eyvind Johnson 168
Strängnäs 30
Sture Chronicles 36ff, 45, 48f
Sture, see Nils Bosson Sture/Sten Sture d. ä.
Stöde church, Medelpad 148
Sund, Åland 146
Sundog picture in Stockholm City Church 35
Svante Nilsson Sture (Natt och Dag), Governor of the Realm (d. 1512) 49
Swart, see Peder Swart
Svarte, Eggert, carver 116
Swedish Chronicle by Olaus Petri 36, 45
Särkilax Chapel, Norrbotten 144

T
Tallinn (Reval) 106, 110, 120f, 137
Tavastland 144, 146
Theodor, Byzantine soldier saint 17, 18, 20, 80, 96
Three Crowns, palace, castle in Stockholm 35, 67
Three water-lily leaves, Sten Sture's coat-of-arms 42, 50, 56, 61, 67, 71, 108, 125, 147
Thönnies Hermensson, Notkes journeyman 135
Tiamat, dragon 11
Tillberg, Peter, artist 164
Tillinge church, Uppland 152
Tillinge reliefs 152ff
Tintoretto (Jacopo Robusti), Italian painter (1518–1594) 21
Tord, master mason 71
Torne river 144
Tortuna church, Västmanland 148
Tott (lineage/bearings) 35, 50, 63, 67, 72, 151; see also Ingeborg Åkesdotter, Ivar Axelsson, Laurens Axelsson, Åke Axelsson
Tournai 107, 108
Triumphal Crucifix in Lübeck 106, 112–118, 137, 139f
Trolle (lineage) 35, 37, 72
Trotskij, Leo, Russian politician 165
Trotte Karlsson till Eka 35
Tsereti, Zurab, Russian artist 165, 166

U
Uccello, Paolo (Paolo di Dono), Italian Renaissance painter (1397–1475) 21, 24
Ulysses, Greek hero 168
Ulysses, novel by J. Joyce 168
Unicorn, creature of fable 57
Uppsala 30
Uppsala Cathedral 39f, 48, 49, 123ff, 128
Uppsala university 39
Uther, J. Baptista von, painter (16th century) 32

V
Vadstena abbey church 128
Valencia 9

Vallentuna calendar 29
Vallentuna church, Uppland 29
Vasa (lineage) 35, 105
Vatican archivea 46
Vendel church, Uppland 30, 31, 133
Veta church, Östergötland 157, 158
Victoria and Albert Museum, London 9
Victoria, goddess of victory 162
Vika church, Dalecarlia 143, 146, 149
Visborg 151f
Visby 16, 30, 150ff
Visby Cathedral, see Saint Mary's Church, Visby
von Klausenburg, Martin and Georg, bronze castings in Prague 20, 22
Voronet, church i Romania 22, 23
Vårdsbergs church, Östergötland 158
Västerås 30
Vättlösa church, Västergötland 29
Vätö church, Uppland 147
Völsungasagan 14

W
Wall paintings 29, bl.v. 30, 31, 38, 39
Weyden, Rogier van der, Flemish painter (1399–1464) 106
Wikander, Hjalmar, consul 163
Wilsing, Henrik, sculptor 109, 134, 135

Z
Zeus, Greek god 13
Zorn, Anders, artist (1860–1920) 163

Å
Åbo 30, 147
Åke Axelsson (Tott; d. 1477) 151
Århus 106, 120
Århus Cathedral 119f, 121, 133

Ä
Ängsö castle, Västmanland 154
Ängsö church, Västmanland 30, 152, 154

Ö
Öland 48
Örbyhus castle 133
Örjansvisan 36, 54, 145, 164
Ösmo church, Sörmland 28
Övertorneå church, Norrbotten 144, 168, 170